JAMES STEPHENS BULLOCH
Aristocratic Southern Gentleman

JAMES STEPHENS BULLOCH
Aristocratic Southern Gentleman

Connie M. Huddleston

Interpreting Time's Past Press
2020

James Stephens Bulloch:
Aristocratic Southern Gentleman

Published by:
Interpreting Time's Past Press
Crab Orchard, Kentucky

Text copyright © 2020 by Connie M. Huddleston
All rights reserved. No part of this book may be used or reproduced in any manner whatsoever without written permission except in the case of brief quotations embodied in critical articles and reviews. For information, please address Connie Huddleston at Interpreting Time's Past Press, 450 Old Richmond Road, South, Crab Orchard, KY 40419.

Cover design by Interpreting Time's Past Press
Cover photograph courtesy of Bulloch Hall, Roswell, Georgia

ISBN-13: 978-1-7328333-4-0
Library of Congress Control Number: 2020900488

Photographs of Midway Congregational Church, JSB's gravestone, and Charles Bulloch's gravestone photographed by and are property of the author. Photograph of Georgia Elliott's gravestone and Founder's Cemetery courtesy of Toby Silver.

Bull Street, Savannah, Georgia The Miriam and Ira D. Wallach Division of Art, Prints and Photographs: Print Collection, The New York Public Library. "Bull Street [Savannah, Georgia]." New York Public Library Digital Collections. Accessed January 16, 2020. http://digitalcollections.nypl.org/items/510d47db-a06d-a3d9-e040-e00a18064a99

Table of Contents

List of Illustrations 7
List of Tables 7
Dedication I
Introduction . . . . K
Chapter I: America's First James Bulloch 1
Chapter II: Georgia's President Archibald Bulloch 9
Chapter III: Captain James Bulloch 25
Chapter IV: Setting the Stage for JSB 43
Chapter V: The Professional Life of JSB 55
Chapter VI: The Marriages of JSB 89
Chapter VII: JSB's Life in Transition 111
Chapter VIII: Legal Matters 125
Chapter IX: The Roswell Decade 131
Chapter X: Death of JSB 155
Endnotes 163
Sources Cited 181
Appendix A 189
Appendix B 219
Appendix C 229
Appendix D 243
Index 251
About the Author 261

List of Illustrations

Bull Street, Savannah, Georgia	m
Map of Georgia Parishes	4
Archibald Bulloch	8
Entitled "At Savannah Georgia"	19
Archibald Bulloch and family	24
Midway Congregational Church	30
Map of Savannah	32
Runaway from the Subscriber	34
Strayed from the Commons	35
Scheme of a Lottery	49
Bulloch and Sadler Advertisment	59
SS *Savannah* by Hunter Wood	69
SS *Savannah* Postage Stamp	76
1832 Gold Lottery Map	109
Cedar Hill Plantation	113
Bulloch Hall	130
Gravestone of Charles Irvine Bulloch	138
Georgia Elliott's gravestone	154
Original James S. Bulloch gravestone	156

List of Tables

Bulloch Family Tree	n
Dunwody Family Tree	45
Elliots of Georgia	47
Stewarts of Georgia	50

Two amazing friends
provided much of the support
needed during the research and completion
of this work.
I could never have accomplished
this biography without
Sherron Lawson
and
Gwendolyn Koehler
You have my eternal thanks!

INTRODUCTION

The miniature of James Stephens Bulloch, enclosed in a gold locket, on the cover was presented to Bulloch Hall in 1974 by the Theodore Roosevelt Association. The reverse side of the locket holds a curl of James' brunette hair wrapped in gold threads and decorated with seed pearls. The letter that accompanied the indefinite loan stated the miniature had been passed down to Mrs. Anna Roosevelt Cowles, daughter of Mittie Bulloch Roosevelt. Cowles' son inherited the miniature from his mother, and he gave it to the Theodore Roosevelt Association. It has been attributed to artist Thomas Sully, according to a 1973 appraisal, and is believed to have been painted in 1816. James would have been twenty-three years old.

Some eleven or twelve years ago, I began research into the life of James Stephens Bulloch. After hearing Bulloch Hall's docents and staff speak mostly of his two marriages and his having built Bulloch Hall, I realized James' story was mostly absent from their dialogue, for it seemed little was known about James' life. For about five years, I pursued this line of research when time and opportunity arose. I discovered a great deal of information about his life considering he left behind no journals, no ledgers, and few letters.

Soon I had a mass of paper, notes, and many word processing files filled with snippets of information about James, his family, and his ancestors. Yet, other projects took priority in my life as an historian and an author. Three other books about James' family kept his presence firmly seated in my mind, always with the idea of writing his story. Over the next seven years, I managed to write the first five chapters of his biography. Only in 2019, did I find time to finish the story.

Presented here is a somewhat typical tale of an aristocratic Southern gentleman. A man of his time and his place. I have heard docents at Bulloch observe how his miniature shows him to be a dandy or fop! Instead I saw a man dressed in the height of English Regency fashion, to which all wealthy men aspired. This was the period of Beau Brummell when trousers were introduced, always with perfect tailoring and unadorned linen. Men wore waistcoats and knee-high boots. Women wore high waisted dresses or a skirt, bodice, and jacket. The natural figure was emphasized, and tight corsets abandoned. Gentlemen and women followed English fashions closely. James dressed just so for his portrait—not as a dandy—as a young man of taste, gentility, and breeding.

Learning about a man's life in so much depth, also led to learning about his ancestors, the first James Bulloch, his son Archibald, and his son James. James

Stephens was the third to be born in America after his great grandfather immigrated from Scotland. I recognized early in my research how much these three men contributed to who James was and what he became. I could not tell his story without telling their stories first. Throughout James' life, others such as his wives, his mother, his stepchildren, and his children appeared and influenced his decisions, for every individual is actually a *being created with and belonging to a family of relations, friends, enemies, and acquaintances.* Therefore, others' stories also appear in this biography, for James' life depended upon and was influence by all these relationships.

One last thought— as an historian I often find myself caught up by history. It overwhelms my sense of reason and restraint. I tend to tell more than I need to or should. I often find a subject, a happening, too enthralling not to relate to my readers in great detail. When writing fiction based on history, my editors tend to "put me back into the story" and insist I delete great hunks of historical detail. In this book, my editors have little choice but to let me tell James' story as I please. After all, what is history without details and understanding?

Some will ask why I put transcriptions of so many legal and period documents into this manuscript. As an historian and amateur genealogist, I understand the difficulties our country's African American population encounters in tracing their ancestors before 1865 due to the overwhelming lack of and complications in finding such documentation. By placing relevant documents here, perhaps I can provide a few researchers with a way to study these documents without going to Liberty and Chatham Counties. Additionally, other historians will have access to the documents related to these families. At some point in time, my copies of the originals will be donated to Bulloch Hall.

Now for a bit of *housekeeping,* I have tried to create endnotes to document facts and statements. I followed Turabian's Sixth Edition the best I possibly could without getting bogged down in formatting. Also, almost every document, letter, or article presented here was transcribed by me. Any mistakes are mine and mine alone. When I could not decipher a word or phrase, I placed an underline to indicate a missing word or words. If I could make a reasonable guess, I often placed [?] beside the word in question. Also, I did not correct archaic spellings. Sometimes I missed putting [sp] beside such words. Please note that *Negroe* was the accepted word and accepted spelling in the time of James' life. If someone else transcribed the historical document, I have used their transcription as presented to me.

As always, I read and respond to all emails. So, if I have a serious error or you just wish to comment, please contact me. It is with great appreciation for my readers and the staff of Bulloch Hall that I give you this biography.

Connie M. Huddleston

Bull Street, Savannah, Georgia, circa 1860

Bullochs of Georgia
(relevent descentants only)

James Bulloch
abt. 1701 in Scotland
married abt. 1728
Jean Stobo
abt. 1710-1750

married
Anne Ferguson
unknown-by 1758
(no issue)

married in 1758
Ann Graham
unknown-1764
(no issue)

married
Mary Jones
1730-1795
(no issue)

Children of James Bulloch and Jean Stobo

Archibald Bulloch 1730-1777, *married in 1764* Mary Olivia DeVeaux 1747-1818

Jean Bulloch 1730-1771, *married in 1750* Josiah Alexander Perry 1727-1773

Christina Bulloch 1746-1779, *married in 1774* Henry Yonge, unknown

Children of Archibald Bulloch and Mary Olivia DeVeaux

Capt. James Bulloch 1765-1807, *married in 1786* Anne Irvine 1770-1831

Archibald Stobo Bulloch 1767-1859, *married in 1793* Sarah Glen 1775-1859

Jane Bulloch 1768-1787, *married* James Benjamin Maxwell 1751-1805

William Bellinger Bulloch 1776-1852, *married in 1807* Mary Young 1782-1768

Children of Capt. James Bulloch and Anne Irvine

John Irvine Bulloch 1787-1827, *married in 1814* Charlotte Glen

Jane Bulloch 1788-1856, *married in 1808* John Dean Dunwoody 1786-1758

see Dunwoody Family Tree

James Stephens Bulloch 1793-1849, *married in 1817* Hester Elliott 1797-1831

married in 1832 Martha Stewart Elliott 1799-1864

Anne Bulloch 1793-unknown

Children of John Irvine Bulloch and Charlotte Glen

William Gaston Bulloch
James Powell Bulloch
Jane D. Bulloch Colburn

Children of James Stephens Bulloch

John Elliott Bulloch 1819-1821
James Dunwoody Bulloch 1823-1901

Anna Louisa Bulloch 1833-1893
Martha "Mittie" Bulloch 1835-1884
Charles Irvine Bulloch 1838-1841
Irvine Stephens Bulloch 1842-1898

Chapter I
America's First
James Bulloch

With the exception of full-blooded Native Americans, Americans' ancestors arrived from either Europe, Africa, or Asia or a combination thereof, with a few Australian Aboriginals thrown in here and there. In the middle to the last part of the 1700s, the majority of free men arriving in the colonies came from Britain and the European mainland. England, Scotland, and Ireland provided more new colonists than any other location, including enslaved Africans.

The colonies offered advancement, opportunity, and land to those willing to risk all. Many immigrants arrived with little or no funds, little education, and no marketable skills. Some arrived and immediately were placed on the auction block to serve as indentured or bonded servants for a period of five to seven years. This servitude paid the cost of their crossing. If lucky, they received training in an occupation or craft. If lucky, their masters treated them with respect. Few proved lucky. After their period of indentureship ended, these men and women found themselves on their own, often with little or no money, facing the trials of a new life in the New World.

Scots arrived in great numbers beginning in the late 1600s. After the first and second Jacobite risings (1715 and 1745) the numbers increased. After the Jacobite uprising of 1715 and the uprising of the Highland Chieftains in 1719, the English Crown's repressive measures against Scottish gentlemen led to the emigration of many such men to the new American colonies. The 1715 rising, also known as Mar's Rebellion, occurred as a result of the death of the last Stuart monarch, Queen Anne, and the accession of George I of the Hanoverian line. Jacobites supported James Francis Edward Stuart VII of Scotland (known as James II in England) as their rightful and Catholic king. James is a derivative of the Latin name *Jacobus* (Iacobus), hence the term Jacobites. Harsh terms by the English upon those who took part in the rising created little opportunity for any Scot whether Catholic or Presbyterian (Protestant).

The English transported many who'd fought for Scotland's freedom. These men, and a few women, had a choice - transportation to the colonies, prison, or execution. Along with political prisoners of rebellions, paupers, petty thieves, and criminals were also transported. Still other Scots came because of poverty. They had no hope of ever breaking out of their set place in the class-system which strongly existed in Britain. In America, a man could step up in society regardless of his background.

Scotsman James Bulloch

James Bulloch (1701-1780) arrived in the new English colonies, circa 1725. Unlike many who emigrated to the colonies seeking advancement and a new life, this James Bulloch, a Scotsman, arrived in America an educated clergyman, after receiving a liberal Glasgow education that included Greek and Latin.[1] Most Bulloch family genealogical scholars list James' parents as William Balloch and Jean Reid who married in 1687. The Bulloch/Balloch family were members of a Sept of Clan MacDonald, Lord of Isles. The family can be traced back to Baldernock, Sterlingshire, Scotland, circa 1591 and Donald Balloch MacDonald. The name *Bulloch* for the Gaelic Balloch, or *beadach* means an outlet of a lake or glen and is an uncommon Scottish name.[2]

James entered the family some fourteen years after his parents' marriage, indicating he may have been one of the family's younger sons and would not inherit. However, James did receive an education and preparation to make his way in the world.

Despite his education, there existed little opportunity in James' homeland. Therefore, in his early twenties, James immigrated to the Carolinas. Although trained for the pulpit, there is no record he ever served in that capacity once in the colonies. Instead, he became active in the colony's government. He was elected a King's Justice of the Peace in Colleton County in 1735 and again in 1737. By this time, now in his thirties, James owned at least one or two plantations.

On 14 December 1738, the *South Carolina Gazette* ran the following advertisement:

> RUN AWAY from Ja: Bulloch's Plantaion, near Pon Pon Bridge, on the 7th of Nov. last, 3 new Angola Negro Men, they speak little or no English, and had when he went away new cloaths fo [sp] white Plains, with a new Duffil Blanket each, branded upon their right Breasts just above the nipple B and are named Fellows, Edinburgh & Humprey, the first viz. Fellow is very remarkable with Bumps on the Joints of his two Knees and Elbows. Whoever takes them up or any of them, whips them according to Law, and brings them home, shall, over and above what the Law appoints, have 40 s paid them by James Bulloch.

In 1740, James served as a Special Agent to the Creek (Muscogee) Indians and became a member of the South Carolina Colonial Assembly in 1754. Along with founding several protestant churches, James occupied his time as a merchant and owned and operated an extensive plantation called Pon Pon near Walterboro.[3] James also owned Oak Grove Plantation (located adjacent to the Retreat Plantation on the Cooper River) in the mid-1740s. This information is based on documents showing him having sold 170 acres of the plantation to a Thomas Dale in 1746.[43] James accomplished all of this before he turned fifty years of age. Considering he most likely came to the United States practically destitute, James' achievements demonstrate a strong will and an excellent mind. His manner of dress, carriage, and speech must have impressed those he met.

Demonstrating his education and wealth, James posted an advertisement, in the *South Carolina Gazette* on 15 December 1837, requesting the return of over fifteen books. James stated in the advertisement "Most of which Books have been out for Several Years, Still expecting the Borrowers (who have now escaped by Memory) wou'd have been so kind as return them..." The listed books included *Salmon's Review of the History of England*, 2 Volumes; *Buchanan's History of Scotland and History of England* (two separate volumes); *Millar's Propagation of Christianity; Paradise regained;* and *The Guardians.*

The Charleston Library Society listed James as a member in 1750. Begun in 1748 by several young gentlemen, the Society raised funds to purchase pamphlets and magazines published in Great Britain. Each member contributed ten pounds sterling. Before the end of 1748, their acquisitions included books as well as pamphlets. Members included such influential names as John Drayton, Charles Pinkney, William Bull, and William Middleton, demonstrating James' circle of friends and acquaintances included those in the top rungs of Charleston society.[5]

James' Marriages

Within his first few years in the colonies, James married for what would be the first of four times. Circa 1728, he married Jean Stobo, daughter of the Reverend Archibald Stobo, a marriage that produced his son, Archibald and two daughters, Jean (1730-1771) and Christina (1746-1779). Like James, Archibald Stobo and his wife Elizabeth Park Stobo had both emigrated from Scotland. James' son Archibald, born 1 January 1730, was the eldest. Both daughters lived to maturity and married. After Jean's death in 1750, James married Anne Barker Ferguson, a Carolina widow. No record of Anne's death has been found. Some thirty years after his first marriage, James married his third wife, another widow, Anne Cuthbert Graham, this time from Georgia. She brought to their 1758 marriage, her successful Mulberry Grove Plantation on the Savannah River about twelve miles outside the city of Savannah. Under the marriage contract, James took ownership of the plantation and moved to Georgia.

Ann Graham Bulloch died in 1764. Her obituary in the *Georgia Gazette* states "On Saturday, the 19th inst. died at Mulberry Grove, Mrs. Anne Bulloch, wife of James Bulloch, Esq. and formerly of Patrick Graham, Esq. late President of this province; a gentlewoman, universally loved and universally lamented."[6] Given her late husband's position and wealth, it seems James married into the top rung of Georgia society.

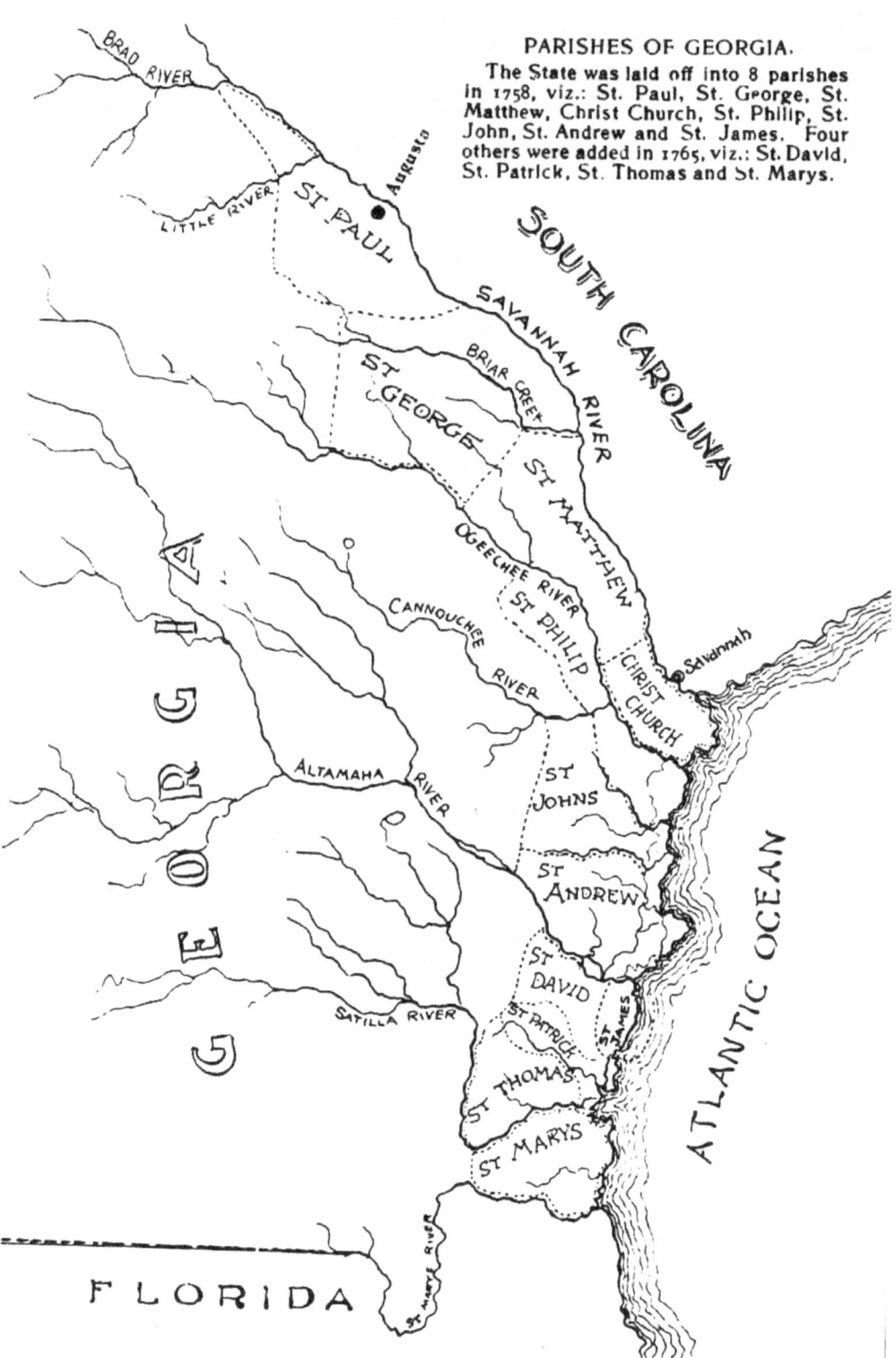

Map of Georgia Parishes as found in *Liberty County: A Pictorial History*

(Note: The use of the term esquire after their names denoted a substantial measure of respect and standing rather than a law degree.)

As in South Carolina, James became active in local and state affairs in his new home colony, serving as Justice of the Peace for Christ Church Parish in 1764 and 1767. He received a grant for 2,000 acres in St. Marys Parish in 1765.[7]

James continued to live on Mulberry Grove Plantation. Bits and pieces about his life from newspapers and other historic documents reveal a series of legal and personal problems. In 1768, James sold forty head of cattle for "ready cash" under order of the provost marshal.[8] This was most likely to settle a debt or a claim against him. That same day's paper contained an advertisement for a missing slave couple.

> Whereas a negroe [sp] fellow called CATO, a cooper by trade, and well known in Savannah, and his wife JUDY, a washer-woman, had a written license from the subscriber to come to town, and there to work for a month from the 13th day of June last, but have not been seen or heard of since, this is therefore to offer a reward of ten shillings sterling, beside all other necessary and common charges, to any person that will take them up, and bring them to the subscriber at Mulberry-Grove, or deliver them into the Work House in Savannah. James Bulloch.[9]

James continued to advertise for the return of Cato and Judy into January of 1769.

Legal problems, perhaps due to a shortage of ready cash, continued to haunt James into 1769 when a newspaper listed him as one of several who had not provided labor for work on the public road in the First North West Division of the Parish of Christ Church.[10]

Not lacking in property, James also owned a house in Savannah, which he advertised for sale on 20 April 1768. The advertisement also showed that James had become involved in some sort of feud with other Savannah residents.

> As the subscriber has removed with his family to his plantation Mulberry Grove, where, and in Carolina, he purposes to spend most of his time for the future, and will have no occasion for a house in Savannah, therefore (and that he may rid himself of some uneasiness and disagreeable treatment which his unhappy connections with a Stewart, a Blake, a Stevens, and some others, more especially with one whom he chuses [sp] not to name, have exposed him to) he means TO SELL HIS HOUSE opposite to Lady Houstoun's, consisting of two tenements, one of which is at present occupied by Mr. Glen, and the other by the subscriber himself. The last may be entered upon immediately, and the other when Mr. Glen's year is up. The subscriber has likewise A FARM LOT to dispose of, about three or between three and four miles from town, near Col. Mulryne's land. James Bulloch[11]

This advertisement noted the subscriber had "removed with his family." At this time, James' family consisted of Archibald, now thirty-nine years of age, who had married four years previously and lived in Savannah. Still at home was Christina, James' youngest daughter, as she did not marry until 1774.[12] His daughter Jean married Josiah Perry before 1757, as their first child was born in that year. Early records show that they lived in Walterboro, South Carolina. Only two years after the above advertisement, in 1770, James sold Mulberry Grove plantation to his son-in-law Josiah Perry.[13] The advertisement to potential buyers in the *Georgia Gazette* read:

> As the subscriber proposes to remove into Carolina early in the Spring, HE WILL SELL HIS PLANTATION, MULBERRY GROVE, containing about 800 acres, of which about 250 are river and upper swamp land, and the rest good corn and timber land, which, for pleasantness of situation goodness of soil, abundance, still, of sawable timber, and its conveniency [sp] to town and a marker, both by land and water, is so well known, that it is stands in no need of recommendation, especially from the seller, which avails but little with the buyer, who will always see and judge for himself, to which therefore I refer him. With the plantation I WILL DISPOSE OF THE STOCK OF CATTLE, HORSES, &c. that are upon it. There is likewise upon it ABOUT EIGHT THOUSAND FIVE HUNDRED FEET OF RANGING TIMBER, and a considerable Quantity of ROUGH RICE, both which I WILL SELL REASONABLY. I have another TRACT OF SIX HUNDRED ACRES on the island opposite to the lands of Purrysburgh, and near to Mr. Zubly's ferry, of a fine rich soil, and abounding with oak and cypress, and A FARM LOT about three or four miles from town, near Col. Mulryne's land; and A GARDEN LOT about a mile from town, on the western road, and A GALLERY FRONT PEW In the CHURCH; All to DISPOSE Of. The buyer of the land may have two or three years credit for two thirds of the purchase money, giving security and interest from the date of the conveyance.   JAMES BULLOCH[14]

Another Marriage

Despite the advertisement's announcement that he would remove to Carolina, James did not return to South Carolina or at least not for any great length of time. Instead, James married again. The marriage date remains unknown. Like his previous marriage, James chose another wealthy Georgia lady. This fourth marriage to Mary Jones (1730-1795), sister of Noble Jones of Wormsloe Plantation, proved as notable and prosperous as his third. Wormsloe, whose ownership remained in the Jones family, and Savannah became his home. This plantation began with a 1736 grant for 500 acres to Noble Jones. Jones constructed a fortified tabby house on the southeastern tip of the Isle of Hope overlooking the Skidaway Narrows on the intra-coastal waterway about halfway between Savannah and the Atlantic Ocean.[15] Ruins of this home and the family cemetery can currently be viewed at Wormsloe State Historic Site.

An Elderly Patriot

In 1775, despite his advanced age of seventy-four, James joined the Revolutionary cause by accepting a seat in the Provincial Congress as a delegate from the Sea Island District. He, like many in Georgia, especially most Scots, cut all ties to the Crown of England and raised a company of Patriots for the protection of the district. James had lived in the colonies for some fifty years by this date, where he enjoyed a relatively prosperous life without the strict oversight of the English crown, unlike what his fellow Scotsmen endured in their home country. The new repressions placed on the American colonies by George III and Parliament in the 1760s, no doubt brought back to James his homeland's struggles and increased his desire to live free of a distant monarch.

In December 1779, the Revolutionary War's First Battle of Savannah ended with the British occupation of the city under the command of Lieutenant Colonel Archibald Campbell, a fellow Scot, who commanded the 71st Regiment of Foot, Fraser's Highlanders.

James Bulloch did not live to see his new adopted country achieve freedom from the repressive English king that had already driven him from his native Scotland. He died and was buried at Wormsloe Plantation on 25 October 1780.[16] James lived the life of a free colonist after his earlier life in the oppressive nature of his native Scotland. He did well for himself, becoming a respected member of genteel society, marrying well, —all four times—and raising three children. His is one of many stories of men and women doing well in the new colonies. James died knowing the role his son Archibald played in the beginnings of the fight for American freedom.

Archibald Bulloch, from a painting by Henry Benbridge, circa 1775

Chapter II
Georgia's President
Archibald Bulloch

James' son, Archibald (1729 or 1730-1777) received his education as a lawyer in Charleston, South Carolina, where he established a practice. In 1757, he accepted a commission as a lieutenant in a South Carolina militia regiment. When his father married Ann Graham and relocated to Mulberry Grove Plantation near Savannah in 1758, Archibald relocated to Georgia. He married Mary DeVeaux (1748-1818) on 9 October 1764 on Argyle Island. Mary's father, James (1710-1785), owned extensive acreage on the island and the adjacent mainland. James DeVeaux served as a senior assistant-judge of Georgia's King's Court. Archibald and Mary settled in Savannah, where he became active in politics.[1] This marriage produced four children, James (1765-1807), Archibald Stobo (1767-1852), Jane (1768-1787), and William Bellinger ((1776-1852).

In 1768, the Lower House of the Royal Assembly chose the newly elected Archibald to serve on a committee that corresponded with Benjamin Franklin. Georgia elected seven Liberty Party candidates, including Archibald, to the Commons House of Assembly. The Party's success heralded the beginning of the call for liberty in the southern colonies. In 1772, this same assembly chose Archibald as Speaker. Just two years later, he took a patriot's stand against the Crown by serving on a committee appointed to sympathize with the residents of Boston. Since 1768, British troops, sent to protect and support crown-appointed colonial officials attempting to enforce unpopular Parliamentary legislation, had occupied Boston. Subsequently, the Boston Massacre of 5 March 1770 in which British soldiers killed five civilian men, increased tensions within the occupied city.[2]

In 1774, having chosen the Patriot cause, Archibald, along with Noble Wymberley Jones (his stepmother's brother), George Walton, and John Houstoun called a meeting of the Patriots at Peter Tondee's Tavern (also known as Tondee's Long Room) in Savannah. Their meeting addressed the "critical situation" resulting from the enactment of the latest taxes on the colonies by the British Parliament, and their meeting served as only the beginning of Archibald's extensive service to the Patriot cause that ended with his untimely death in February 1777.[3]

In 1775, Tondee's Long Room hosted many rebellious Georgians to "celebrate" King George's birthday. They had already erected a liberty pole earlier in the day, then during the evening, about forty Sons of Liberty marched the streets of Savannah with loaded arms and fixed bayonets. On 4 July, Tondee's Long Room hosted the Second Provincial Congress, where delegates created the state's first independent government. They elected members of the Continental Congress and a Council of Safety tasked with restricting trade with Britain, seizing British arms, and persecuting Tories.

Unfortunately, Peter Tondee died in October 1775. Archibald Bulloch administered his estate; however, Tondee's will gave total control of the tavern to his wife Lucy. [Appendix A] She carried on in her husband's absence, running the tavern, and supporting the Patriot cause. In 1782, when Georgia's revolutionary government returned at the end of the British occupation of Savannah, the Patriots again met at Tondee's Long Room.

In November 1775, the Patriots appointed Archibald to the Secret Committee of the Continental Congress charged with approaching foreign nations for the purpose of importing war materials for the coming revolution. Early the next year, Archibald took up arms and served under Colonel Lachlan McIntosh, a fellow Scot, in the Battle of the Rice Boats, which occurred in Savannah's harbor. Due to increased Patriot activity, in January 1776, British warships arrived in the Savannah River, prompting the Patriot's Council of Safety to anticipate a British incursion. The Council placed the British Governor Wright under house arrest and Colonel McIntosh in charge of Savannah's defenses. By late February, hostilities had escalated, and when British warships in Savannah's harbor seized merchant ships carrying rice from the plantations to market, the Council urged action. The Battle of the Rice Boats occurred on March second and third, after which the British fleet sailed off in defeat with the rice, the fugitive Governor, who had escaped his captors, and his chief councilors.[4]

Archibald continued to serve in a military capacity in late March when he led an expedition to Great Tybee Island to destroy British facilities located there. Bulloch's detachment consisted of riflemen, light infantry, fusiliers, volunteers, and even a few Creek Indians. They burned the military materials and all the houses except one sheltering an ill woman and several children. The Patriots killed two British marines and one Tory, taking several more captives with no injuries to their own party. Archibald having taken military action against the King's troops would have been tried and hung for treason if captured.[5]

Without a British government in place, the Georgia Provincial Congress elected Archibald as *President* of the Georgia Provincial Congress, one of five men to serve Georgia at the Continental Congress in Philadelphia, and Georgia's military Commander-in-Chief. As the colony's president, Archibald refused the posting of Georgia Grenadiers as guards at the door of his office, stating his belief that he served "for a free people, in whom I have the most entire confidence, and wish to avoid on all occasions the appearance of ostentation." He forbade swearing in the streets of Savannah, "especially on the Sabbath," and set aside a day of prayer "to implore His divine goodness to restore our Adversaries to reason and Justice, and thereby to relieve the United States from the distresses of an Unnatural War."[6]

In April 1776, Archibald charged Georgia's representatives to the Second Continental Congress writing:

> Gentlemen :—Our remote situation from both the seat of power and arms, keeps us so very ignorant of the councils and ultimate designs of the Congress, and of the transactions in the field, that we shall decline giving any particular instructions, other than strongly to recommend it to you that you never lose sight of the peculiar situation of the province you are appointed to represent; the Indians, both south and northwestwardly, upon our backs, the fortified town of St. Augustine made a continual rendezvous for soldiers in our very neighborhood; together with our blacks and tories with us; let these weighty truths be the powerful arguments for support. At the same time we also recommend it to you, always to keep in view the general utility, remembering that the great and righteous cause in which we are engaged is not provincial, but continental. We, therefore, gentlemen, shall rely upon your patriotism, abilities, firmness, and integrity, to propose, join, and concur, in all such measures as you shall think calculated for the common good, and to oppose such as shall appear destructive.
> By order of the Congress.
> Archibald Bulloch,
> President.
> Savannah, April 5, 1776.[7]

Less than one month after the above, on 1 May 1776, Georgia's Provincial Congress saluted their first Republican President saying:

> May it Please Your Excellency:
>
> The long session of the late Congress, together with the season of the year, called particularly for a speedy recess: and the House having adjourned while you were out of town, it becomes more particularly necessary for us to address your Excellency. All, therefore, with unfeigned confidence and regard, beg leave to congratulate not only your Excellency on your appointment to, but your country on your acceptance of, the supreme command in this Province.
>
> It would be needless and tedious to recount the various and yet multiplying oppressions which have driven the people of this Province to elect that which they have called upon you to see executed. Suffice it thus to declare that it was only an alternative of anarchy and misery, and, by consequence, the effect of dire necessity. Your Excellency will know that it was the endeavor of the Congress to stop every avenue of vice and oppression, lest the infant virtue of a still more infant Province might, in

time, rankle into corruption; and we doubt not that by your Excellency's exertions all the resolutions made or adopted by Congress will be enforced with firmness without any regard to any individual or any set of men; for no government can be said to be established while any part of the community refuses submission to its authority. In the discharge of this arduous and important task your Excellency may rely on our constant and best endeavors to assist and support you.[8]

President of Georgia Archibald Bulloch replied:

Honorable Gentlemen:

I am much obliged to you for your kind expression of congratulation on my appointment to the supreme command of his Colony. When I reflect from whence the appointment is derived, — that of the free and uncorrupt suffrages of my fellow-citizens, —it cannot fail to stimulate me to the most vigorous exertions in the discharge of the important duties to which I am called by our Provincial Congress. While I have the advice and assistance of gentlemen of known integrity and abilities, I doubt not but that I shall be enabled to enforce and carry into execution every resolve and law of Congress. And, as far as lies with me, my country may depend I will, with a becoming firmness and the greatest impartiality, always endeavor to cause justice in mercy to be executed.[9]

Several documents survive from this period that relate to Archibald's presidency and reveal his ardent support of the Patriot cause including this one to John Adams:

Savannah in Georgia

May 1st. 1776

Dear Sir

As a Multiplicity of public Business prevents my revisiting Philadelphia, I have embraced an Opportunity by Major Walton of enquiring after your Welfare; and as he is capable of giving you the amplest Account of the State of this Province, I wou'd take the Liberty of introducing him to your Notice and Acquaintance. I make no Doubt but it will afford you the highest Pleasure to see one irresistible Spirit of Freedom, animating all the Inhabitants of this great Continent. The Ministry never conceived that the Infant Colony of Georgia wou'd so daringly oppose their iniquitous Measures, and notwithstanding the great Number amongst us, under the Influence of Government, that we shou'd so ardently and successfully follow the glorious Examples of our Northern Brethren. From the present Disposition of the People here, their Readiness to expose themselves on every Occasion, and their great Desire of preserving the Grand American Union, there is little Prospect of Success to the Attempts either of our secret or open Enemies. We are determined in all Things to look up to the Continental Congress: On their Wisdom and Prudence we rely; and tho' our local Situation exposes us to many Difficulties, and Dangers, yet we have, and shall continue to pursue at the Risque of our Lives that great Object of our Wishes, the free Enjoyment of our Liberties. The Continental Battalion granted this Province hath made a great Progress in recruiting, and will undoubtedly be very usefull in aiding and supporting the constitutional Authority of this Country. The News that the Ministerial Troops have evacuated Boston hath diffused a general Joy among the People. Such a series of Victory having attended the American Arms, emboldens us further to trust in Providence, that has so remarkably interposed in our behalf, and we cannot but entertain the most sanguine Hopes, of still preserving our most invaluable Liberties. Wishing you Health, and all Manner of Happiness I remain Dear Sir Your affectionate Friend & very hum: Servant

Arch: Bulloch[10]

George Walton (c.1749-1804) had been elected as a Georgia delegate to the Continental Congress in February 1776. For an unknown reason, his arrival in Philadelphia was delayed until late June. He carried this letter from Archibald directly to John Adams as a means of introduction. Archibald had served in the Congress in the Fall of 1775 and was reelected. However, his duties in Georgia prevented him from attending in 1776. George Walton, Lyman Hall, and Button Gwinnett, Georgia's three representatives to the 1776 Congress, signed the Declaration of Independence later that year.

While others traveled to Philadelphia, Archibald took up the reins of leadership and spoke to Georgia's congress on 20 June 1776. His speech can be found in Principles and Act of the Revolution, a document printed in 1822. Archibald directed congress saying:

Mr. Speaker, and gentlemen of the congress—

The state of the province at your last meeting made it absolutely necessary to adopt some temporary regulations for the preservation of the public Peace and safety; and your appointment of me to carry these things into execution, at a time so critical and important to the welfare of this country, requires an exertion of the greatest prudence and abilities.

At a time, when our rights and privileges are invaded, when the fundamental principles of the constitution are subverted, and those men whose duty should teach them to protect and defend us, are become our betrayers and murderers; it calls aloud on every virtuous member of the community to stand forth, and stem the prevailing torrent of corruption and lawless power.

The many and frequent instances of your attachment towards me, and an ardent desire to promote the welfare of my country, have induced me to accept of this weighty and important trust; for your interest only I desire to act; and relying on your aid and assistance in every difficulty, I shall always most confidently expect it.

Some venal disaffected men may endeavor to persuade the people to submit to the mandates of despotism; but surely every freeman would consider the nature, and inspect the designs and execution of that government, under which he may be called to live. The people of this province, in opposing the designs of a cruel and corrupt ministry, have surmounted what appeared inseparable difficulties; and notwithstanding the artifice and address that for a long time were employed to divert their attention from the common cause, they, at length, by imperceptible degrees, succeeded, and declared their resolutions to assert their liberties, and to maintain them, at all events, in concurrence with the other associated colonies. For my part, I most candidly declare that, from the origin of these unhappy disputes, I heartily approved of the conduct of the Americans. My approbation was not the result of prejudice or partiality, but proceeded from a firm persuasion of their having acted agreeable to constitutional principles, and the dictates of an upright disinterested conscience.

We must all acknowledge our great obligations to our ancestors, for the invaluable liberties we enjoy; it is our indispensible [sp] duty to transmit them inviolate to posterity; and to be negligent, in an affair of such moment, would be an indelible stain of infamy on the present era. Animated with this principle, I shall think myself amply rewarded, if I can be so fortunate as to render any service to the cause of freedom and posterity.

Mr. Speaker and gentlemen of the congress—

Being sensible that colony matters of great importance will claim your attention at this meeting, I will not take up too much of your time from the public business. Some further regulations respecting the courts of justice, the state of the continental battalions, and the better ordering of the militia of this province, will necessarily be the subject of your disquisitions. You must be convinced of the many difficulties we labor under, arising from the number that still remain among us, under the shelter of an affected neutrality. The arguments alleged for their conduct, appear too weak to merit a refutation. This is no time to talk of moderation: in the present instance it ceases to be a virtue. An appeal, an awful appeal, is made to Heaven, and thousands of lives are in jeopardy every hour. Our northern brethren point to their wounds, and call for our most vigorous exertions; and God forbid that so noble a contest should end in an infamous conclusion. You will not, therefore, be biassed [sp] by any suggestions from these enemies of American liberty, or regard any censure they may bestow on the forwardness and zeal of this infant colony.—You must evidently perceive the necessity of making some further laws respecting these nonassociates; and though there may be some who appear at present forward to sign the association, yet it becomes us to keep a watchful eye on the motive and conduct of these men, lest the public good should be endangered through this perfidy and pretended friendship.

By the resolves of the general congress, the inhabitants of the united colonies are permitted to trade to any part of the world, except the dominions of the king of Great Britain; and in consequence of which, it will be necessary to fix on some mode of proceeding, for the clearance of vessels and other matters relative thereto; and perhaps you may think it further requisite, to appoint proper officers to despatch [sp] this business, that the adventurers in trade may meet with as little obstruction as possible. And I would at the same time recommend to your consideration, the exorbitant prices of goods, and other necessaries of life, in the town of Savannah, and every part of the province. This certainly requires some immediate regulations, as the poor must be greatly distressed by such alarming and unheard of extortions.

With respect to Indian affairs, I hoped to have the pleasure of assuring you, from the state of the proceedings of the commissioners, that they were in every respect friendly and warmly attached to our interest, and that there was the greatest reason to expect a continuance of the same friendly disposition; but I have received some accounts rather unfavorable. As this is of the highest consequence to the peace and welfare of the colony, I would here suggest, whether it would not be necessary to enter, into some resolves, in order to prevent any future misunderstanding between them and our back settlers; and to this I think I may add, that the putting the province in the best posture of defence [sp], would be an object very requisite at this juncture.

The continental congress have always been solicitous to promote the increase and improvement of useful knowledge, and with the highest satisfaction contemplating the rapid progress of the arts and sciences in America, have thought proper to recommend the encouraging the manufactory of salt-petre, sulphur, and gun-powder — The process is extremely easy, and I should be very glad to see any of the good people of this province exerting themselves in the manufacture of these useful and necessary articles. If they once consider it is for the public good, they will need no other inducement.

Mr. Speaker and gentlemen of the congress—

Remember in all your deliberations you are engaged in a most arduous undertaking. Generations yet unborn may owe their freedom and happiness to your determination, and may bestow blessings or execrations on your memory, in such manner as you discharge the trust reposed in you by your constituents. Thoughts like these will influence you to throw aside every prejudice, and to exert your utmost efforts to preserve unanimity, firmness and impartiality in all your proceedings.

Archibald Bullock. [sp][11]

Several weeks later, Archibald received this reply to his John Adams letter [presented as originally written]:

Philadelphia

July 1. 1776

Dear Sir

Two Days ago I received, your Favour of May 1st. I was greatly disappointed, Sir, in the Information you gave me, that you Should be prevented from revisiting Philadelphia. I had flattered myself with Hopes of your joining Us soon, and not only affording Us the additional Strength of your Abilities and Fortitude, but enjoying the Satisfaction of Seeing a Temper and Conduct here, Somewhat more agreable to your Wishes, than those which prevailed when you was here before. But I have Since been informed, that your Countrymen, have done themselves the Justice to place you at the Head of their Affairs, a Station in which you may perhaps render more essential Service, to them and to America, than you could here.

There Seems to have been a great Change in the sentiments of the Colonies, Since you left Us, and I hope that a few Months will bring Us all to the Same Way of thinking.

This Morning is assigned for the greatest Debate of all. A Declaration that these Colonies are free and independent States, has been reported by a Committee appointed Some Weeks ago for that Purpose, and this day or Tomorrow is to determine its Fate. May Heaven prosper, the new born Republic,—and make it more glorious than any former Republic has been.

The Small Pox has ruined the American Army in Canada, and of Consequence the American Cause. A series of Disasters, has happened there; partly owing I fear to the Indecision at Philadelphia, and partly to the Mistakes or Misconduct of our Officers, in that Department. But the small Pox, which infected every Man We sent there compleated our Ruin, and have compell'd us to evacuate that important Province. We must however regain it, sometime or other.

My Countrymen have been more successful at sea, in driving all the Men of War, compleatly out of Boston Harbour, and in making Prizes of a great Number of Transports and other Vessels.

We are in daily Expectation of an Armament before New York, where, if it comes the Conflict must be bloody. The Object is great which We have in View, and We must expect a great Expence of Blood to obtain it. But We should always remember, that a free Constitution of civil Government cannot be purchased at too dear a Rate; as there is nothing on this Side of the new Jerusalem, of equal Importance to Mankind.

It is a cruel Reflection that a little more Wisdom, a little more Activity, or a little more Integrity would have preserved Us Canada, and enabled Us to Support this trying Conflict at less Expence of Men and Money. But irretrievable Miscarriages ought to be lamented, no further, than to enoble and Stimulate Us to do better in future.

Your Colleagues Hall and Gwinn[ett], are here in good Health, and Spirits, and as firm as you yourself could wish them. Present my Compliments to Mr. Houstoun. Tell him the Colonies will have Republics, for their Government, let us Lawyers and your Divine Say what We will. I have the Honour to be, with great Esteem and Respect, Sir, your, sincere friend, and most humble Servant.[12]

[signed] John Adams

John Houstoun previously served with Archibald in the Second Continental Congress. He earned his living as a lawyer and advocated the Whig cause. Adam's mention of the "Divine" referred to John J. Zubly, Presbyterian minister (Independent Presbyterian Church of Savannah), who served as the other Georgia representative in 1775. Zubly, however, favored reconciliation with Britain. Although he wrote a series of pamphlets and letters supporting the Patriot demands, he continued to believe the revolution was an unlawful act. John Adams reported that Zubly had declared, "A Republican Government is little better than a Government of Devils. I have been acquainted with it from 6 Years old."[13]

Zubly became a loyalist upon his return to Georgia, where the citizens of Savannah branded him a traitor to the Cause. On 1 July 1776, just as Adams wrote to Archibald, Georgia's Council of Safety ordered Zubly's arrest, stormed his home, and threw his library into the Savannah River. Zubly escaped to South Carolina, where Loyalists protected him until the British retook Savannah in 1778. He returned to the city and again took up his pen, writing a series of nine essays under the name *Helvetius* using the Bible and international law to support his views before dying in 1781.

On 8 August 1776, a copy of the Declaration of Independence arrived in Savannah.[14] Archibald Bulloch read the document aloud to the Council of Safety. Most reports of the events that followed indicate Archibald repeated his reading to Savannah's citizens gathered in Reynolds Square two days later in a hastily arranged celebration. In 1892, *Harper's New Monthly Magazine* carried a story entitled "How the Declaration Was Received in the Old Thirteen."[15] The description of the Georgia celebration came last with its author Charles D. Deshler stating:

> Savannah (in Georgia), August 10, 1776, A Declaration being received from the Honourable John Hancock, Esq., by which it appeared that the Continental Congress, in the name and by the authority of their constituents, had declared that the United Colonies of North America are, and of right ought to be free and independent States, and absolved from all allegiance to the British Crown, his Excellency the President and the honourable the Council met in the Council Chamber and read the Declaration. They then proceeded to the Square before the Assembly House, and read it likewise before a great concourse of the people, when the Grenadier and Light Infantry Companies fired a general volley. After this, they proceeded in the following procession to the Liberty Pole: The Grenadiers in front; the Provost Marshall on horseback with his sword drawn; the Secretary with the Declaration; His Excellency the President; the honourable the Council and gentlemen attending; then the Light Infantry and the rest of the Militia of the town and district of Savannah. At the Liberty Pole they were met by the Georgia Battalion, who after reading of the Declaration, discharged their field pieces and fired in platoons. Upon this they proceeded to the Battery, at the Trustees Gardens, where the Declaration was read for the last time, and the cannon of the Battery discharged. His Excellency and Council, Colonel Lachlan McIntosh, and other gentlemen, with the Militia, dined under the Cedar Trees, and cheerfully drank to the United, Free, and Independent States of America. In the evening the town was illuminated, and there was exhibited a very solemn funeral procession, attended by the Grenadiers and Light Infantry Companies, and other Militia, with their drums muffled, and fifes, and a greater number of people than ever appeared on any occasion before in this Province, when George the Third was interred before the Count House in the following manner:

> "Forasmuch as George the Third, of Great Britain, hath most flagrantly violated his coronation oath, and trampled upon the Constitution of our country and the sacred rights of mankind, We therefore commit his political existence to the ground, corruption to corruption, tyranny to the grave, and oppression to eternal infamy, in sure and certain hope that he will never obtain a resurrection to rule again over these United States of America. But, my friends and fellow-citizens, let us not be sorry as men without hope for tyrants that depart; rather, let us remember, America is free and independent! That she is and will be, with the blessing of the Almighty, great among the nations of the earth! Let this encourage us in well-doing, to fight for our rights and privileges, for our wives and children, for all that is near and dear to us. May God give us his blessing, and let all the people say, Amen!"[16]

Another retelling of the reading of the Declaration of Independence, written in 1908, by Lucian Lamar Knight gave a much more colorful version. A small excerpt reads:

Entitled "At Savannah Georgia" from
Harper's New Monthly Magazine, 1892

Together with the Executive Council, he then repaired to the public square and read the document again to the assembled populace of Savannah. It was received with acclamations of great enthusiasm. But still again the document was read, ere the sun intoxicated by the musical accents lit the western horizon into sympathetic flames.

This time it was read to the Georgia battalion at the Liberty Pole in front of Tondee's Tavern, the historic rendezvous of the patriots. It fired the hearts and steeled the nerves of the soldier boys, who were soon to make the lusty echoes ring on the battlefield. At the command of Colonel McIntosh thirteen volleys were fired indicative of the fair sisterhood of sovereign States which comprised the Continental union. Later in the day the tables were spread in the open air and the dignitaries dined under the cedars.

But the final ceremonies took place after nightfall, when the bonfires were kindled- and the mortal ashes of King George were consigned in effigy to the dust. The red glare of the torch, the sharp flash of the bayonets and the struggling moonbeams' misty light, recalled the burial of Sir John Moore. It was an evening never to be forgotten.

But Archibald Bulloch soon fell asleep; and the Declaration of Independence sealed the lips of the old patriot who presided over Georgia's first secession convention.[17]

Demonstrating Archibald Bulloch's extensive correspondence, an early letter from Archibald Bulloch spoke to a controversy between General Charles Lee (1732-1782) and the Georgia colony. Lee, an officer for the British during the Seven Years War, had also served in the Polish army. He moved to the Virginia colony in 1773, became a planter and volunteered in 1775 to serve the patriot cause. He desired the post as commander in chief and took severe offense at the appointment of George Washington to that post. In 1776, his forces repelled a British attempt to capture Charleston, South Carolina. Later in the year, Lee was captured by British cavalry under Banastre Tarleton and held prisoner before being exchanged in 1778. His misguided attack during the Battle of Monmouth later in 1778 led to his court-martial. Many considered Lee a difficult man to deal with due to his resentment over not being given the high command he sought.

> Savannah, 23 August, 1776
> Sir,
>
> We have just received your favour, and, on perusing the Contents, we are apt to imagine some officious Person hath been making false representations to your Excellency. We never entertained any other Idea than that it was your Excellency's Intention to put this Province in a State of Security, & to use your utmost exertions for the safety & protection of the united Colonies. We would not desire to know any thing that may be inconsistent with your honor to communicate, for our real Intentions were ever to afford your Excellency every assistance in our power, at the executive part of the

Constitution, & to render your residence among us, as comfortable & agreeable as possible.

Your Excellency never made any Requisitions that we have not complied with, and, therefore, we apprehend that your request relative to Messrs. Bryan & Joyner must have arisen from some wrong Information. We know of no counter Orders, but on this Principle – that from a further Conference with your Excellency we should be enabled to ascertain, what might yet remain wanting to compleat [sp] your Intentions & we are infinitely concerned that any misapprehension should happen, as we have only acted consistent with our duty to our Constituents, & always meant most heartily to concur with you in every measure that appear to us calculated for the welfare & support of the common Cause.

Some are happy in having your Excellency Presence among us, we would desire not to be understood to interfere in your department, but we would observe, that being answerable for our Conduct to the People, we are obliged in all our proceedings to conduct ourselves in such manner, as to justify our Conduct to them, as Guardians of their rights and Privileges, for which our fellow Citizens have and are daily bleeding.

Before we received your Letter, we had issued 2 orders to Captain Thomas Morris, V & ___ Capt. Joyner will assist him, we shall be obliged to him & think that these two Gentlemen will be sufficient to the Service.

          We have the honor to be
          your Excellency's most obedient
          Servant
          Arch: Bulloch[18]

In 1913, William Harden in *A History of Savannah and South Georgia* revealed some details left out of the Harper's article. For example, more than a year before the Declaration of Independence, Savannah's Patriots, led by Archibald Bulloch, John Houston, Noble W. Jones, and George Walton had erected the Liberty Pole at Tondee's Tavern, located at the corner of Broughton and Whitaker Streets on 5 June 1775,[19].

Archibald Bulloch's influence and leadership, during the years before the American Revolution as the Patriot Cause gained momentum, united the colony in a dream of political freedom. In 1907, one of his descendants wrote "A Biographical Sketch of Hon. Archibald Bulloch, President of Georgia, 1776-77." J. G. B. Bulloch began his sketch with this statement:

> THOUGH there were many men of sterling integrity, bravery and worth during the Revolutionary period, there came a time, as often happens, when one was needed who could steer the barque through shoaly places, avoid

sunken rocks and safely guide her between Scylla and Charybdis. The people of the infant colony of Georgia were divided and it required a man who could unite all parties and safely pilot through many a tortuous channel the young, struggling colony. Apparently there was but one man who could accomplish this task and only one who could keep clear of the breakers and land her in a port where she could be, though with difficulty, anchored in a safe harbor. This man was Archibald Bulloch.[20]

Like his father, James, Archibald Bulloch died before the battle for independence was won. He was buried in Colonial Cemetery in Savannah.[21] His death came only eight months (22 February 1777) after taking office. He was only 47 years of age. The cause of death has never been determined. Many historians have postulated he was poisoned. The inscription on his monument reads:

First President of Georgia 1776-1777

Archibald Bulloch

Born in South Carolina 1730

Georgians! Let the memory of

Archibald Bulloch live in your breasts,

tell your children of him and let them

tell another generation.[22]

Unlike Declaration of Independence signer Button Gwinnett, who died as the result of a duel only weeks after Archibald, Bulloch's name is little known outside of his adopted state. Early patriots and many years later his great-great-grandson President Theodore Roosevelt considered him a Patriot of standing beside John Adams, Thomas Jefferson, and Nathan Hale.

Archibald left a will dated 12 February 1775. This document provided directly for Mary and made her executrix of his will and includes his son James as executor.

> Also, I give, devise, & bequeath to my dear Wife Mary Bulloch, all my Furniture, Goods, household stuff, utensils & implements whatsoever in or belonging to my dwelling house or dwelling houses whatsoever at the time of my death. Also, I give and bequeath to my said dear wife and to all my children that may be alive at the time of my death, all the rest and residue of my personal Estate to be equally divided between them share and share alike, but it is my Will and I do hereby give my said dear Wife full power to name any four of my Negroes to be included in her share in portion the respective share of each child or children to be respectively delivered to them upon their obtaining their ages of years or days of marriage which shall first happen, and it is my further will that the proceeds of my said estate, after the maintenance of my said Wife and Children is deducted be laid out

in Land or Negroes or both as my Executor herein after mentioned shall think fit and most for the benefit of my Estate. But I do order and direct and it is my Will that no part of my Estate be sold. _____ And I do hereby nominate and appoint my said dear wife Mary Executrix and my friends James Deveaux and Joseph Clay - Esquires and my dear son James to be Executors of this my will. But it is my will, and I do hereby order and direct my saidExecutors not to interrupt my said Wife in the management of my Estate and education of my Children as long as she continues my widow,

       Archibald Bulloch. (Appendix A)

Archibald Bulloch and family painted by Henry Benbridge, circa 1775
From left: Archibald Stobo, Mary DeVeaux Bulloch, Jane, Archibald, and James
(only known image)

Chapter III
Captain James Bulloch

Today's history scholars associate the American Bulloch family name more with the American Civil War than they do with the American Revolution. However, a third American generation of Bulloch men carried on the Revolutionary cause just as they carried on the line of distinguished Bullochs. Archibald's children were James (1765-1807), Archibald Stobo (1767-1852), Jane (1768-1787, who married James Benjamin Maxwell), and William Bellinger (1776-1852). Archibald's death, at age 47, left Mary with four children including a newborn. For the next few years, Mary and her children lived either in Savannah or at her father's home at Shaftesbury Plantation on Argyle Island. James DeVeaux, a successful rice planter, owned several plantations on Warsaw and Skidaway Islands as well as Argyle. Evidence that Mary relied on her father during the war for their welfare and safety resides within James' codicil to his will, dated 7 December 1785, in which he cancelled certain obligations due him by Mary. James DeVeaux died before the end of 1785.[1]

The Revolutionary War

In the year following Archibald's death, 1778, Archibald's eldest son, James, enlisted in the Revolutionary cause. Leaving Savannah before the city fell to the British on 29 December 1778, thirteen-year-old James joined (Muter's) Virginia State Garrison Regiment. Earlier in that year, Virginia established this regiment for the protection of Williamsburg, the colony's capital. Comprised of eight companies of sixty men each, the Virginia State Garrison troops patrolled the Tidewater area of Virginia with troops stationed at Hampton, Yorktown, and Williamsburg. It is unrecorded why young James traveled so far to join the cause as he had relatives in South Carolina. Still, by 1780, fifteen-year-old James had risen to the rank of captain.[2]

Mary and her remaining three children continued to support the Patriot Cause providing the new government with various supplies. After the war, Mary appealed to the legislature for restitution of expenses and received, on 10 February 1784, £11.7.3 "for provisions supplied for the use of the Troops." On 14 March 1788, the State of Georgia paid the "Ballance due to Mary Bullock {sp} and settled by order of the House of Assembly, £99-0-8 1/4." The two amounts listed equal approximately $13,646.00 in today's currency.[3]

After the defeat of General Charles Cornwallis in late 1781 and the British withdrawal from Savannah in early 1782, Captain James Bulloch resigned from the Virginia militia and returned to Savannah, where he became active in the Georgia Troops, serving during operations to repel hostile Indians until the war's end with the Treaty of Paris in 1783. After the war, James enjoyed an honorary membership in the Society of the Cincinnati in the State of Georgia and served as captain of the East Savannah Company, 1st Regiment, Georgia Militia from 1786-1789.[4]

Public Service and Family Matters

Obviously, a man of influence and standing, James ran for Chatham County court clerk as early as 1785 at age 20. He won the election. Only four years later, he won the election for superior court clerk in Savannah.[5]

In early 1786, James became heavily involved in the probate of his father's will. Although Archibald had died nine years earlier, the war for independence interfered with many legal matters of the time. Archibald penned his will in 1775 just as he became more and more involved in the Patriot Cause. [Appendix A] Unusual for the time, he made his wife Mary *Executrix* of his estate and left her all of his household furniture and personal goods, as well as four slaves. Except for his real estate, all of his personal holdings went to Mary for her income and to support his children. His real estate holdings were to be divided among his sons. At the division of Archibald's property in 1786, James, age 21, and Archibald Stobo, age 19, had reached their majority while William Bellinger was only 10 years old. James, as the eldest, received first choice of which property he was to inherit. Archibald's children were to receive four slaves each at either their marriage or reaching maturity. His daughter, Jane married James Benjamin Maxwell on 17 February 1786.

Attorney William Stephens verified Archibald's will on 1 March of that same year. William had married Mary's sister, Margaret. His grandfather, the successor to James Oglethorpe, Georgia's founder, had been a proponent of allowing women to inherit. Early Georgia Trustees' policy, commonly called *tail-male land tenure*, prohibited daughters from inheriting land so as to ensure that all freeholders could be soldiers and eligible to defend the colony. Stephens numerous attempts to change the policy failed. However, during this period, many men's wills left personal estates of money, stocks and bonds, and other non-real estate wealth to their wife as *Executrix*. Archibald's will went so far as to instruct his executors "I do hereby order and direct my said Executors not to interrupt my said Wife in the management of my Estate and education of my Children as long as she continues my widow."

At the probate of Archibald's estate, Mary enumerated 36 slaves, 18 men and 18 women. She provided names and values in British pounds. At a total value of £1,880, these enslaved individuals amounted to approximately $238,900 in wealth. At the bottom of the listing of slaves, Mary noted nine head of cattle at a value of

£20 or approximately $2,546.[6] As Archibald left Mary all of his household goods, furniture, etc., none of these items were listed in the probate (Appendix A).

Marriage and Family

On 13 April 1786, James married Anne Irvine (1770-1833), daughter of Dr. John Irvine of Savannah, a Loyalist, originally from Aberdeen, Scotland. Dr. Irvine's family had returned to England during the Revolutionary War where he served as a physician to King George. After the war, the family again journeyed to Georgia where Dr. Irvine helped create the Georgia Medical Society and served many years as a physician in Savannah. Like many Loyalists, Dr. Irvine and his family slowly assimilated back into Georgia society, where after a while, he and his family were once again accepted.[7]

As would be widely reported many years later when Theodore Roosevelt became president, the Irvine line has been researched back to Robert III, King of Scotland (1337-1406) and before him Robert the Bruce (1274-1329), King of Scotland. This lineage continued back for another 200 years or so to Robert de Beaumont, Earl of Leicester (1104-1168) under Henry II of England.[8]

James and Anne named their first child, John Irvine Bulloch (1787-1827) for her father. Another child, Jane joined the family in 1788. Jane would form the family's direct connection to the Dunwody family with her marriage.

In 1793, Anne bore her second son and her second daughter. No record of the exact day of birth for either James Stephens or Anne has been uncovered.[9] They may have been twins or simply born within the same calendar year. James middle name Stephens probably originated with William Stephens (1671-1753) who served as the colony's secretary under James Edward Oglethorpe and later president after Oglethorpe departed Georgia. Stephens was highly regarded among early colonists. His grandson, also named William (1752-1819), married Mary DeVeaux Bulloch's sister Margaret (1759-1807).[10] As brothers-in-law, Archibald and William no doubt discussed such things as inheritance practices. This uncle, through marriage, may have also been an influence upon the young Bulloch children after their father's untimely death.

In November of 1788, James advertised the sale of the personal estate of James Bulloch, his grandfather, listed in most records as "James Bulloch of Wormsloe (James last home)."[11] The ten year delay in the closing of this estate resulted from the intervening war which ended in 1783, and the slow process of establishing governments and courts in the years after the war.

Little is known about Captain James and Anne's life other than their children were raised in Savannah and at times in Liberty County. While James inherited property from Archibald Bulloch, the location and size of this property has not been discovered. Indirectly, he may have received property as part of an inheritance from the first James Bulloch.

James and Ann's two boys received their initial education at the Sunbury Academy near Midway, Georgia. Their names appear on the Academy's list of students for 30 July 1807. Also shown as students are sisters Hester and Matilda Elliott, along with John Law; these three children would join the extended Bulloch family through marriage in the coming decades. It is not known if the Bulloch daughters, Jane and Anne, also attended Sunbury Academy.[12]

By 1781, Sunbury boasted of more than one thousand residents on three hundred acres on the Medway River. After being granted the land by King George II, Mark Carr established the town and sold lots. Carr designated that each of the 496 lots would measure 70 by 130 feet. The town had three squares, King's Square, Meeting Square, and Church Square. The lots along the river housed five wharfs. The Sunbury Academy stood adjacent to King's Square in a two-and-a half story building. In February 1788, the state legislature appointed five commissioners for the academy, Abiel Holmes, John Dunwody, John Elliott, Gideon Dowse, and Peter Winn. These five men were granted the power to raise money for the construction of a suitable house for the school.[13] For over thirty years, beginning in 1793, the Reverend William McWhir, a friend of President George Washington, reigned with an iron hand as the school's Irish headmaster. Boys, who attended from too great a distance to travel each day, lived in a nearby boarding house.[14]

The Sunbury Academy was widely acclaimed and somewhat expensive. A *Columbia Museum and Savannah Daily Gazette* advertisement, dated 26 February 1802, stated the Academy's rates as "For Reading and Writing 25 dollars, For English Grammar [sp], Arithmetic, or Geography 30 dollars." A follow-up announcement on 4 March 1803, in the same newspaper, added "higher branches of mathematics, Belles Letters, or Learned Languages, 35 dollars." Belles letters often refers to the study of literature, in particular, poetry and oratory and may include instruction in writing of both. Yearly tuition rates for the Academy exceeded $600 in 2018 purchasing power, making schooling a very expensive expenditure for the family.[15] Local prominent citizens, John Elliott and James Dunwody, both of whom had close ties to the Bulloch family, served on the Academy's board during those years.

As no real estate records for Captain James Bulloch have been found in Liberty County records, it is possible James rented a home in Sunbury for his family.

Three signers of the Declaration of Independence held ties to Sunbury. Dr. Lyman Hall owned a house on the river front as well as Hall's Knoll Plantation. Button Gwinnett served as the Justice of St. Johns Parish and transacted his private business from the town. George Walton's connection was much more dire as during the Revolutionary War, he was wounded and paroled at Sunbury until his wound healed.[16]

The Bulloch family attended Christ Church when in Savannah where James served as vestryman. When in residence in Liberty County, the family attended the Midway Congregational Church.[17] In 1754, in a log meeting house, a group of Congregationalists established the Midway Society and Church. The nature of the church's teachings was closely related to Presbyterianism and all its ministers were Presbyterian. The first permanent meeting house was built in 1756 but destroyed by the British during the Revolutionary War. In 1792, the congregation built a New England style replacement and painted it red to prevent decay of the wood.[18]

The Bullochs, like most of the wealthier coastal Georgia families, fled Savannah during the summer to escape yellow fever and other seasonal epidemics. Those who could afford the journey often traveled north to Connecticut and other coastal New England states. Others simply retreated to their rural plantations where they hoped to avoid the plagues brought on by Savannah's miserably hot and humid summers.

Setbacks in Life

James ran for re-election to the post of Clerk of the Superior Court in 1795. He posted the following notice in the *Georgia Gazette* on 24 September.

> To the Electors of the County of Chatham. The subscribed, trusting that he has to the utmost of his abilities, and with integrity, executed the duties of his office and finding that several have offered themselves as candidates for the appointment he holds, is induced thus to come forward and request the suffrages of his fellow citizens at the ensuing Election as Clerk of the Superior Court of this county. He returns his sincere thanks for their former countenance and favor, and assures them, that whenever he is possessed of the means of decently supporting himself and his family, he will not impose on them but freely and with happiness resign to him whom they may choose to succeed him.

This was a difficult time in a new country. James had little education and a wife and four children to support. It seems he depended upon his position as his only means of income. Things would only get worse for him and his family.

In late 1796, the Bulloch family lost their Savannah home to fire while they were absent from town. Two widespread fires occurred within days of each other, the first on 26 November and the second on 6 December. The first was described in an editorial printed in the *Columbian Museum and Savannah Advertiser* on 29 November.

> On Saturday the 26th instant this City exhibited a scene of desolation and distress, probably more awfully calamitous than any previously experienced in America, Between six and seven o'clock in the evening a small Bakehouse belonging to a Mr. Gromet, in Market Square, was discovered to be on fire. The citizens, together with the officers and crews of the vessels in the

Midway Congregational Church

harbor, were soon convened; but, unfortunately, no immediate and decisive measures were adopted by which the fire could be stopped at its beginning. The fortunate escape from the destructive element which the City for many years past experienced had greatly lulled the vigilance of its inhabitants, and prevented suitable preparations for such a calamity. The period when such prevention and the united efforts of actual exertion could have been useful was, however, of very short duration. The season for two months previous to this incident had been dry; the night was cold, and a light breeze from N. N. W, was soon increased by the effect of the fire. The covering of the buildings being of wood, were, from the above circumstances, rendered highly combustible. Several of the adjoining houses were soon affected, and then almost instantly in flames. The wind now became strong, and whirled into the air, with agitated violence large flakes of burning shingles, boards and other light substances which, alighting at a distance, added confusion to the other terrors of the conflagration. The use of water was now rendered totally vain, its common extinguishing power seemed to be lost. Torrents of flames rolled from house to house with a destructive rapidity which bid defiance to all human control, and individual exertions were from this time principally pointed towards the securing of private property. The direction of the fire being now committed to the wind its ravages were abated only when, by its extending to the common, it found no further object wherewith to feed its fury. On the north side of Market Square, and thence in a southeasterly direction, the inhabitants were enabled, by favor of the wind, to save their houses and limit the conflagration. On the other hand, by the time it had extended on the Bay, nearly to Abercorn street, the prodigious quantity of heat already produced in the centre of the city began to draw in a current of air from the east, and enabled some of the most active inhabitants and seamen to save a few houses in that quarter, after having been in imminent danger. Between twelve and one the rage of the fire abated, and few other houses from this time took fire. The exhausted sufferers of both sexes had now to remain exposed to the inclemency of a cold frosty night, and to witness the distressing spectacle of their numerous dwellings, covered with smoke and flames, tumbling in ruins. Thus was the little City, soon after emerging from the ravages of a revolutionary war, and which had lately promised a considerable figure among the commercial cities of our sister States, almost destroyed in a single night. The number of houses (exclusive of other buildings) which are burned is said to be nearly three hundred, but of this (together with an estimate of property destroyed) a more particular statement than we can now furnish is expected shortly to be offered to the public. We can now only say that two-thirds of the city appears in ruins, in a direction from the corner of Market Square along the Bay to Abercorn street, thence in a southeast direction, taking the whole centre of the city to

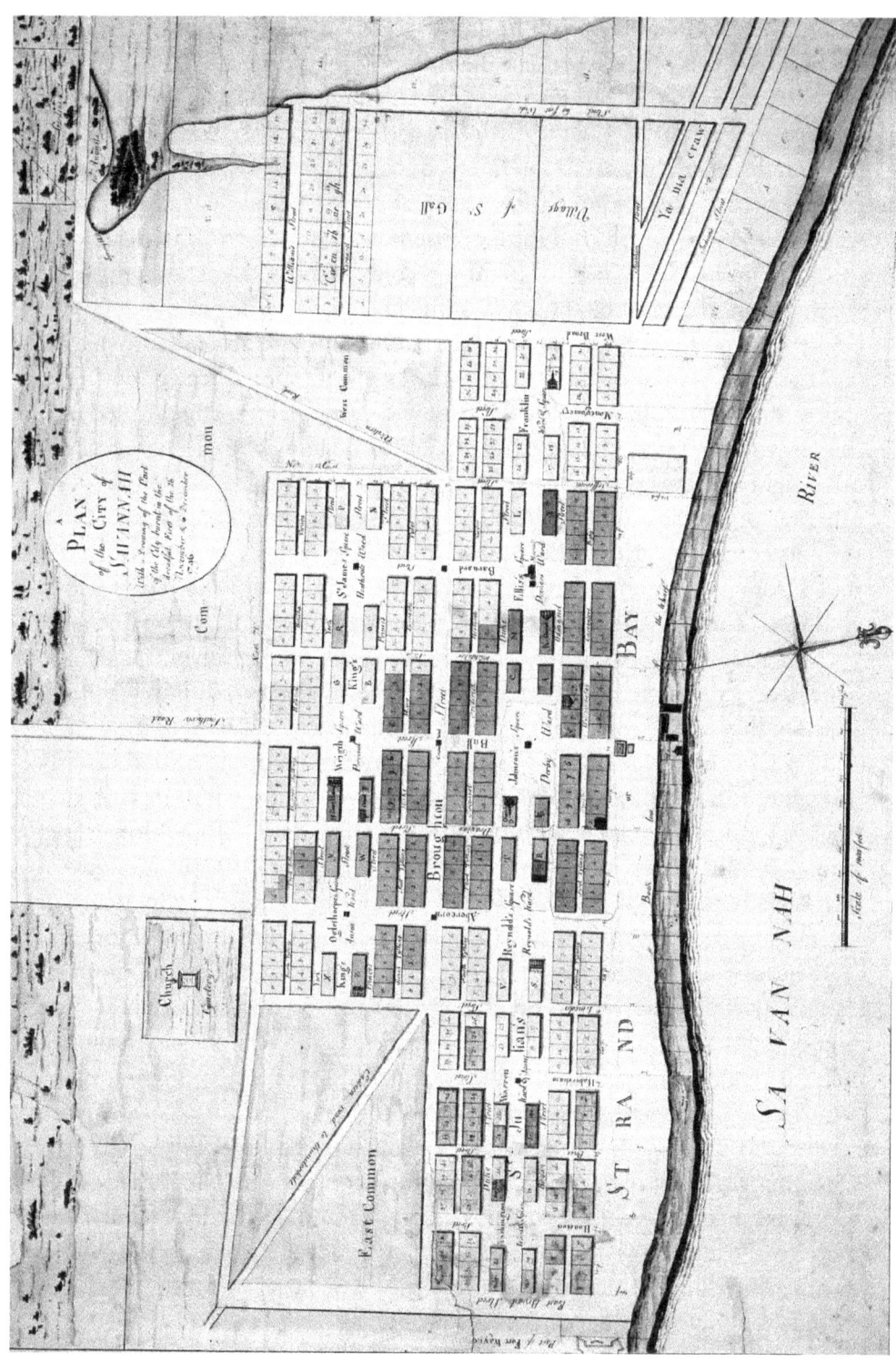

Map of Savannah showing areas burned (darker gray) in 1796 fire.
Marian S. Carson Collection (Library of Congress)

the south and east commons, a few houses quite in the southeast part only excepted. Tis said that three or four white men and two or three negroes lost their lives in rendering assistance during the fire, and whether any more is not yet ascertained. The following statement is just handed, as this paper is going to press : During the conflagration on Saturday night last in four hours 229 houses, besides out-houses, &c., were burnt, amounting to One Million Dollars, exclusive of loose property. Three hundred and seventy-five chimneys are standing bare, and form a dismal appearance—one hundred and seventy-one houses only of the compact part of the city are standing—upwards of four hundred families are destitute of houses. Charities are solicited.

More houses burned on the evening of 6 December, along with Christ Church, located on Johnson Square. The congregation began rebuilding in 1803, yet in 1804, an immense hurricane destroyed the incomplete structure. The second Christ Church was not consecrated until 1815.

After these fires, James placed an advertisement in a local newspaper in search of his desk which had been removed from his burning house during the fire and placed in Church square.

The subscriber and family were absent when the unfortunate event of fire took place, and did not return until some days after. Every article, almost belonging to him, was burned, or are still out of his possession, but particularly his Desk, containing his papers, some deeds, which he had recorded when in the Office of Clerk of the Court, all the cash he owned, and all two hundred and odd pounds, Georgia paper medium. It was in a small mahogany desk, had been much used, but not very much injured, though one foot was defective, and small piece broken off the door. I will be under great obligation to any person, who will give me any information referring to it. My brother, Mr. William Bulloch, thinks it was placed in the Church square.[19]

Historical documents have not revealed if the desk was recovered; however, no further newspaper requests for its return could be found. Most early historic Savannah maps will not show *Church Square*; however, several historic documents revealed it to be the common name used by many early residents for Johnson Square. This square, the first and largest of the original squares, was laid out in 1733. On the east side is Christ Church. The Bulloch home's exact address has not been determined.

A search of Savannah newspapers revealed James' name occurred many times. Most often these were court-related announcements. More personal notices proved difficult to find. However, several newspaper notices indicated James seemed to have trouble keeping up with two personal pieces of property, not counting his desk, for James constantly lost both slaves and horses. The first advertisement for his missing manservant Abraham appeared in December 1787. This advertisement from the *Georgia Gazette* appeared on 9 December 1788.

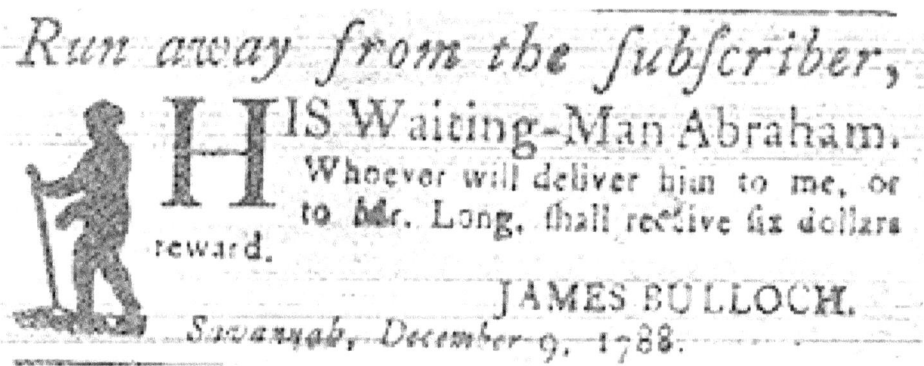

It seems Abraham ran away on numerous occasions, for the advertisements appeared periodically until 1792. The *Gazette* printed this more detailed account on 5 December 1789. It may be that Abraham returned to his Skidaway Island home and family on each of these occasions.

> RUNAWAY
>
> From the subscriber, his waitingman ABRAHAM, the same who was run away and advertised in this paper some time since; he is about five feet ten inches high, of a yellowish complexion, and rather knock knee'd; he was formerly the property of the Hon. Henry Yonge, Esq. deceased, and since his death on the division of his estate, fell to and became the property of Mrs. Christiana Yonge, of Skidaway; he is of the race of old Simon and Phebe, who, with their descendants, were called and known on the main island of Skidaway by the name of the Royal Family. Whoever will deliver unto the custody of Mr. Long, goaler of the county, the said Abraham, shall receive the above mentioned reward.
>
> Tuesday, December 5, 1789   James Bulloch

Interestingly, the advertisement failed to mention the amount of reward to be paid.

It seems that James had just as much trouble keeping up with his horses, for he placed several advertisements for a missing bay horse in 1789, and then, in 1790, for a missing black horse. This notice appeared in the *Georgia Gazette*. Again, historical documents fail to advise if James recovered either horse.

Very little can be gleaned from historical documents about the last years of Captain James Bulloch's life. In May of 1797, in need of office space after the previous year's fire, he leased the east tenement belonging to Mr. George Ash, at 9 Broughton Street, and opened his office there as clerk for the superior court. Office hours were listed as eight o'clock in the morning until two o'clock in the afternoon.[20] Number 9 Broughton Street was located between Drayton and Whitaker Streets. While James

> **STRAYED**
> From the Common,
> A BLACK HORSE,
> About 14 and an half hands high, with a docked tail, rather slender made behind, branded on the mounting shoulder something like a fleur de lis and a heart. Whoever will deliver him to the shall receive two dollars.
>
> James Bulloch.
>
> Savannah, August 17. 1790.

continued to serve as court clerk, he also provided a more official service for his new state. In 1798, Georgia ratified its constitution and reorganized its Superior Court. The first case was filed on 6 March 1799 with the signature of Judge David B. Mitchell and James Bulloch, clerk.[21]

Debts

Savannah's newspapers and court records serve as the only testaments of James' life during the Federal period. Beginning in 1798, Court of Aldermen records, now available on Ancestry.com, indicate James was sued numerous times over outstanding debts. The following contains a summary of findings from 1798 to 1806. While the sums James owed seem to be mostly trivial amounts to readers in the twenty-first century, each amount was exceedingly more in early nineteenth century spending power. To demonstrate the real value in each the 2018 Consumer Price Index purchasing value for each amount is also listed.[22]

30 August 1798 - Thomas Smith vs James Bulloch - JB paid $31.40 (2018 CPI = $661.)

7 February 1798 - Jeremiah Cuyler vs James Bulloch - dismissed

July 1799 - Court of Aldermen - Benjamin Sheftall - $38.62 for writing[?] (asked for damages of $50) - JB ordered to appear on 4th Tuesday in July - withdrawn (2018 CPI = $814.)*

1799 - Ambrose Gordon - $30.40 for a note dated 7 Sept. 1799 - JB ordered to appear on 4th Tuesday in October - JB paid 22 October (2018 CPI = $640.)

1799 - Court of Aldermen - Sarah Cusak, executrix for John Cusak - $4.32 for tailor work - sheriff served copy to James on 10 November - judgement for Cusak on 26 October 1799 (2018 CPI = $91.)

31 December 1799 - Court of Aldermen - Roderick & Norman McLeod (merchants) - indebted for various goods at $100.00 (asked for $200 in damages) - JB ordered to appear on 4th Tuesday in February (2018 CPI = $2110)*

8 December 1800 - JB paid $65.00 to William Burke (2018 CPI = $1,340.)

10 February 1802 - Court of Aldermen - Seymour Tue_olhopten - for $94.80 for printing advertising and James' subscription to the *Columbia Museum* newspaper (2018 CPI = $2,290.)

February 1803 - Court of Aldermen - Thomas P. Chapman - $42.00 for services as a clerk at James' office (asked for $80 in damages) - JB appeared and accepted judgement on 11 April (2018 CPI = $962.)*

February 1803 (directly below Chapman entry) - Court of Aldermen - Ann Lesimger - $54.25 for a dinner provided and breakage (asked for $60 in damages) - JB ordered to appear on 4th Tuesday in April (2018 CPI = $1,240.)*

1803- Court of Aldermen - James Johnston - $92.81 for printing and materials since 1 January 1799 (asked for $100. in damages) - JB ordered to appear on 4th Tuesday in June - James appeared on 18 June and confessed judgement (2018 CPI = $2,130.)*

28 June 1806 - Court of Aldermen - William Camp - JB paid court costs and produced Kenneth Irvine as his security for the payment of the debt.

28 June 1806 - Court of Aldermen - H. Kneeland & Co. - JB paid court costs and produced Kenneth Irvine as his security for the payment of the debt.

* based on initial amount, does not include damages requested as the judgements do not indicate if damages were to be paid.

Based on the dates and amounts owned in this list, (assumed to be incomplete due to age of records and inconsistencies in recognizing names in digitalized records), James appears to have been deeply in debt, beginning not long after the loss of his Savannah home. One might assume that James was simply a poor record keeper, although since he was a court clerk this seems unlikely. Also, his need for a security agent in 1806 strongly indicates he truly was in financial trouble for the last part of his life.

In June of 1804, James offered his house and lot for lease, identified in the *Columbia Museum and Savannah Daily Gazette* advertisement simply as "where I reside." Newspaper accounts show James still serving as Inferior Court Clerk and Justice of the Peace in December of 1804.[23]

Death of Captain Bulloch

Several family genealogical studies list James' death date as 1806; however, the *History of the Georgia Militia* cites Dr. Joseph Gaston Baillie Bulloch's application for membership in the Sons of the American Revolution with a death date of 8 February 1807.[24] James Bulloch died young, being only 41 or 42 years of age. The Register of Deaths for Savannah, dated 8 February 1807, listed his cause of death as "debility, died suddenly. Died at his House." Debility generally is interpreted as unable to walk or get out of bed and is considered an age related illness.[25] However, this sudden death from debility can be interpreted as the result of several illnesses and conditions, either long term or sudden which would bring about bodily weakness, such as a stroke. James was still actively serving as the Chatham County Superior Court clerk, having been recently reelected. Newspapers of the day, carried legal announcements with his signature for several months after his death, indicating that he was carrying out court business shortly before the day of his demise. In this case, *debility* appears to have been used, as it often was, when the cause of death could not be determined.

On 12 February, the *Patriot* carried an announcement for the election of his successor to be held on Monday, 2 March. On 19 February 1807, an announcement listing Thomas Whitefield, Esq. as a candidate for the office appeared in the *Patriot*. The position seems to have been one deemed highly desirable as the article ends with this statement:

> If industry, integrity, and capacity, are qualifications necessary to the due and faithful execution of the appointments sought for, this candidate will yield to none, who have or may after; nor would the present publication have been deemed necessary, if other candidates and their friends, had observed the same delicacy in their conduct.

Two last bits of information about Captain James Bulloch appeared in local newspapers. The first, gathered from this same page of the *Patriot* where an advertisement for his replacement appears reads:

> Sales for House Rent. WILL BE SOLD, At the dwelling house lately occupied by James Bulloch, Esq., dec., in Jefferson street, [illegible] in the south common, near Mr. John Eppinger's between the hours of 10 and 3 [illegible] on Monday next, the 23rd inst.

> Mahogany Dining and Tea Tables, one Mahogany Desk, 2 pair elegant fire dogs and tender, a mahogany chest of drawers, one do [ditto] elegant sideboard, one do bed stead, plated and brass candlesticks, one mahogany knife case, and knives, China glass, and crockery [illegible] Windsor chairs, kitchen furniture, and a variety of other articles distrained on to satisfy John Eppinger, for House Rent. Conditions cash.[26]

Such an advertisement appearing so soon after James' death leads to the impression that his estate did not include sufficient cash for payment of his immediate debts including rent of his Savannah residence. James left behind a young wife and four children, ages thirteen to nineteen.

The second newspaper announcement, dated 23 October 1807, showed James' sudden death also left other affairs unsettled. The article reported the possible discharge from "the Goal of said County" of one "George, alias Charles White" a freeman who was accused on 2 January of that year of "attempting to enveigle [sp] away a negro girl, the property of James Bulloch."[27] No doubt, the case was dismissed after James' death due to his inability to continue the suit.

Ann and the children may not have resided with James in Savannah at the time of his death as indicated by the sale of household items listing only one bed. Given Savannah's climate and the need for the children to be near the Sunbury Academy for schooling, the household appears to have been divided with only James residing almost full time in Savannah. A divided household might also be the reason for the immediate sale of the Savannah residence's household goods. Anne would not need these items, had need of the cash they would bring, and/or no direct means of support. However, archival searches of Liberty County land records have not revealed their exact place of residence nor that James and Anne owned any property in the county.

The Chatham County Tax Digests beginning in 1809 listed a *Mrs. Bulloch* as owning no real estate; however, she did own five slaves for which she paid $2.25 in tax that year and the following one. She either rented a house or quarters for her family during this period. In 1811, the last year she was listed, she owned only four slaves and paid $5.00 in tax. However, this Mrs. Bulloch may be Anne or Mary, James' widowed mother. Little is known about James' family until 1810 when Anne Bulloch remarried on 13 November. She married James Thomas Powell, Jr., a wealthy Liberty County planter. James Powell died in early 1816. John Dunwody served as one of three executors of his will.[28]

Ann Bulloch?

There is a record of another marriage in Liberty County in 1810, containing the name Bulloch. Ann Bulloch married Imla Keep on 20 December 1810. Could this be James' sister? Ann was born in 1793, the same year as James, and was now seventeen years of age. To determine if this was James' sister it was necessary to research Imla Keep.

Dr. Keep, born 31 July 1785 in Groton, Massachusetts, had married Susanna Sylvester on 13 March 1808 at Townsend, Middlesex, Massachusetts. Susanna bore Imla a son, Edwin Sylvester, on 1 May 1808. After this time, Susanna appears to have disappeared from historical records. After Imla married Ann, they moved west toward Texas. One has to assume that Ann died during their journey west, sometime before 1818; for in that year, Imla married for a third time, in Louisiana. This woman, surname Williams, bore Imla a son, Calvin Williams Keep.[29]

By 1820, the Keep family had arrived in Texas as the 1820 to 1829 tax lists for Stephen Austin's colony show Dr. Imla Keep as a resident. Imla marries yet again in Louisiana in 1828. This fourth wife, Leah Hannah was only thirteen years old. She bore three children, two of whom lived to their maturity. In 1837, the Texas Republic's Congress appointed Dr. Keep to its Board of Medical Censors indicating that he still resided in the Republic of Texas. Dr. Keep died in 1854 in Vicksburg, Mississippi, where he had been a resident since at least 1850. While Imla can be traced through census and marriage records, Ann's fate remained unknown after this initial research. Additionally, none of James' personal correspondence, retained in the historical record, nor any of the repeated family stories mention James' sister Ann.

A more recent Ancestry.com search revealed this article which fills in some of the missing information:

> According to the *Descendants of the Keep Family in America*, Imla Keep studied medicine and had set up a practice in Townsend, Mass. where he met his first wife Susanna Sylvester. "…believing that the south would provide better opportunities, he desired to move to the south. His father-in-law objected to Susanna being so far away from her family…" they separated.
>
> Imla traveled south into South America and for a time was a surgeon in the army of General Bolivar. Returning to the United States he married for a second time, Ann Bullock [sp] of Georgia. About a year into the marriage Ann fell from a carriage sustaining injuries that killed her.
>
> His third wife unknown (Williams) O'Neill died from complications from the birth of Calvin Williams Keep in Alexandria, Louisiana. After his marriage to his fourth wife, Leah Hannah Terry, daughter of Champness Terry, a Virginian, he moved his family to Vicksburg, Mississippi where he established a medical practice and accumulated a considerable amount of property. He lived in Vicksburg for the rest of his life.[30]

At this time, it has not been firmly established that the Ann Bulloch who married Imla Keep was James' sister. There were other Bulloch families living in Liberty County during those years; however, no daughters with the name Ann or Anne have been found that fit the time frame or historical record, despite numerous and exhaustive searches of family records.

Death of Mary Bulloch

On 26 May 1818 at seventy years of age, Mary DeVeaux Bulloch, widow of Archibald Bulloch, died of *billious fever* at her home situated on the corner of Broughton and Abercorn streets. The diagnosis of bilious fever by Dr. Soor was one often applied to any fever that exhibited the symptoms of nausea and/or vomiting along with an increase in internal body temperature and strong diarrhea. That Mary was buried that same day indicates the suspicion of contagion. The death index for 26 May 1818 lists five deaths from fever, including Mary.[31]

Her will stated that her estate was to be divided between her two sons, Archibald and William who "shall pay in money in Equal proportion; to the widow & children of my deceased son James Bulloch, one fourth part of the amount of the Valuation & appraisement of my estate, real & personal."

Mary's will noted that she had sold the plantation on Skidaway Island she had inherited from her father James DeVeaux to her son William B. Bulloch for a sum of $2000. The appraisal of her estate dated 4 June 1818 listed thirteen slaves, eight of which are women for a total value of $7,500. One male African slave named John was at $800. *Therysa* [spelled Teresa elsewhere] was noted as "with Mrs. James Bulloch which she may keep at the appraisement at the time of my decease." Another notation gave to "my G.D. [granddaughter] Ann D. Bulloch - my sisters Stephens and M. __ Stephens." The enslaved Diana and Peggy are the only sisters noted in the inventory and appraisement other than Teresa and Charity.[32]

The surname Stephens used by Diana and Peggy may indicate these two women once belonged to Margaret, Mary's sister, who married William Stephens and died in 1807. Enslaved Africans often took their master's surname as their own. However, much may have changed from the writing of Mary's will in 1808 until her death in 1818. She had made two additions, one about the sale of her Skidaway Island plantation and another much more personal about her private belongings.

> My wearing apparel, such as are good, the others to my attendances on my Last & gold watch I leave to my GD Ann D. Bulloch, my sister Stephens & Wm Stephens picture I leave to my niece Mrs. Belcher - Brother and Mrs. Deveaux to my Niece Mrs. Alger - Mr. & Mrs Algers to My Niece M. O. Deveaux. My family p^s [pieces or portraits] to my Eldest son or only son if it should be so at my death - to the longest liver at any rate. All my others to my son William B. Bulloch - unless my unfortunate G S Will B Maxwell should be alive and wish for one - then let him have one if he is fit to have it - all only to say I have not forgot my nieces - am sorry I don't think it in my power to do better - My D. Jane Dunwody must take something to say was mine- and with most ardent wished to meet you all in Heaven. I conclude yours ____ M. Bulloch[33]

From colonial times into the beginning of the new republic, the Bulloch family rose to the forefront of Georgia society by making the most of new opportunities and marrying into the most prominent and wealthy families. By the fourth generation, the third born in North America, Bulloch had become a recognized and notable name. Captain James Bulloch served bravely in the American Revolution, following in the footsteps of his grandfather and father. Unfortunately, historic records leave much unknown about his life.

Chapter IV
Setting the Stage for JSB

Born in 1793, James Stephens Bulloch's birth occurred in the new state of Georgia only seventeen years after the Colonies declared their independence from England. For some twelve years since the end of the Revolutionary War, and six since the signing of the Constitution creating the United States of America, this new nation struggled to find its way as a republic and to establish its place in the world order. Many formal and legal documents of the time still enumerated the new republic's age following the official date.

In the year 1793, George Washington began his second term as president and declared this nation's neutrality in the conflict between France and England. On 10 June, Washington, District of Columbia, became the nation's new capital replacing Philadelphia. As the government continued to settle in Washington, yellow fever struck Philadelphia. Beginning in July and raging well into October, the fever spread rapidly and killed over 2,000 and sickened thousands more of the first capital's residents.

This year also saw two events occur that would directly affect James Stephens Bulloch's life. In February, Congress passed, and President Washington signed into law "An Act respecting fugitives from justice, and persons escaping from the service of their masters." Commonly known as the 1793 Fugitive Slave Act, this law ensured that slave owners would be able to recover their slaves in any state, whether free or slave holding. The other event occurred closer to Bulloch's home, when in early 1793, Eli Whitney invented the cotton gin, a machine that greatly reduced the work needed to process short-staple cotton fibers. This gin, patented in October, automated the separation of cottonseed from the cotton fibers. Whitney carried out his work at the Georgia plantation called Mulberry Grove, once owned by Revolutionary War hero Nathaniel Greene and even earlier by James Stephens Bulloch's great grandfather.

European events in 1793 included the beginning of France's Reign of Terror, which changed forever the way the world viewed the aristocracy and began the creation of modern France's democratic-style government. Much of western Europe was already involved in the French Revolutionary Wars, when the Reign of Terror began in July. Events occurring at this time would lead to the War of 1812.

Three generations of patrician coastal Georgia families created each of James Stephens Bulloch's two marriages. James first married Hester Elliott, daughter of Senator John Elliott. The deaths of Hester and John Elliott led directly to his second marriage to Martha Stewart Elliott. An understanding of the histories and relationships of three prominent coastal Georgia families is necessary to appreciate the fascinating and often confusing interrelationships created by each of James' marriages and his relationship with so many prominent families of Georgia. It is the connections between these families that established the Bulloch's legacy and ultimately led to the birth of America's twenty-sixth president - Theodore Roosevelt.

The Dunwody Family of Georgia[1]

Like the Bulloch family, the Dunwody clan began in Scotland; however, the Dunwodys of Georgia immigrated first to Pennsylvania about 1730. This first American John Dunwody died in 1776, leaving a wife, Susannah, and eight children, three boys and five girls, many of them married with children of their own. Susannah moved south, led there by her oldest son, James, a doctor, who'd settled previously in Liberty County, Georgia. In 1776, he and his brother John were elected to the Council of Safety and the First Executive Council of Georgia.[2]

Dr. James Dunwody married the widow Esther Dean Splatt, who had inherited Arcadia Plantation, near Midway. James served alongside Daniel Stewart and John Elliott as a commissioner of the Sunbury Academy. The family attended the Midway Congregational Church.[3] The couple raised two sons and one daughter, Esther, who married John Elliott in 1795. Her brother John Dean Dunwody graduated from Yale in 1807 and married Jane Bulloch, in 1808. Jane was James S. Bulloch's oldest sister. John Dean Dunwody made his living as an attorney, a factor, and partnered with James S. Bulloch in business for many years. John inherited Arcadia Plantation upon his father's death in 1809. John and Jane had five sons and one daughter.

John D. Dunwody served with Charles Colcock Jones' association for the religious education of the Negro population by serving as superintendent at one of the Sunday school stations organized by the association of planters. At Walthourville, near his plantation, John organized seven teachers, including his wife Jane Bulloch Dunwody. They taught the Bible and religious principles to slaves, who walked to services each Sunday from nearby plantations.[4]

John Dunwody sold Arcadia Plantation to Charles Colcock Jones in 1845. Located near the Midway Church, John had already developed its 1,996 acres and was known for the rice grown in the swampy areas. According to Erskine Clark in *Dwelling Place: A Plantation Epic*, at Arcadia "a fine plantation home stood at the end of a straight, oak-lined avenue that ran perpendicular to the main road. . . The settlement [slave dwellings], located close to the road, was to the left of the avenue as one approached the plantation house and helped to provide not only an impressive entrance but also, for those who lived there, easy access to a wider world."[5]

Dunwody Family Tree in America
(relevent descentants only)

John Dunwody
abt.1680 in Ireland-1749 in Pennsylvania
married
Ann (unknown)

John Dunwody 1707-1776
married
Susanna Cresswell/Criswell 1721-1819

- **Robert Dunwody** abt.1740-1798 — *married* Mary Cresswell
- **Dr. James Dunwody** 1741-1809 — *married* Esther Dean Splatt 1746-1812
- **Margaret Dunwody** abt.1744 — *married* Alexander Maghan
- **John Dunwody** 1745-1824 — *married* Jane Hamilton abt.1750
- **Mary Dunwody** abt.1746 — *married* John Euart
- **Susanna Dunwody** abt.1750 — *married* William Hamel
- **Rebecca Dunwody** abt.1755 — *married* Hugh McWilliams
- **Sarah Dunwody** abt.1755

Children of Dr. James Dunwody and Esther Dean Splatt:

- **Esther Dean Dunwody** 1775-1815
- **Col. James Dunwody** 1782-1833 — *married* Elizabeth West Smith 1794-1879
- **John Dean Dunwody** 1786-1858 — *married* Jane Irvine Bulloch 1788-1856

Children of John Dean Dunwody and Jane Irvine Bulloch:

- **Rev. James Bulloch Dunwoody** 1816-1902
  - *married in 1842* Laleah Georgiana Wood Pratt 1823-1853
  - *married abt. 1856* Ellen Galt Martin 1823-1857 (no issue)
  - *married in 1859* Caroline Indiana Havgood 1837-1894
- **John Dunwody, Jr.** 1818-1903 — *married in 1849* Elizabeth Clark Wing 1825-1898
- **Jane Marion Dunwody** 1821-1885
  - *married in 1840* Rev. Erwin Stanhope 1821-1840 (no issue)
  - *married in 1851* Dr. William E. Glen 1800-1853 (no issue)
- **Dr. William Elliott Dunwody** 1823-1891 — *married in 1846* Ruth Ann Atwood 1823-1891
- **Henry Macon Dunwody** 1826-1863 — *married in 1852* Matilda Elizabeth Maxwell 1829-1902
- **Charles Archibald Alex. Dunwody** 1829-1905 — *married in 1852* Ellen Rice 1827-1895

The Elliott Family of South Carolina and Georgia

With his family, Captain John Elliott (1730-1765) moved from the Dorchester - Beech Hill area of South Carolina to Georgia's Midway region [now Liberty County], in 1754, as one of the original grant holders. Early records, dated 5 March 1756, show grants of 500 acres in the District of Midway and 300 acres in the District of Newport. Other grants added 50 additional acres in the District of Midway on a branch of the Medway River and 250 acres in St. Johns Parish.[6] From the beginning of his residence in Georgia, John is identified as "Captain John Elliott"; however no record of military service, including militia, has been found. Elected as a representative to the General Assembly on 31 January 1755, John also served as one of the founders/trustees of the town of Sunbury in 1758. He died on 30 July 1765.[7]

The second John Elliott (1750-1791) joined the revolutionary cause, receiving his commission on 9 July 1777, as a lieutenant colonel in the 1st Battalion, Third Regiment, Georgia Militia. He was elected colonel around March of 1778. His service to the Cause included, in particular, the defense of the small villages of Sunbury and Midway along with the remainder of St. Johns Parish. On 30 January 1783, he took the oath of office for Georgia's House of Representatives representing Liberty County.[8] Later, he served on the board of commissioners for the Sunbury Academy, a school constructed in 1788.

Colonel John Elliott married Rebecca Jane Maxwell (1752-1781) of Midway in 1770, who gave birth to the third John Elliott in 1773. Four additional children resulted from this union with only John and Daniel Roberts (1779-1810) living to maturity. After Rebecca's death, Colonel John married Mary Bliney (1751-1789) in 1782. They had four children, none of whom lived more than three years. After Mary's death, Colonel John married Amarintha Renchie Norman Quarterman (1771-1807) on 1 July 1790. Renchie, only 19 years old at the time, had married Thomas Quarterman in 1787. Thomas died in 1788 leaving her with a small child, also named Thomas (1788-1857). Renchie and John Elliott had one child, William. William and his father both died in 1791. Renchie married Reverend Cyrus Gildersleeve of the Midway Congregational Church after John's death.[9]

The Colonel was one of three representatives from the county to the 1788 convention in Augusta that ratified the new Federal Constitution.[10] John and his family were related through marriage to many of the prominent families in Liberty, Chatham, and Burke counties. Colonel John Elliott died on 7 June 1791.[11] An appraisement of John's estate showed that he owned 57 slaves, including 18 *fellows*, 13 *wenches*, 13 *girls*, and 13 *boys*. [Appendix A]

The third John Elliott, born on 24 October 1773, studied law at Yale University receiving his degree in 1794. After completing his degree, John practiced in Sunbury. He ran for and was elected state representative in 1798 and again in 1800, representing Liberty County. He also owned extensive land holdings in Liberty,

Elliotts of Georgia
(relevent descendants only)

Captain John Elliott
1730-1765
married
Elizabeth Way
1720-1785

Children of Captain John Elliott and Elizabeth Way:

Colonel John Elliott
1750-1791
married
Rebecca Jane Maxwell
1752-1781

Thomas Elliott
1757-1797
married
Ann Baker
1759-unknown

(Two additional marriages, see text for names)

Amarinthia Elliott
1759-1826
married
Daniel Roberts
1750-by 1785

married in 1785
Capt. John Whitehead

Ann Elliott
1746-1771
married
Gideon Dowse

William Elliott
unknown-1769

Children of Colonel John Elliott and Rebecca Jane Maxwell:

Ann Elliott
1771-1772

Senator John Elliott
1773-1827
married in 1795
Esther Dean Dunwody
1775-1815

Thomas Elliott
1776-unknown

Elizabeth Elliott
1776?-unknown

Daniel Roberts Elliott
1779-1810
married
Betsy Hayward Thecher
1752-1781

Children of Senator John Elliott and Esther Dean Dunwody:

Carolina Matilda Elliott
abt. 1796-before 1827

Hester Amarinthia Elliott
1797-1831
married
James S. Bulloch
1793-1849

John Elliott
1801-1803

Rebecca Jane Elliott
1803-1804

Jane Elizabeth Elliott
1809-1829
married
Dr. John Law

John Elliott
1807-1813

Corinne Louisa Elliott
1813-1838
married
Robert Hutchinson
1802-1861

Charles James Elliott
1816-1817

Children (third marriage):

married in 1818
Martha Stewart
1799-1864

John Whitehead Elliott
1818-1820

Susan Ann Elliott
1820-1905
married
Hilborne West
1818-1907

Georgia Amanda Elliott
1822-1848

Charles William Elliott
1824-1827

Daniel Stewart Elliott
1826-1862
married
Lucinda Ireland Sorrell
1829-1903

JSB - 47

Glynn, and Burke counties, holding in 1801 some 1,556 acres. In 1804, John purchased Cedar Grove Plantation on the Medway River near Sunbury which contained some 894 acres for $3,000.[12]

On 27 February 1809, John acquired three additional plantations in Liberty County. John purchased Fairlawn, Rural Felicity, and Butler's Tract from Dr. Charles W. Rogers and his wife Ann for $4,500. The three plantations contained some 1,123 acres. The same deed recorded the sale of 28 slaves for "consideration of $11,150." John's purchases for a total of $15,650 in 1809 equaled roughly $330,000 in 2018.[13] John continued to add to his holdings, obtaining 150 acres of Hester's Bluff from William Maxwell, Sr., in February of 1811, and 150 acres of the same plantation from John Maxwell in May of that year. A bill of sale also transferred five slaves from John Maxwell to John Elliott on the same date.[14] On 4 July 1814, John purchased for $3,600 additional lands in Liberty County.[15]

On 1 October 1795, he married Esther Dunwody (d.1815), daughter of Dr. John Dunwody. John and Esther maintained homes on his Laurel View Plantation and in Savannah. They had several children, including, Caroline Matilda (baptized 11 December 1796, died between 1822 and 1827), Hester Amarinthia (born 2 December 1797, died 1831), John (born 1801, baptized 4 April 1802, died 7 September 1803), Rebecca Jane (born July 1803, died 1804), John (baptized 13 December 1807, died 30 October 1813), and Jane Elizabeth (born June 1809, died 1829). Midway Church records also list a daughter born in 1813; other sources reveal this to be Corinne Louisa (1813-1838). An additional child, Charles James (baptized 25 February 1816, died 6 August 1817, probably by the same fever that took so many of the small congregation) was listed as "son of John" in the baptismal records of the Midway Church. John's wife Esther had died in 1815, probably due to or shortly after the birth of Charles James. His delayed baptism occurred after a period of mourning, following his mother's death.[16]

In 1811, John ran unsuccessfully for a U.S. Representative seat on the Federalist ticket. The Federalist Party, or First Hamiltonian Party, founded in 1789, believed in a strong national government to promote economic growth and friendly relationships with Great Britain. The party opposed the revolutionary forces in France. That same year, Liberty County elected John to the Georgia legislature, where he was assigned to the committee on privileges and elections.[17]

John Elliott served with Daniel Stewart and James Powell as Commissioners of the Cemetery at Midway Meeting House (later called the Midway Congregational Church). On 12 January 1811, an advertisement appeared in Savannah papers announcing a "Scheme of a Lottery" for the purpose of raising $1,500 to erect an enclosure around the burial ground adjacent to the Midway church. The advertisement ran in various papers for several weeks.[18]

John Elliott served in the military and was instrumental in establishing defenses for Sunbury during the War of 1812. He served with Revolutionary War General Daniel Stewart on the Committee of Safety, which called upon the county's inhabitants for its defense. This committee directed the rebuilding of Sunbury's fort. Elliott and Stewart's relationship from this time greatly impacted the future of their offspring.

John remarried in January of 1818. Elected by the Georgia Legislature to the U.S. Senate in March of 1819, John served one term, 1819 to 1825. Assigned to committees on military affairs and pensions, Senator Elliott voted for the Public Lands Act of 1820 which eliminated the purchase of public land on credit. This law also reduced the minimum size of such tracts from 160 to 80 acres, making its cost more obtainable, encouraged westward expansion, and limited squatter's rights. John also voted for the Missouri Compromise and gave "perhaps the finest speech of his career" in opposition to the tariff bill of 1824[19]. After his term ended in 1825, the family returned to Savannah, where John became the director of the Planter's Bank and resumed his role as a planter in Liberty County.

The Stewart Family of South Carolina and Georgia

The first Stewart came from South Carolina to settle in the Sunbury-Darien-Midway area in about 1756. Differing sources place the family's origins in Scotland and England; however, recent research confirms the family to be of Scots origin. The first emigrant John Stewart (died 1763) and his wife, Jerusha (died 1762) disembarked in the new world in North Carolina and had settled in the Dorchester area of South Carolina by 1723. A second John Stewart, of whom little is known, married a woman

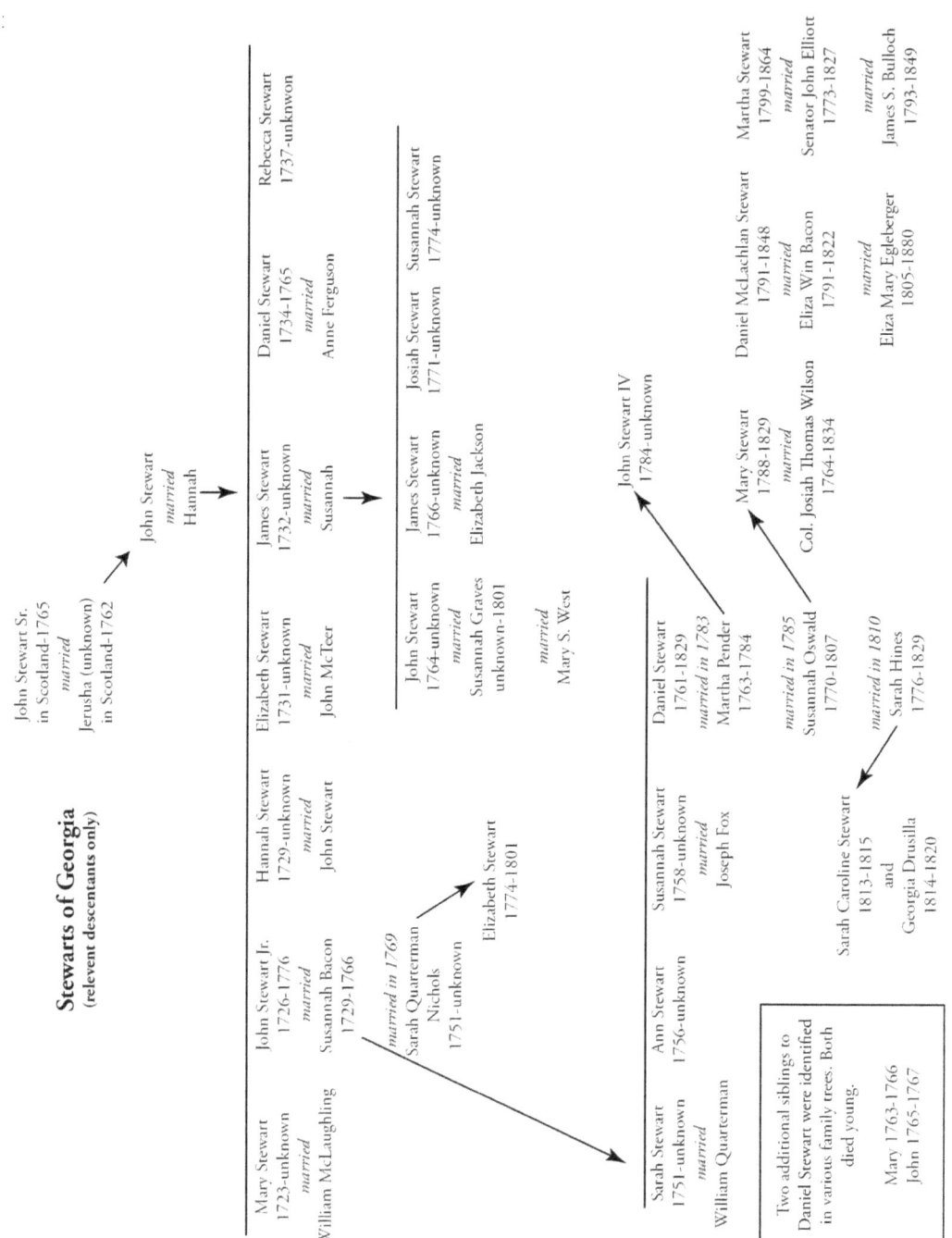

Dorchester and received the land grant that brought the family to the Midway area. In Georgia, John and Susannah established Tranquil (sometimes called Tranquilla) Plantation on the New Port River and were among the founders of the Midway

Congregational Church. They had at least six children; however, daughter Mary and her mother Susannah, both died in 1766. John Stewart III died in 1767. Susannah's death left John with three surviving children; Sarah, born 1750, Susannah, born 1758, and Daniel, born 20 December 1761.[20]

In 1769, John, Jr., married Sarah Quarterman Nickols. They had one child, Elizabeth, born in 1774. John Stewart, Jr., briefly served as a militia officer in the Revolutionary cause before his death on 6 September 1776. That same year, fifteen-year-old Daniel enlisted in the Georgia militia and served under the command of Colonel John Baker's Continental Light Horse of Liberty County. For two years, this unit attempted unsuccessfully to rout the British from Georgia and Florida.[21]

In 1778, Daniel, now a member of a unit organized for the defense of Charleston, South Carolina, was wounded and captured by the British. While held aboard a British prisoner-of-war ship in Charleston harbor, Daniel escaped, along with several other prisoners, and swam to shore. Afterward, while hiding with South Carolina relatives, he met his first wife, Martha Pender (1763-1784). They married on 20 February 1783; however, she died in childbirth, leaving behind their son John, born 21 March 1784. Meanwhile, promoted to colonel, Daniel established a cavalry brigade, the Minutemen of Georgia, and served as their commander.[22]

After the war, Stewart returned to Liberty County and resided at Tranquil Plantation. In 1785, he married Sarah Susannah Oswald (1770-1807) and sent for his son, who had lived under the care of South Carolina relatives since birth. This marriage produced three surviving children, Mary in 1788 (d.1829), Daniel McLachlan in 1791 (d.1848), and Martha in 1799 (d.1864). Three additional children, two daughters and a son, died either as infants or young children.[23]

Daniel served as a state representative from 1785 to 1787, Liberty County sheriff from 1795 to 1797, and state senator for three terms between 1802 and 1811. He continued as a planter, served in various military positions, and was active in Masonic rites and veterans' meetings and affairs. In 1809, Stewart was promoted to brigadier general in the Georgia Militia and commanded a cavalry brigade during the War of 1812. Again, using his military acumen, Stewart was involved in resolving the Creek Indian wars and the defense of nearby Sunbury, Georgia.[24]

Daniel's second wife died in 1807, and in 1810, he married Sarah Hines Lewis (1776-1829). Her father gave the couple Cedar Hill Plantation as a wedding gift. This third marriage produced one son, Edmond, who died in June of 1817,[25] and two daughters, Sarah Caroline (1813-1815) and Georgia Drusilla (1814-1820). Both died very young and were buried in the Midway cemetery. Their tombstones lie next to their parents and place their births at the General's Tranquil Plantation.

General Daniel Stewart died at his Cedar Hill Plantation near Sunbury on 27 May 1829. Charles Colcock Jones with his wife-to-be and cousin Mary Jones were by Daniel's side, having stopped to see the General before their journey north, as Charles planned to study at Princeton. Charles and Daniel had made their profession of faith together, some seven years earlier, before the congregation of the Midway Church. Charles recorded in family letters that he "reminded him [General Stewart] of Christ's gracious promises, and watched his father's hunting friend and brother-in-law close his eyes in death."[26]

In 1915, the U.S. Congress erected a monument in the Midway cemetery in honor of Generals Daniel Stewart and James Screven. The monument reads:

East Face: *Reared by the Congress of the United States as a Nation's Tribute to Brigadier Generals James Screven and Daniel Stewart*

West Face: a copper relief of Midway Church

South Face: *1759-1829 Sacred to the History of Brigadier General Daniel Stewart A Gallant Soldier in the Revolution and an Officer Brevetted for Bravery in the Indian Wars*

North Face: *1750-1778 Sacred to the memory of Brigadier General James Screven, who Fell, Covered with Wounds, at Sunbury, Near the Spot, on the 22nd Day of November, 1778. He Died on the 24th Day of November, 1778 from the Effects of his Wounds.*

Daniel Stewart and his wife Sarah's personal tombstones read as follows:

Gen. Daniel Stewart, died May 27th 1829: aged 70 years. An honest man. This Stone Marks the Spot Where, Beside His Wife and Children, Repose the Remains of Brigadier General Daniel Stewart in Recognition of Whose Life and Services the Congress of the United States Has Reared a Monument in This Cemetery. He was one of the Youthful Patriots Who Fought to Achieve the Independence of America, and Who Later Rendered Signal Service to His Country, Being Brevetted by the Legislature of Georgia for Bravery in the Indian Wars.

Sacred to the Memory of Mrs. Sarah Stewart, who was born in N.C. 7th October 1776, & died at the Sand-Hills in this county after a distressing illness of ten days, Oct. 7th 1829. aged 55 years. Blessed are the dead which die in the Lord from henceforth: Yea, Saith the Spirit, that they may rest from their labours; and their works do follow them.

An Intermingling of Families

By 1812, the United States had experienced the continued rise of the Federalist and the Democratic Republicans and put into office John Adams (1797-1801) and Thomas Jefferson (1801-1809). In March of 1809, James Madison, another Democratic Republican came into office.

In Savannah, James Stephen's oldest sister, Jane, married John Dean Dunwody during the summer of 1808 at twenty years of age. John and Jane's family remained active in the life of James Stephens until his death. John and Jane raised five sons and one daughter to maturity. Their eldest son was named James Bulloch Dunwody. James Stephens would later name his second son, James Dunwody Bulloch.

James Stephens' older brother John Irvine remained at home until 1814 when he married Charlotte Glen, daughter of John Glen, Chief Justice of Georgia, from 1776 to 1778, and Sarah Jones, daughter of Dr. Noble Wymberly Jones. Sarah was the step-grandniece of John's great grandfather, the first James Bulloch in America. John Irvine served as an attorney in Savannah and became active in politics. John and Charlotte parented two children that lived to maturity.[27]

Both of James' paternal uncles, Archibald Stobo Bulloch and William Bellinger Bulloch, took an interest in James and his siblings after their father's untimely death in 1807. James, only fourteen at his father's death, seems to have been influenced and guided by these men. While historical evidence of their legal obligations has not been uncovered, it seems likely that one or both men were appointed legal guardians of Captain James Bulloch's children to protect their inheritance and provide them with fatherly advice as was common during this age when women were seen as unfit to handle money. As Captain James Bulloch left little money or property, it is possible these two men helped support the family.

While some sources state Archibald Stobo Bulloch (1775-1859) served as a naval officer during the War of 1812, the alphabetical card index to the compiled service records of volunteer soldiers who served during the War of 1812 list him as "Private, 1st Regiment (Johnston's) Georgia Militia." He later served in the Savannah Heavy Artillery. His professional interests included buying and selling real estate as well as a successful factorage and commission business. He participated in Savannah politics and was elected to and appointed to various positions. Archibald served as the tax collector for the port of Savannah and invested in the *Steamship Savannah*.[28]

Savannah's citizens elected William Bellinger Bulloch (1777-1852), a lawyer, mayor from 1809 to 1812. During the War of 1812, he served in the Savannah Heavy Artillery. After Senator William H. Crawford's resignation, William filled his vacated U.S. Senatorial seat for five months in 1813, before serving as city alderman in 1814 and again in 1824.[29] Like many of Savannah's elite, William owned extensive agricultural land along with other real estate. William's banking career spanned twenty-seven years, after being a founding member of the State Bank of Georgia. He held the position of president from its founding until 1843.

Chapter V
The Professional Life of a Southern Gentleman

Accounts of James Stephens Bulloch's professional life, revealed in several popular books about his descendants and recent biographical sketches, fall far short of its actuality and each seems to contain various inaccuracies. His careers involved a wide range of interests and pursuits, as did those of many southern gentlemen during the early nineteenth century. James occupied himself at various stages in life as a military officer, factor, attorney, investor, banker, and plantation overseer/owner, and politician. Like many of his day, he excelled in some realms, dabbled in many, and failed at several.

JSB - Military Officer

In December 1807, President Thomas Jefferson asked Congress for, and received, a bill ordering an "embargo on all ships and vessels in the ports and harbors of the United States" following a period of impressment of American sailors and disruption of commerce by Great Britain.[1] This action resulted from several years of unrest between the new nation and Great Britain, where "the great and increasing dangers with which our vessels, our seamen and merchandise are threatened on the high seas and elsewhere, from the belligerent powers of Europe."[2] The embargo followed a year of Jeffersonian statements that riled a nation into action, especially citizens of port cities. Already, in 1807, the citizens of Savannah had formed a military company, the Republican Blues. On 9 July 1807, a special meeting of council recommended the removal of thirteen casks of gunpowder from the city's magazine to prevent its being "removed from the magazine for improper purposes."[3] Fourteen-year-old, James Bulloch stood witness to these events during a tumultuous year that began with the 8 February death of his father.

The Republican Blues continued to organize and recruit, as hostilities between the two nations climbed, and many foresaw the coming of yet another conflict to secure the young nation's independence. On 22 May 1812, Savannah's city council resolved to invite the city's citizens to meet at the "Court house on Saturday, the 30th inst. [instante mense, meaning a date of the current month] At 12 o'clock for the purpose of taking into consideration the present situation of their country, of expressing their opinion thereon, and of adopting such other business as their patriotism may dictate."

On 3 June, the city recognized "the grievances against both England and France, which they deemed sufficient to cause war, and calling for the seizure by the United States of East Florida."[4]

Like his father and grandfathers before him, James felt the need to serve his country. Along with a group of Savannah's young men on 17 June 1812, James joined in a meeting for the sole purpose of receiving subscriptions for the formation of a volunteer company. James' name is first on the list of those assigned to elicit and receive subscriptions.[5] Unfortunately, no additional newspaper notices of this subscription drive have been uncovered, and there is no other reference to a military company being formed at that time. At 18 or 19 years of age, James most likely continued his education by reading the law under one of his uncles or perhaps John Dunwoody, his brother-in-law. It is also possible that James attended a university at this time; however, no evidence for such has been uncovered.

Many young men of Savannah answered the call; many enlisted that day in early June and encamped at the South Common where they remained until 21 June. On that day, they struck their tents and marched off to war in heavy rain "accompanied by the best wishes of their fellow-citizens who had assembled in crowds on the shore for the purpose of taking leave."[6] Escorted and saluted with cannon fire by the Chatham Artillery and the Chatham Rangers, they proceeded down the river in gunboats. As no actual fighting occurred around Savannah, the regiment saw no action.

On 2 September 1814, Savannah's city council called its citizens to action to defend the city against imminent attack. They urged residents to assist in the building of breastworks. James' uncle, William Bellinger Bulloch, a city alderman, served on one of the council's committees for specific action. Various groups worked with the military officers, while another called the citizens to action and requested funding (donations) for the city's defense. Slave owners received requests for their male slaves to provide labor for the building of the defensive works. Yet another committee worked to "guard against the introduction of suspicious characters into the city, and to have weekly returns from all taverns, lodging and boarding-house keepers of the numbers, names and business of such persons, and to act towards them as the law and ordinances direct, and they are required to aid in ascertaining the earliest information of the approach of the enemy by land or water."[7]

The war progressed far from Savannah until the Battle of New Orleans on 8 January 1815, which occurred despite the signing of a preliminary treaty in Ghent Belgium on 24 December 1814. While General Andrew Jackson took on the British outside New Orleans, Admiral Sir George Cockburn landed on Cumberland Island, off the coast of Georgia on 10 January. Cockburn planned to tie up forces in Georgia to prevent their reinforcement of Jackson's forces in Louisiana. An American battery at Point Peter, on the mainland across from Cumberland, became Cockburn's next objective. A running battle occurred between these forces, resulting in Cockburn taking the small town of St. Marys.

As this occupation became known, James signed with the 60th Battalion, 1st (Johnston's) Regiment, Georgia Militia, as an ensign (lowest commissioned officer within a unit)[8] His active service began on 22 January and ended on 23 February. In early February, Cockburn became informed of the treaty signing and withdrew after the ratification of the treaty on 17 February. James short term of service came during a period of increased military preparation for the defense of Georgia.

James continued his military service with the Georgia Militia, despite the end of hostilities. Militia regimental history for the 60th Battalion, 1st Regiment, Georgia Militia shows that James, commissioned captain in July of 1816, rose to the rank of major on 9 August 1817 when he took command of the 60th. He was commissioned as major on the 20th of that month, and served until 1822.[9] During those intervening years, James served as the commander of 3rd Beat Company, also called the Courthouse Company.[10] At some point, James joined the Chatham Artillery, as the *Savannah Georgian* newspaper notice of his service to this organization reports his election as first lieutenant on 4 February 1826. Despite this notice, a notice of the Savannah Georgian on 3 August 1824 named him "Major of the Regiment."

The Chatham Artillery served as Savannah's elite militia during the early 1800s and a gentleman's club as a military unit. Recognized as Georgia's oldest military organization, the unit organized on 1 May 1786, with its first duty occurring the following month, when the unit provided funeral honors for General Nathanael Greene, who then resided at Mulberry Grove Plantation, the one-time home of James' great grandfather. The residents of Georgia had gifted the plantation to the General after the war. The Chatham Artillery participated in the Oconee wars from 1789 until 1793. In 1791, in appreciation for services, President George Washington presented the unit with two cannons, one captured at Yorktown and one given by France.[11] In 1815, during the War of 1812, the unit was federalized and assigned to Fort Jackson on Savannah River. They again served as an honor guard in May of 1825 during the Marquis de Lafayette's fifteen-month tour of the new American nation. No doubt, James participated in these celebrations, for in August of 1824, James was noted as Major of the Regiment.[12]

James' service in the Texas War of Independence (1832-1836) remains widely reported in books and articles, in particular those about President Theodore Roosevelt. Despite extensive research into this action and Georgians who actually did participate, no evidence of such service has been uncovered. Further evidence of this story being nothing more than family lore, is James' documented presence in Savannah during these war years. Newspaper articles refer to his activities as a factor, politician, and businessman during the war's four-year period.[13]

JSB's Education

Exhaustive research has uncovered no formal education for James Stephens Bulloch except for his attendance at the Sunbury Academy. However, it is quite possible, James studied law under the auspices of an attorney or continued his formal education during his teens. His formal writings are legible, astute, and knowledgeable on a variety of subjects. As early as 1818, twenty-one-year-old James was listed in at least two newspaper notices as *Attorney* for various individuals, including his mother, Anne Powell, who remarried in 1810 and became widowed a second time in 1816, and his brother-in-law John Dunwody.[14]

Setting for JSB Entereing Business

By the time James, age 22, entered the business world in 1815, James Madison (1809-1817) served as the nation's fourth president; however, King George III still ruled the British Empire. The United States' struggle with England ended on 8 January with the Battle of New Orleans, although a truce had been signed on 24 December 1814. In 1815, Napoleon escaped from Elba and established his 100-day rule. In 1816, the Treaty of St. Louis was signed, and James Monroe elected president. The next year, 1817, saw the beginning of the Seminole Wars in Florida during which James' future father-in-law General Daniel Stewart would distinguish himself. The White House reopened on 1 January 1818 after having been burned by the British during the War of 1812. Mary Shelley published "Frankenstein; or, The Modern Prometheus" while Byron and Keats wrote popular poetry. "Silent Night" was sung for the first time in Austria, and Handel's *Messiah* premiered in Boston.

King George IV replaced George III on 29 January 1820. Early that same year, Congress passed the Missouri Compromise allowing Missouri to join the United States despite slavery still being legal there. Later in the year, the populace reelected James Monroe as president. On 2 December 1823, President James Monroe declared his "Monroe Doctrine." This foreign policy regarding Latin America would affect the growth of the United States for years to come. One year later on 1 December, the U.S. House of Representatives met to decide the outcome of the election deadlock between John Quincy Adams and Andrew Jackson. Despite Jackson winning the popular vote, President John Quincy Adams took office in 1825. The young country prospered during this period while still establishing a foothold in foreign markets.

JSB - Factor

In 1816, if not earlier, James entered the world of commerce, serving as a factor or middle man/wholesaler of plantation crops and goods, as well as merchandise from New York and Philadelphia.[15] As a factor, an agent entrusted with the possession of goods to be sold in the agent's name or a merchant earning a commission by selling goods belonging to others, his responsibilities included purchasing and arranging for the shipment of plantation crops such as cotton, rice, indigo, corn, and lumber, to Savannah and then on to other ports and other buyers. As early as 1818, newspaper notices indicate James was purchasing rice and cotton for resale.[16] James married Hester Elliott, daughter of politician and planter John Elliott, in December 1817. Now with a wife to support, James apparently threw himself into his business ventures.

James first partnership in the factoring business appears to have been with George Sadler. The first mention of this firm appeared on the 7 January 1820 in *The Daily Georgian*. Throughout the late summer and autumn of 1820, the *Savannah Republican* ran the following announcement from the firm:

> Notice. The public are forbid to negociate [sp] the Notes hereafter enumerated, as they have never been legally transferred by the subscriber, via Low, Wallace & Co.s to Bulloch & Sadler, dated 17th March 1820, and due 17th Sept. 1820 for $684 161-1000.
>
> J.P. Williamson to Bulloch & Sadler, dated 26 July, 1820 and due six months from date, $561_9 1-00.
>
> Jas. S. Bulloch

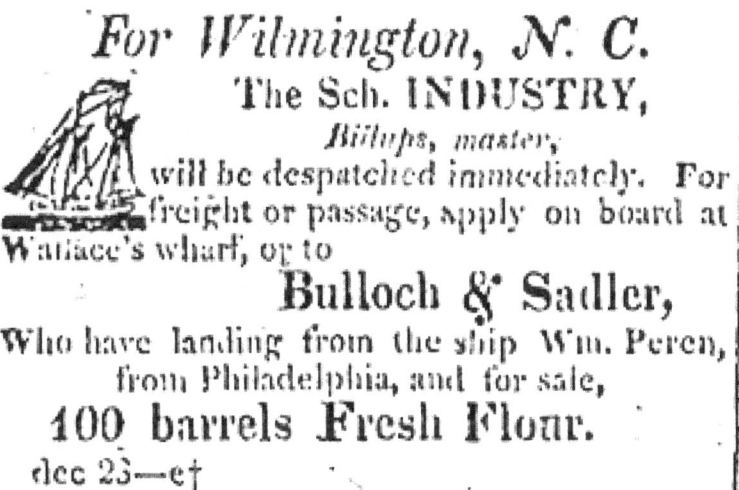

The partners dissolved their business with a notice in the *Savannah Republican* on 9 September 1820 which read:

> The Copartnership of the subscribers is dissolved this day by mutual consent. Jas. S. Bulloch will attend to, and settle the business of the concern. Jas. S. Bulloch, Geo. Sadler
>
> The subscriber will continue the Factorage & Commission business and solicits a continuance of former patronage. Jas. S. Bulloch

James most likely took up the profession of factoring due in part to his father and uncle. William Bellinger Bulloch had previously practiced this profession as did James' father, although for only a limited time and not successfully. James began paying a Savannah tax on his profession as early as 1816 when he paid $3 and an additional $2 for poll tax. He paid the same amounts in 1817.[17]

The profession of factor required capital to establish the business of fronting money to planters, steamship captains, and other business required to furnish the needs of their clients. *The Consequences of Cotton in Antebellum America* states:

> Because the planter lived far from the city and transportation was slow and difficult, the factor, a city resident, performed many services for him. He purchased items needed for the plantation and the planter's household: cloth, groceries, wines, etc. The factor charged these purchases to the planter at higher than market prices and then added his commission of 2.5 percent. Along with this profitable service, the factor also benefitted by charging the planter for monies laid out for such items as costs of transportation of cotton, storage, insurance, drayage, weighing, sampling, and repairing cotton bales.
>
> The factor was, above all, the planter's banker. The plantation system was a credit-capitalist enterprise that was basically speculative. It depended to a large extent upon items that had to be purchased rather than produced, often even food for man and beast.[18]

A factor observed the markets and prepared to move his goods at the right time. His amount of commission substantially depended on the excellence of his judgement. If he could not produce a good price for each plantation product, the planter might move his business to another factor.[19]

Having seen that Captain James Bulloch died, apparently leaving his family almost destitute, the question arises as to how his son James managed to set himself up in business. One answer to this question comes in the form of inheritances James received from family members during these years. In 1818, James received an inheritance from his grandmother, Mary DeVeaux Bulloch, giving him a sum with which to fully establish himself in the business.

To show the extent of his business efforts, the following table lists some of James' business dealings as a factor during his years as a coastal resident. This is an incomplete record and is based entirely on newspaper announcements. Each entry is a listing of cargo assigned to James Bulloch that arrived in Savannah from mostly smaller southern ports. Some of the ships arrived on several dates with like cargo. Not listed are the numerous ships arriving from New York, Philadelphia, and Boston with cargo for James, with the exception of the two pianos on 26 January 1831.

Conveyance	Out of:	Captain	Cargo	Newspaper/Date
1818				
Sloop *Good Intent*	Ogeechee	Allen	rice	SDG 12 Dec.*
Sloop *Niagara*	Charleston	Fowler	coffee, raisins, rum bagging, gin, etc. . .	SDR 5 Dec.
1819				
Sloop *Hesper*	Sunbury	Allen	cotton	SDR 25 Feb.
Sloop *Mercy*	Riceboro**	Bolles	cotton	SDR 5 March
Sloop *Elizabeth*	Darien	Green	cotton	SGR 30 March
Sloop *Sailor's Rights*	Sapelo	Derverger	cotton	SDR 7 April
Sloop *Leopard*	Riceboro	Snow	cotton	SDR 8 April
Sloop *Rosetta*	Darien	Hathaway	cotton	SDR 6 May
Sloop *Mercy*	Riceboro	Bolles	cotton and rice	SDR 16 Dec.
1820				
Sloop *Good Intent*	Ogeechee	Allen	cotton and rice	SDR 7 April
Sloop *Union*	Riceboro	Salowich	cotton	SDR 9 Nov.
Sloop *Union*	Riceboro	Salowich	cotton	SDG 27 Nov.
1821				
Schooner *Two-Sisters*	Osabaw	unknown	cotton and wood	SDG 3 March
1823				
Sloop *Union*	Riceboro	Salowich	cotton	SDR 7 May
Schooner *Flora*	Riceboro & Ossaba	Tomerson	cotton and live oak	SG 19 July
1824				
Sloop *Union*	Riceboro	Salowich	cotton	SDR 15 Jan.
Sloop *Mercy*	Riceboro	Bolles	cotton and rice	SG 16 Jan.
Sloop *Two Friends*	Harris Neck	unknown	cotton	SG 16 Jan.
1826				
Sloop *Union*	Riceboro	Salowich	cotton	SR 6 Feb.
1827				
Sloop *Mariner*	Riceboro	Boles	cotton	SG 24 Feb.
1829				
Sloop *Jno Chevalier*	Charleston	Sisson	goods	SDR 7 March
Sloop *America*	Riceboro	Bolles	cotton	SDR 21 April
Sloop *America*	Riceboro	Bolles	cotton, rice, hides	SDR 21 Dec.

1830

Sloop *Albert*	Riceboro	Lissett	cotton and rice	DSR 7 Jan.
Sloop *Ann*	Sunbury	Selowich	cotton	DSR 16 March
Sloop *Three Brothers*	Darien	Dean	1330 bushels rough rice	SDG 2 Nov.
Sloop *Eliza*	Sunbury	Richardson	Sea Island cotton, hides, tallow, and c.	SDG 6 Nov.
Sloop *Three Brothers*	Darien	Dean	rough rice	SDG 16 Nov.
Sloop *Ann*	Sunbury	Reitz	Sea Island cotton	SDG 20 Nov.
Sloop *E[illegible]*	Darien	Briggs	1300 bushes rough rice & Georgia syrup**	SDG 23 Nov.
Sloop *George Lane*	Turtle River	unknown	wool	DSR 26 Nov.
Sloop *Albert*	Riceboro	Lissett	Sea Island cotton, rice, corn & c.	DSR 27 Nov.
Sloop *America*	Riceboro	Boles	cotton & live oak wood	DSR 29 Nov.
Sloop *Three Brothers*	Darien	Dean	casks of rice & Georgia. syrup	SDG 1 Dec.
Sloop *[illegible]*	Darien	unknown	rough rice & Georgia syrup	SDG 7 Dec.
Sloop *Angelica*	Harris' Neck	Burgo	8 bales S.I. cotton & groundnuts	DSR 8 Dec.***
Sloop *America*	Riceboro	Bolles	Sea Island cotton and rough rice	DSR 16 Dec.***

1831

Sloop *Eliza*	Sunbury	Richardson	Sea Island cotton & c.	DSR 5 Jan.
Sloop *Ann*	Sunbury	Reitz	Sea Island cotton	DSR 5 Jan.
Sloop *Albert*	Riceboro	Lissett	Sea Island cotton	SDG 10 Jan.
Sloop *Augusta*	Harris Neck	unknown	Sea Island cotton	SDG 20 Jan.
Sloop *America*	Riceboro	Boles	Sea Island cotton & rice	DSR 21 Jan.
Sloop *Eliza*	Sunbury	Richardson	Sea Island cotton, bacon, flint corn & syrup	DSR 25 Jan.
Ship *Benjamin Rush*	Philadelphia	unknown	two superior pianos (received on consignment)	SDG 26 Jan.
Sloop *Ann*	Sunbury	Reitz	Sea Island cotton	SDG 31 Jan.
Sloop *America*	Sunbury	illegible	Sea Island cotton & rice	SDG 11 Feb.
Sloop *Albert*	Riceboro	Lissett	cotton, rice, & sugar cane	DSR 15 Feb.
Sloop *Eliza*	Sunbury	Richardson	Sea Island cotton & bees wax	SDG 17. Feb.
Sloop *Derigo*	Darien	Look	cotton & rice	SDG 24 Feb.

Sloop *America*	Riceboro	Bolles	cotton & rice	SDG 1 March
Sloop *Albert*	Riceboro	Lissett	Sea Island cotton & rice	SDG 12 March
Sloop *America*	Riceboro	Boles	Sea Island cotton & rice	SDG 26 March
Sloop *Eliza*	Sunbury	Richardson	Sea Island cotton & rough rice	SDG 6 April
Sloop *Argo*	Darien	Lawton	Sea Island cotton & rice	SDG 22 April
Sloop *Eliza*	Sunbury	Richardson	Sea Island cotton	SDG 26 April
Sloop *Jackson*	Riceboro	Liggett	Sea Island cotton & hides	SDG 10 May
Sloop *Eliza*	Sunbury	Richardson	Sea Island cotton & oats	DSR 13 May
Sloop *Jackson*	___ren's Mill	Liggett	rice	SDG 16 May
Sloop *America*	Riceboro	Bolles	Seal Island cotton	SDG 25 May
Sloop *Eliza*	Sunbury	Richardson	Sea Island cotton	SDG 6 June
Sloop *Jackson*	Riceboro	Liggett	Sea Island cotton & rough rice	SDG 15 June

* SDG - *Savannah Daily Georgian,* SDR - *Savannah Daily Republican,* SG - *Savannah Georgian,* SR - *Savannah Republican,* DSR - *Daily Savannah Republican*

** Georgia syrup is pure cane syrup.

*** Listed as J.M. Bulloch, believed to be a misprint of J.S. Bulloch. No further reference to J.M. Bulloch could be found.

It should be noted that all of James' clients lived in or near Liberty County. Sunbury, Riceboro, and Darien served as the main ports in the county. Riceboro sits on the North Newport River, while Sunbury is located on the Medway River. Darien, which lies at the mouth of the Altamaha River, was during this period a bustling seaport.

By 1824, James had partnered with John Dunwody in the factoring business. That same year, James' uncle, William Bellinger Bulloch, served as executor for Nichol Turnbull's estates until Turnbull's son could come of age. William consigned the following to Bulloch & Dunwody in December.

```
Dec.   9—By proceeds of 4 bales cotton sold
              Bulloch & Dunwoody 1376 lbs. @ 23c        316.48
              By 3 bales cotton ditto 1004 lbs. @13c    130.52
      25—By 2 bales white cotton 399 lbs. @27c
              By 1 bale stained cotton 192 lbs. @13c    120.72
```

Dec. 18	—By 4 Tierces[20] rice 2 frt schooner Thorn	102.00
23	—By 3 tierces rice sold by Bulloch & Dunwoody	56.00
25	—By 39 tierces rice 23604 lbs. @3.00 cask 50c	727.62
	By 1 half cask rice 364 lbs. @3.00 cask 50c	11.40
		$1,464.74[21]

Accounting simply for the commission on these sales, Bulloch & Dunwoody cleared approximately $37, which equals about $950 in today's purchasing power.[22]

To demonstrate the extent of his factor business, one notice in the *Savannah Daily Georgian*, dated 7 October 1830, advertised:

> For Sale. 200,000 Sugar Cane, of first quality for seed, delivered at $7 per M. At the landing places. Vessels can be had to take it to Charleston or any intermediate place in Carolina at $5 per M. And to Savannah for $3. James S. Bulloch

Until 1831, shipping deliveries in the newspaper rarely included weights or amounts. In 1831, in those shipments where cotton bales were enumerated, James received 840 bales. In this period, based on numbers seen in Savannah records, a bale of cotton weighed between 200 and 350 pounds. This equals approximately 252,000 lbs of cotton delivered to James' warehouse for him to sell as a factor or wholesaler to northern or European mills. Cotton sold for approximately 0.08 cents per pound in 1831 making the value approximately $20,160.[23] The value of this commodity in today's terms is $604,000. James most likely charged the usual 2.5% fee, providing himself with a tidy income of $504 on this small percentage of the cotton he traded in 1831. In 2018 purchasing power, James' $504 would equal approximately $15,100.[24]

James' business dealings also included serving as a factor for *Smith's Fire Proof Stores*. The first notice of his involvement with this agency appeared in the *Savannah Daily Georgian* on 18 February 1831. The advertisement offered brown sugar and salt in sacks, brown sugar in barrels, and Liverpool Ground Salt in four-bushel sacks. That same day, another advertisement offered hay and oats at James Bilbo's plantation on the Thunderbolt Road near the city. The advertisement advised those interested to contact Joseph Hanham at the plantation or "James S. Bulloch, Factor."

James must have been successful from the beginning based on taxes paid in Savannah. While in 1816 and 1817, he paid only professional and poll taxes; by 1819 James owned Lot 17 with buildings in Washington Ward, 2 slaves, 1 carriage, and 1 *top chair* (a type of small, two-wheeled carriage), all with a value of $7000. By 1821, he owned 3 slaves, and his property values were $6000. The 1824 tax digest showed James owning Lots 37 & 38 in Washington Ward with buildings, six slaves, and a carriage on which he paid taxes. His property was valued at $4250. In 1826, James owned Lot 37 in Washington Ward, four slaves and a carriage. His holdings increased by one slave in 1827. In 1829, he owned 8 slaves and added a gig (small carriage) to his holdings and continued to be listed at the same address. In 1831, James owned seven slaves, and the gig disappeared from his holdings. This is the last year he paid taxes on his profession. In 1832, James no longer owned lot 37 Washington Ward. His only holdings in Savannah were seven slaves. The final listing for James is 1839. At that time, he owned "2____ and 6 other slaves, four wheel carriage" in Savannah. The illegible word appears to be an abbreviation of either mulatto or mechanic.[25]

JSB - Investor

On 22 May 1819, when the Steamship *Savannah* sailed for Liverpool, England, James, only 26 years of age, served as one of the company's directors. Initially financed by William Scarbrough, the *Savannah* launched in New York in 1819 with engines installed soon thereafter in New Jersey. The *Savannah*, though only 98 feet long, became one of the most important vessels in maritime history as the first steamship to cross the Atlantic Ocean. President James Monroe and Secretary of War John C. Calhoun toured the ship in Savannah and were treated to a short cruise along the Savannah River to view the city's forts and defenses. No doubt James interacted with Monroe and Calhoun during this historic cruise and during their stay in Savannah. Afterwards, President Monroe suggested the government buy the ship and use her along the coast of Florida which was beleaguered by pirates from Cuba.[26]

William Scarbrough of Savannah served as the principal financial promoter of the project. A leading citizen, known as the *Merchant Prince* of this great southern seaport, Scarbrough's family had also emigrated from Scotland, where he had returned in his youth to study at the University of Edinburgh. His wife, Julia Scarbrough, often dubbed "the Countess" and considered one of the beautiful women of Savannah, gave frequent lavish parties, often entertaining as many as 300 guests in their home located at the corner of Pine and Broughton streets. One Savannah resident reported, "Every room in a large house was newly furnished for the occasion, the beds, etc. sent out; refreshments handed round from garrett [sp] to cellar through the night."[27]

Just before the *Savannah* sailed, the Scarbroughs moved to their William Jay designed mansion on West Broad Street.[28] Jay, a young English architect, who had arrived in Savannah only two years earlier, made his name very quickly in the city. For the arrival of President Monroe, Jay oversaw the construction of a "Pavillion [sp] of very great extent in the church square . . . It is lined with red baize or flannel, with festoons and pilasters of white muslin . . . and by candlelight will look most superbly."[29]

Funding or capital for the Steamship *Savannah* consisted of $50,000 divided into 500 shares of 100 dollars each. Each investor paid ten percent down at the time of subscription and the remainder at the time designated by the committee appointed for the preliminary arrangements for the company's organization. No investor could purchase more than 10 shares; therefore, James' investment was limited to $1000, approximately $17,400 today.[30] The notice of the investment opportunity appeared in the *Columbia Museum and Savannah Daily Gazette* on Thursday, 7 May 1818. By noon of that day, the subscription books for the newly created Savannah Steam Ship Company had closed; however, a limited number of *investment opportunities* had been set aside to permit those living in outlying areas to join the new enterprise.[31]

Many Savannah investors had already seen their $100 shares in the Steam Boat Company of Georgia leap to $800 and regularly received dividends of twenty-five percent. Coincidentally, the Savannah Steam Ship Company's offering premiered on the same day as the newly formed Savannah River Navigation Company's. Financed at the time for $600,000, the Navigation Company's stock offering foreshadowed that of the newly formed steamship company.[32] Several days later, the *Westchester Herald* reported the investments as "a bold enterprize [sp]; and if it succeeds, Atlantic steamboats ought to be called *Savannahs*, in honour [sp] of the place whose public spirit introduced them."[33]

Incorporation of the new company listed twenty-one individuals and one company. In the order listed in the Acts of Incorporation and apparently in value of investment order were:

William Scarbrough

Major Abraham B. Fannin (Savannah cotton merchant)*

Joseph P. McKinnie (Scarbrough's partner)

Samuel Howard (prominent steamboat owner)

Charles Howard (agent for the Steamboat *Charleston*)

John Haslett (unknown)

Moses Rogers (SS *Savannah's* captain)

Archibald S. Bulloch (merchant of means and James' uncle)

John Bogue (head of a Savannah mercantile firm)

Andrew Low and Company (wealthy London merchant who resided in Savannah)

Robert Isaac (member of the Low firm and Scarbrough's brother-in-law)

Isaac Minis (wealthy Savannah merchant)

Captain Sheldon C. Dunning (Savannah merchant and importer)

J. P. Henry (relative of the Minis family)

John Speakman (attorney who dabbled in mercantile business)

Robert Mitchell (a Scotsman known more for social activities)

Robert and Joseph Habersham (sons of one of Savannah's famous early families)

James Stephens Bulloch (merchant)

Gideon Pott (partner of Joseph P. McKinnie, resided mostly in New York)

W. S. Gilbert (unknown)

Samuel Yates (old Savannah name but unknown individual)

* identifications provided by author

Governor William Rabun signed the Act of Incorporation stating its purpose as "making a laudable and meritorious experiment" on 19 December 1818.[34]

James' grandmother, Mary DeVeaux Bulloch, had recently passed away at the age of 70. Her will left one fourth of her estate to the wife and children of her deceased son James; therefore, James Stephens Bulloch had recently come into an inheritance of some value. While her estate documents do not show an exact amount for her estate's assessment, her slave holdings alone were valued at $7,250, approximately $148,000 in today's money (Appendix A).[35] Twenty-five-year-old James would have come into a substantial amount, of which it seems he quickly invested a portion into this new venture.

A 25 February 1819 meeting of the Savannah Steam Ship Company stockholders elected five of the incorporators as directors. A local newspaper reported on the meeting the next day and listed the directors as William Scarbrough, Robert Isaac, S.C. Dunning, James S. Bulloch, and Joseph Habersham.[36]

During these events of early 1819, the South continued to suffer from a business slowdown that began in the early months of the year. This was a continuation of the financial panic that began on 23 March 1815 shortly after the end of the War of 1812. Bank notes rapidly depreciated because of inflation. Several years of mild depression followed this panic before a major financial crisis that involved widespread foreclosures, bank failures, unemployment, a collapse in real estate prices, and a slump in agriculture and manufacturing occurred.[37] In 1819, the South suffered the collapse of several banks and a large drop in cotton prices.

After leaving New York on 28 March 1819, the *Savannah* sailed under steam and sail for her home port in Georgia. For her gala arrival, the *Savannah* steamed into her sponsoring city's harbor on a Tuesday morning amidst cheering crowds. One account read:

> The elegant Steam Ship *Savannah*, arrived here about 5 o'clock yesterday evening. The bank of the river was lined by a large concourse of citizens, who saluted her with shouts during her progress before the city. She was also saluted by a discharge from the revenue cutter *Dallas*. Her appearance inspires instant confidence in her security. It is evident that her wheels can be unshipped in a few minutes, so as to place her precisely in the condition of any other vessel, in case of a storm or rough seas. Our city will be indebted

to the enterprise of her owners for the honor of first crossing the Atlantic in a vessel propelled by Steam.[38]

After spending the night in the harbor, near where General Oglethorpe had landed and within sight of many of Savannah's residents, she moved to a pier about six in the morning to begin a week of tours and celebrations in honor of her arrival and her coming attempt to cross the Atlantic under steam power.

The Steamship *Savannah* was described as:

> . . .350 tons burden; length overall 110 feet; beam 25.8 feet, or over the paddle wheels 36 feet. Her draught [sp] was 13 feet. She carried three tall masts, was wooden hulled with a raked curved stem and a plain square transom. Her bowsprit was steeved and well upward. The mainmast and foremast were set rather far apart giving ample room for the machinery that was to supply her auxiliary power.[39]

Built in Francis Fickett's shipyard at Corlears Hook, New York, the *Savannah* was originally designed as an elegant coastal packet. Touring the shipyard, Captain Moses Rogers saw her as a full-rigged sailing ship and brought to William Scarbrough, the idea of sailing her across the Atlantic. Often described as *elegant* in both New York and Savannah newspapers, she held thirty-two berths, all of which were staterooms "fitted up in the most tasty manner."[40]

Another early viewer described her staterooms as "commodious, and to have resembled those of a pleasure yacht rather than a steam packet."[41] Her cost was $50,000, about $1,020,000 in 2018.[42]

In the spring of 1819, President Monroe proceeded south on a tour of the southern coastal states, planning to travel as far south as Savannah. Scarbrough, learning of the Presidential tour, decided to send the *Savannah* back north as far as Charleston to deliver an invitation to the President to make his southern journey on the elegant new steamship. After placing notices in all of Savannah's newspapers about this short excursion, Captain Rogers sailed for Charleston, on 14 April, at ten o'clock in the morning, traveled the sixteen miles to the gateway of the Atlantic, and anchored off Tybee Island at one o'clock that afternoon. The following letter which appeared in the *Daily Georgian* on 20 April, demonstrated the awe and wonder shown by the ships' first passengers.

> Dear Sir,
>
> It is with no small degree of gratification that I transmit to you, according to promise, a partial description of my first voyage in the *first Steam Ship that was ever launched*; and in that sentence, the proprietors blend their own honor with that of the nation. As a native, I confess that a glow of pride animates my heart, at every step the genius of my country makes in the wide ways of emulation; her progress to improvements is marked by gigantic

SS *Savannah* by Hunter Wood, 1819

strides, and perfection seems to promise its accomplishment to their energetic and all-grasping hand. When patriotic feelings come in contact with enthusiasm, their statement alone I trust is an apology for digression — But to the purpose of my epistle.

You are aware that a fresh breeze and a rapid flood opposed the commencement of our voyage from Savannah; yet we were propelled by the steam power against wind and tide, at a rate of five miles (nautical) per hour; when you take into consideration the opposing powers of those elements, the difficulties arising from the slower motion of new engines at starting — the weight of the hull, 300 tons burthen [burden, in particular a ship's burden], spars, rigging, machinery, etc., this rapidity appears almost incredible. The apparent smallness of the paddles also, with their distance from each other, serves to heighten the astonishment. We soon arrived abreast of Tybee light, and the weather wearing a tempestuous aspect it was the opinion of our pilot, that it would be of little use to proceed, until next morning. On such occasion the responsibility rests upon himself, and of course his will is law.[43]

The S.S. *Savannah* passed two weeks in Charleston, where her decks were cleaned and polished and thronged with visitors curious about this new form of travel.

Captain Rogers enjoyed the city life, where he was well known, attending parties and entertaining others on board the new steamship, all while awaiting the arrival of President Monroe. Charleston's residents decorated their city with flags and pennants for the Presidential party's arrival by coach on 26 April, and upon his arrival, held a gala reception. At some point, Captain Rogers delivered, in person, an invitation to the president to travel to Savannah upon his vessel. Monroe declined the invitation, probably because the people of Charleston did not want the president to leave their city on a Georgia conveyance. However, given the then current views on steamship travel, it is just as likely that President Monroe was advised against traveling on a ship that had already been nicknamed "Fickett's Steam Coffin." Many believed sparks from the fire would set her ablaze. Others believed the paddle wheels which were removed while the ship was under sail alone and lashed to the deck, would be hazardous in a storm. Monroe did promise to visit the ship during his stay in Savannah. Through Rogers, Scarbrough also extended an invitation for the president to reside in his new dwelling during his stay in Savannah.[44]

At this time, not knowing when President Monroe would appear in his home city, Scarbrough decided to send the *Savannah* to New York and back if there was enough interest. Response to his advertisement in the *Columbia Museum* garnered only three passengers, resulting in the trip's cancellation.[45]

On 8 May, President Monroe arrived in Savannah by carriage after crossing the Savannah River on "an elegant barge." Savannah greeted him with a cannon salute from the Chatham Artillery using the brass six-pound cannons given them by President George Washington. Upon his arrival, Monroe enjoyed a superb reception at Scarbrough's home, for which the city had appropriated $5,000 to defray costs.[46] A supper and ball followed that evening in the Jay-designed, Johnson Square pavilion described as "unpolished" on the exterior but "truly magnificent and beautiful on the interior."[47]

Tuesday, the eleventh of May, dawned with light breezes as the President and his entourage, which included Secretary of War John Calhoun, five generals, and two judges along with five others boarded the Steamship *Savannah* for a tour of the Savannah River forts and defenses. Savannah's dignitaries, who sailed that day, were not listed. The ship's galley served both breakfast and lunch aboard. Lunch included a "succession of fine dishes with the best of wines and liquors." It was during this voyage that the president "expressed himself greatly pleased with the vessel and told Mr. Scarbrough that when she came back from her trip across the Atlantic to bring the vessel to Washington." The idea was expressed that the government would no doubt purchase the ship to employ her as a cruiser on the coast of Cuba.[48]

The *Savannah Daily Republican* carried the following story of the 11 May events:

Public Dinner

Yesterday morning the President with the gentlemen who accompany him, the secretary of war, general Gaines, colonel Clinch, general Floyd and staff, general McIntosh, general D.B. Mitchell, general Hugar of South Carolina, the reverend doctor Kollock, Judge Berrien, colonel Marshall and staff, the committee of reception, judge Charlton, Charles Harris, esq. and Dr. Waring, and a number of our most respected citizens, both civil and military, went down to Tybee in the elegant steam-ship *Savannah*. The wind being from the north-west the sails were but partly used against the flood tides, but the wheels were the essential powers that forced her through the water—and with the utmost majesty she proceeded down the sound, until she came opposite the light house—when she cast anchor for a few minutes to enable our distinguished guest to take a more certain view of our harbour, the different bearing and distances of either the impediments to the navigation which might be distinguished by beacons, or points which might be made capable of defence (sp).

The anchor was then weighed and then she proceeded up the river, accompanied by the steam-boat Altamaha, and two barges manned by a picked crew and steered by two experienced masters of vessels. On going by the Patriot brig *La Fortuns*, lying near Long-Island, the American colors were hoisted at her foremast, and those with the national flag of the brig were lowered as the steam-ship passed—— a salute was then fired from her and three loud cheers acknowledged the respectful esteem of foreigners to our beloved chief magistrate. The tide having fallen too low for the ship to come farther up, the whole party went on board the steam-boat, and partook of a collation prepared for the occasion.

We are happy to learn that Mr. Monroe was very much pleased with the attention paid him on the pleasant excursion.

On the steam boat passing the Revenue cutter *Dallas*, commanded by captain Jackson, laying opposite the town, handsomely dressed with colours, a salute of 21 guns was fired by her. The boat proceeded to the steam boat wharf, when Mr. Monroe, landed amidst a large concourse of our population, whose loud acclamations evinced their respect and admiration for talents and virtue.

About half past 5 o'clock the President was waited on by the committee of arrangements, and with Mr. Calhoun, and Mr. Governeur, escorted by them to the Dinner Booth, erected at the East end of the bay, for the occasion, where a numerous company awaited his arrival. On his way to the booth, the Cutter again fired a salute of 21 guns, and the band played the National Air of "Hail Columbia." Many distinguished persons attended as guests. The chair was filled by James M. Wayne, esq. Mayor, and Wm. B. Bulloch, Charles Harris, Matthew McAllister, and John Eppinger, esqrs. Officiated as Vice Presidents. Never did so large a body demean themselves with propriety. The booth was ornamented with wreaths and branches of laurel. At the head of the table was an arch composed of laurels beautifully decorated with roses so disposed as to form the name of James Monroe.

The company having dined, the following Toasts were announced from the chair, accompanied with appropriate music from the band. During the toasts the *Dallas* fired to them, her commander having obligingly tendered his services for the occasion. On the President retiring from the table a grand national salute was opened which made the welkin ring. [welkin means to raise a loud sound unto the heavens]

1. Our Country.—In her infancy, she is mighty in the first class of nations: what will be the meridian of her life? 2 guns—3 cheers.

2. The Federal Union.—May the head be accursed, that shall insidiously plot its dissolution: the arm withered that shall aim a blow at its existence. 2 guns—3 cheers.

3. The Constitution of the United States.—framed by the wisdom of sages; may our statesmen and our posterity regard it as the hallowed ark of political safety, never to be abandoned. 2 guns—3 cheers.

4. The Military, Naval, Legislative, and Diplomatic Worthies of the Revolution.—It is our duty and delight to honor them, and to tell their deeds with filial piety. 2 guns—3 cheers.

5. Gen. George Washington.—Revered be his memory! Let our statesmen and our warriors obey his precepts, our youth emulate his virtue and services, and our country is safe. 2 guns—3 cheers.

6. The Cession of the Floridas.—honorable to the administration, and useful to the United States; "it completes the form of the republic." 2 guns—6 cheers.

7. Maj. Gen. Andrew Jackson.—The hero of New Orleans, the brave defender of his country and vindicator of its injured honor. 2 guns—9 cheers.

8. Adams, Jefferson, and Madison.—They have withdrawn from public duty, and illustrious by their virtues and services, carry with them a nation's gratitude. 2 guns—3 cheers.

9. The Navy.—Imperishable fame accompanies the star spangled banner. In the last war we coped with Britain on the ocean; now we bear no search, no impressment. 2 guns—3 cheers.

10. The Army.—Our pillar of protection on the land: their valor and patriotism won the victories of York and of Erie, of Chippewa and of Niagara. 2 guns—3 cheers.

11. The Militia.—Yet the bulwark of our country. Invincibles fell before them in the battle of Baltimore and of Plattsburg, of the Thames and of New Orleans. 2 guns—3 cheers.

12. Concord between the North and the South, the East and the West.—May unanimity till the end of time, falsify the timid fears of those who predict dissolution. 2 guns—6 cheers.

13. The American Fair.—May they always be mothers to a race of patriots. 2 guns—3 cheers.

Volunteers [unplanned toasts presented by those attending]

By the President of the United States.— The People of the United States-They constitute but one family: may the bond which unites them together as brethren and freemen be eternal.

By John C. Calhoun, Secretary at War.—The freedom of the Press and the responsibility of (illegible) the noble (illegible) of American liberty.

By Major-General Gaines.—The Memory of Jackson, Tattnall and Telfair—The choice, the pride, and ornament of Georgia.

By Mr. Middleton.—The Memory of General Greene, who conquered for liberty.

By Major-General Floyd.—Our Country—May its prosperity be as lasting, as its government is free.

After the President and Secretary at War retired.

By the Mayor.—The President of the United States.

By William B. Bulloch, esq. Vice-President.—Mr. Calhoun, Secretary at War—The distinguished statesman, the virtuous citizen.

By General John McIntosh.—Peace with all the world so long as they respect our rights–disgrace and defeat to the power who would invade them.

By Colonel James E. Houstoun.—The Memory of General Lacklan McIntosh.

By General Mitchell.—The late War—a practical illustration of the energy of our republic.

After the Mayor retired.

James M. Wayne, Mayor of the City

By Colonel Marshall.—The Governor of the State of Georgia—a virtuous man and zealous chief magistrate.

After the Vice-President retired:

William B. Bulloch—Our respected citizen.

By Colonel Harden.—The assistant Vice-Presidents of the day, Charles Harris, Matthew McAllister, and John Eppinger, esq'rs.

By John H. Ash.—Colonel James Marshall—A skillful officer, and the friend of his country.

By Major Gray.—We are a free and happy people; and, while enjoying every blessing, let us not forget the great author from whom all good emanates.

By Josiah Davenport.— The union of our country—May the last trump alone dissolve it.

―――

The President, this morning, attended by a number of gentlemen, civil and military, rode down to Coston's bluff, Thunderbolt and other points which were thought to be assailable. He returned at about 12 o'clock, and we understand intends visiting the Academy at ½ past one. He will leave us to-morrow morning at an early hour, for Augusta. He does not intend to go by water as we stated yesterday; but he will proceed by land.

―――

The Ball

In honor of the President of the United States, will be given THIS EVENING, in the building prepared for the occasion, in Johnston's square.—The entrance will be at the southern door, and carriages are required to drive in on the western and out on the eastern part of the space from which the railing has been removed, passing round on the outside of the enclosure towards the church and bank.

Subscribers are required to call for their tickets on Joseph S. Pelot, esq. treasurer, as none will be admitted without them.

Wm. Scarbrough,

Moses Sheftall,

T. N. Morel,   Managers

Steele White,

W.T. Williams,

While there is no official record of their involvement, it seems very likely that James Bulloch and his wife Hester attended the reception for President Monroe as well as the supper and ball that followed. No doubt, as one of the original investors and a director of the company, James sailed with the president and his delegation aboard the Savannah. This exposure and experience for a young man, only 25 or 26 years of age, must have made quite an impression.

In the subsequent nine days, the *Savannah* suffered minor squall damage, the death of *Savannah* crewman John Weston due to drowning when he fell from a plank while passing to shore, and several crewmen injured in various accidents. Despite all this, the ship left her namesake city right on schedule.[49] On 20 May 1819, the elegant Steamship *Savannah* began a 10,000-mile, six-month-long voyage that would take her to Liverpool, Stockholm, St. Petersburg, Copenhagen, and Arendal, Norway. It is one of those coincidences of life that Liverpool would one day become the home of James' son James Dunwody Bulloch, who served as the Confederate States naval agent and remained in England, making it his home, after the end of the War Between the States.

Once again, the *Savannah Daily Republican* posted news of the Steamship *Savannah* on 24 June 1819, when they carried a report from the *Newburyport* (Massachusetts) *Herald* from 10 June.

Steam Boat at Sea

Capt. Livingston of the schr. *Contract*, who arrived here Saturday, saw 20th ult. lat. 27.30, long. 70, a vessel ahead to the eastward, from which he observed volumes of smoke issuing judging it to be a vessel on fire stood for her, in order to afford relief "but (observes capt. L,) to or astonishment found she went faster with the fire and smoke than we possibly could with all sail set—it was then we discovered that what we supposed a vessel on fire was nothing less than a steam-boat crossing the Western Ocean, laying his course, as we judged for Europe; a proud monument of Yankee skill and enterprise. Success to her."

[This is undoubtedly the steam-ship Savannah, capt. Rogers.—*Newburyport Herald*, 10th inst.]

On 28 August, the *Savannah Daily Republican* once again reported on the *Savannah*.

The citizens of Liverpool were gratified and astonished by the arrival, at that port, on the 21st of June, of the beautiful steam ship Savannah, captain Rogers, in 26 days from Savannah and 21 from land to land. She was five days in the channel, before she got up to Liverpool, and worked her engine eighteen days of the passage. She is the first ship, on this construction, that has undertaken a voyage across the Atlantic. She was built in this city, and is 350 tons. The London papers will have it that she is going to St. Petersburg as a present from the United States to the emperor of Russia.

The London papers were mistaken as the *Savannah* continued her tour and arrived back in her home port on 30 November 1819. However, the ship's steam power proved to be too costly to operate, as carrying enough coal to fuel her engines for long journeys severely limited her cargo space. Upon her return to the United States efforts were made to sell the unique vessel.

Following yet another devastating fire in urban Savannah, financial difficulties for the Savannah Steam Ship Company forced the sale of the ship, now stripped of all her steam-related machinery. Scarbrough suffered such a severe setback that he lost his Jay-designed home in 1820 to satisfy a judgement held by Andrew Low and Co.[50] The *Savannah* sailed again as a commercial vessel hauling passengers and cargo along the eastern seaboard, before she sank off Fire Island, New York, in a gale on 5 November 1821, a total loss.[51]

James' initial investment and losses resulting from his investment in the Steamship *Savannah* remain undiscovered. The *Savannah*, while never a commercial success, stands as the first steam-powered vessel to cross any ocean. A great celebration was held in Savannah in 1919 to celebrate the centennial of her sailing. Two memorial tablets commemorating the event were unveiled, and Alexander R. Lawton, Jr., grandson of the Confederate general of that name, delivered a speech at City Hall in Savannah on 21 April to immortalize the venture, the investors, and the *Savannah*.[52] In 1944, the United States Postal Service recognized her contribution to America's developing technology with the issuance of a commemorative stamp bearing her likeness.

JSB - Executor/Attorney

A notice of James serving in a different legal capacity appeared in the *Savannah Daily Georgian* on 10 February 1820 when James acted as executor for the estate of Peter Groves. In 1825, James partnered with an attorney named Goodwin [first name illegible] in offices located at the Counting Room of Bulloch & Dunwody, suggesting his factor partnership with brother-in-law John Dunwody began as early as 1820. Based on newspaper notices, some of their work centered on settling estates. In the Fall of 1825, the firm sold on the courthouse steps "a Negro man slave named Adam, being part of the personal estate of Mrs. C. Yonge, late of Chatham County, dec., to be sold for the benefit of the heirs and creditors of said estate." Some notices contained the name of the firm Bulloch & Dunwody, while others, such as this one ended with *Jas. S. Bulloch, Esq.*[53]

By the 1820s, Bulloch & Dunwody appeared to be a successful venture based on the number of legal notices in various Savannah papers.[54] The firm conducted all types of factor/legal work. For example, in 1822, the firm advertised the sale of a "gang of twenty-six prime NEGROES. They will be disposed of in families to suit purchasers."[55]

That same year, James' name, along with those of Archibald Stobo Bulloch (1767-1859) and Alexander Hunter (1789-1829), appeared on documents prepared and presented to the United States Congress. James' uncle Archibald served as Collector for Savannah's port while Alexander Hunter served as Surveyor of the Customs for Savannah's port. The documents listed James as the legal representative/administrator for Alexander Irvine (1781-1821), noted as "late of the city of Savannah, naval officer." Alexander Irvine was the ninth child of Dr. John Irvine and Ann Elizabeth Baillie Irvine and the younger brother of James' mother Anne. James served as his executor.

All three of these men held important positions in the United States Customs Service, created in 1789, the first federal enforcement agency. Bulloch served as Collector; Alexander Hunter served as Surveyor; and Irvine as Naval Officer. Each had specific duties for the Customs Service. Each received a commission signed by the sitting President and the Secretary of State. The official statute related to their duties stated:[56]

> Collector: That the duties of the respective officers to be appointed by virtue of this act, shall be as follows: At such of the ports to which there shall be appointed a collector, naval officer and surveyor, it shall be the duty of the collector to receive all reports, manifests and documents made or exhibited to him by the master or commander of any ship or vessel, conformably to the regulations prescribed by this act, to make due entry and record in books to be kept for that purpose, all such manifests and the packages, marks and numbers contained therein; to receive the entry of all ships and vessels, and of all the goods, wares and merchandise imported in such ships

or vessels, together with the original invoices thereof; to estimate the duties payable thereon, and to endorse the same on each entry; to receive all monies paid for duties, and to take all bonds for securing the payment of duties; to grant all permits for the unloading and delivery of goods, to employ proper persons as weighers, gaugers, measurers and inspectors at the several ports within his district, together with such persons as shall be necessary to serve in the boats which may be provided for securing the collection of the revenue to provide at the public expense, and with the approbation of the principal officer of the treasury department, store-houses for the safe keeping of goods, together with such scales, weights and measures as shall be deemed necessary, and to perform all other duties which shall be assigned to him by law.

Naval Officer: It shall be the duty of the naval officer to receive copies of all manifests to estimate and record the duties on each entry made with the collector, and to correct any error made therein, before a permit to unload- or deliver shall be granted; to countersign all permits and clearances granted by the collector.

Surveyor: It shall be the duty of the surveyor to superintend and direct all inspectors, weighers, measurers and gaugers within his district, and the employment of the boats which may be provided for securing the collection of the revenue; to go on board ships or vessels arriving within his district, or to put on board one or more inspectors, to ascertain by an hydrometer, what distilled spirits shall be of Jamaica proof rating all distilled spirits which shall be of the proof of twenty-four degrees as of Jamaica proof and to examine whether the goods imported are conformable to the entries thereof; and the said surveyors shall in all cases be subject to the control of the collector and naval officer.

Their petition, delivered in January of 1822, to the United States Congress referred to an 1819 case involving the Portuguese Schooner *Montevediana* which arrived in Savannah with one African to be sold as a slave. The importation of slaves had been declared illegal by Congress with the law taking effect on 1 January 1808. According to the petition, Bulloch, Hunter, and Irvine had been responsible for prosecuting the case and had entailed expenses in this process that had not been repaid by the United States government. The case involved a forfeiture of $1176.70 paid by the *Montevediana's* owners. Bulloch, Hunter, and Irvine asked for this money or "of such other sum as may seem right and just" to repay their losses. There are two reports from the Treasury Department sent to the Claims Committee that affected the judgement. One of these inferred that the United States government had never received the $1176.70 owed by the second judgement against the *Montevediana*. The resolution said "That the prayer of the petitioners ought not to be granted" or to *lie on the table*. [The entire document related to their petition is presented in Appendix A.

Note, the original petition was placed at the end of the finding in the Congressional Proceedings.]

An 1825 legal notice for Bulloch & Goodwin indicated the firm still occupied the counting rooms used by James Bulloch's factor concern. The notice read:

All persons having demands against Major Charles Stephens will present them at the Counting Room Bulloch & Dunwody. James Bulloch [illegible] Goodwin, Attornies [sp].[5576]

While no notice has been found for the dissolution of Bulloch & Goodwin, Attornies, Bulloch & Dunwody ended their partnership in the Fall of 1830. The announcement in the *Savannah Daily Georgian* on 10 October read:

Notice: The co-partnership of Bulloch & Dunwody is this day dissolved by mutual consent, and they thus publicly return their thanks for the liberal support uniformly bestowed upon them, and sobeit (sp) a continuation of it for James S. Bulloch, who will settle the affairs of the current and continue to devote his time and best exertions for the interest of his customers. James S. Bulloch   John Dunwody

Half a year later, on 7 September 1831, the *Savannah Daily Georgian* ran the following announcement:

Notice: The undersigned begs leave to inform his customers and the public, that he has this day declined Factorage and Commission Business and thus publicly returns his sincere thanks for the kind and liberal support he has received for the past sixteen years. All persons are requested to bring in their accounts for settlement to day. For sale: Counting Room. Desks. Copying Machine, Dearborne's Patent Balances. James S. Bulloch. Savannah 1st July 1831.

From this announcement, it is evident that James began his factoring business in 1815 at twenty-two years of age. James' sale of his counting room with all its related equipment indicates his total withdrawal from all factoring concerns.

JSB - Pirate?

In 1818, James' and his uncle Archibald Stobo Bulloch's names were associated with a piracy case that ended with an 1820 review by the United States Supreme Court. The basic details of the case as presented by University of Maryland law student Justin L. Sieffert are as follows:

On April 11, 1818, Ralph Clintock served as the second lieutenant of the *Young Spartan*, a privateering vessel sailing under a foreign commission from a revolutionary government seeking independence from Spain. The *Young Spartan* engaged and seized a prize in the form of the Danish vessel

Norberg. At the direction of written instructions of James S. Bulloch, the *Young Spartan* committed fraud utilizing false Spanish papers to legitimate the seizure. Abandoning the crew of the *Norberg* on an island, the *Young Spartan* sailed back to the port at Savannah, Georgia, with the *Norberg* and impersonated the proper owners of the *Norberg*, entered the port unmolested by the Collector, Archibald Bulloch, and sold the cargo accordingly. The Federal government deemed the seizure of the *Norberg* to be an act of piracy and prosecuted Clintock for his involvement. Piracy was a significant problem for the United States, and prosecuting piratical acts was one method used to address the problem.[58]

A search of Savannah newspapers during this period found a couple of short references to the case of the *Young Spartan* and some follow up articles about Ralph Clintock. The latter most articles referred to his punishment, or lack thereof. Sieffert's review of this case appears well documented and mentions a letter that Clintock supplied to the court from James S. Bulloch that "provided written instructions to Captain Smith for the voyage and how to return a captured prize to Savannah." He also claimed Archibald was part owner of the *Young Spartan*.[59]

However, no such letter was presented to the court during the trial. Clintock asserted that the Bullochs had used their personal connections to secure the letter and remove it from evidence. Sieffert's article mentions Clintock's extensive correspondence with John Q. Adams, Secretary of State, under President James Monroe, and Adams' acceptance of Clintock's view of the crime. Yet, the Bullochs were never indicted, and their names do not appear in the Federal case notes of the Supreme Court decision.[60]

Several questions now arise when trying to understand this case. Were James and Archibald actually guilty of piracy? Did such a letter exist? Or was Clintock simply trying to justify his crimes and push the blame onto two persons heavily involved with port operations in Savannah? At the time of the crime and the trial, James and Archibald were heavily invested in the SS *Savannah*, and other financial proceedings in Savannah. James served as alderman, on the board of at least one bank, and as factor/attorney/executor for numerous local planters and businessmen. Archibald continued to serve as Port Collector for many more years. As stated previously, the Savannah newspapers remained silent about any involvement of James or Archibald in the court case and/or trial.

While fighting for Clintock's release in January of 1819, Georgia's District Marshall John H. Morel stood surety for Archibald's bond of office, some $10,000. One might question if Morel believed Clintock's claim against the Bullochs? Was he working with them to insure Clintock's release, all the while taking care not to implicate James and Archibald? After calling for a personal review of the trial and documents, President Monroe pardoned Clintock, and he was released from jail in July of 1821.[61]

Sieffert's conclusion of the Monroe document states:

> Monroe also acknowledged the connection of James Bulloch to a United States Senator, indicating his awareness of the political implication of the situation calling the senator a man he was "personally acquainted [and] entertained for him great consideration." He then referred the case and sent all case documents to Attorney General William Wirt for a report for the proper action to take, if any, against James Bulloch, Archibald Bulloch, and John Bulloch.[62]

The Senator mentioned would have been John Elliott, James' father-in-law. Sieffert's reconstruction of the case mentions that John Bullock, Georgia Clerk of Court, was dismissed from the case being as he was Archibald's brother. Yet, Archibald did not have a brother named John. Who made this mistake is not apparent from the documents presented in Sieffert's analysis.[63]

JSB - Banker

Only a few years after his investment in and the sailing of the Steamship *Savannah*, the city's business interest recognized James' financial adroitness and elected him to posts at several banks. In December of 1821 and again in 1822, he served as one of two directors of the Planter's Bank.[64] His position was one of two appointed by the Georgia Legislature to serve, "on the part of the state." John Dunwody was one of five appointed by the legislature to serve as director for the Bank of Darien. Although both gentlemen were appointed by the legislature to serve, their nominations for the postings came directly from the local community.

In 1818, James served as one of five commissioners of the Building and Insurance Bank. The other four commissioners were William Scarbrough, B. Burroughs, Robert Isaac, and J.P. Henry, of which only Burroughs did not invest in the Steamship *Savannah*. The bank failed and the subscription money collected at $2 per subscription was returned in December of that year.[65]

In 1822, the *Savannah Daily Georgian* announced James' election to a one-year term as director of the Savannah Marine and Fire Insurance Office. This concern operated a bank which had its own paper currency in later years. Interestingly, a *Savannah Republican* notice about actions of the Georgia Legislature dated 26 November 1816, noted "A Bill is before the Senate to *double tax* the 'Savannah Marine and Fire Insurance Company.' We cannot see why this institution should be taxed more than the Banks in this state."

A national crisis occurring some ten years later would again propel James to the forefront in Savannah banking interest. In 1816, President James Madison authorized the Second Bank of the United States' tenure for a period of twenty years. Consequently, the bank carried out much of the nation's business until the arrival of

President Andrew Jackson, who opposed the bank based on his support of Thomas Jefferson's idea of an *agricultural republic*. Jackson believed the Bank improved the fortunes of an "elite circle" of commercial and industrial entrepreneurs at the expense of farmers and laborers. Jackson remained convinced that the bank concentrated the nation's financial strength into a single institution which could be controlled by foreign interests as well as exercising too much control over members of Congress. Jackson recognized the bank's favoritism of the northeastern states over the southern and the ever-expanding western states. In 1832, Jackson succeeded in revoking the bank by vetoing its 1832 re-charter. His actions led to the banking crisis of that year and additionally to the Panic of 1837, which threw the national economy into a deep depression.[66]

During this banking crisis, the Federal government closed the Second Bank of the United States and redistributed its monies. Local, regional, and even state banks sprang up to cover the needs of the populace. State governments took over the job of supervising the banks, but the crisis often required action both by local citizens and governments. Banks of the period issued loans in their own currency using notes that could be converted, on demand, to cash—that is gold or silver. Bank examiners were appointed to visit banks making sure they had enough cash on hand to redeem outstanding currency or notes. During the crisis, many banks did not hold sufficient funds to support their outstanding paper notes, leaving many bank note holders stuck with worthless paper. It became difficult and often impossible to detect which notes were sound and which were not, because of their staggering variety and a lack of state oversight.[67]

In August 1832, James was "called to the chair" by the citizens of Savannah, at a public meeting, to deal with the banking crisis. The article read:

> At a meeting of the citizens of Savannah, held at the Exchange, on Friday the 10th inst. For the purposes of taking into consideration, the present state of the money market, James S. Bulloch, Esq. was called to the chair, and William Remshart, appointed secretary, when the following preamble and resolutions were offered and adopted.
>
> Whereas, the large amount of issues of the Country Banks of this State, having become the circulation medium of this city, to the almost total exclusion of the notes of our Banks, and thereby subjecting the trading part of this community to heavy losses, the discount at this time being on Branch and Country Bank Notes 4 to 10 per cent.
>
> Be it therefore resolved that from and after Monday next, the 13th inst. that we will not receive in our respective business transactions the notes of *any Bank* but such as will be received on deposit by the Banks of this city, or at such a discount as will be fixed upon by the brokers of this place, or until arrangements are made by the President and Directors of the respective up-

country banks, with the President and Directors of the banks of this city, to have their bills redeemed here.

Resolved, That a committee of three be appointed to wait on the officers of the Banks of this city, with a copy of the resolutions adopted by this meeting, and request their co-operation in carrying the same into effect, and that the Chairman appoint the committee, when Levi S. D'Lyon, Aaron Champion, and S. Philbrick were appointed that committee.

Resolved, That the proceedings of this meeting be published in the Gazettes of the city.
J.S. Bulloch, Chairman
W.M. Remshart, Sec'ry [68]

Subsequently, several newspapers printed additional notices about the committee's actions associated with the bank crisis, which resulted in James remaining extremely active in Savannah's financial circles.

During the next decade, James received an appointment as one of five directors of the Branch Bank of Darien.[69] The Bank of Darien had branches in Savannah, Augusta, Marion, Dahlonega, and Auraria. Both Dahlonega and Auraria were in the gold mining region of north Georgia, and in each, the bank had representatives available to purchase gold. Roswell King had been on a mission from the Bank of Darien when he rode by Roswell's Vickery Creek and realized its potential as power for a manufacturing center.[70]

JSB - Civic Leader

Beginning with the arrival of the first James Bulloch in the colonies, public service occupied a portion of the life of each male descendant. Bulloch men served as community leaders, and as such were recognized for their values and beliefs that made them respected in their communities. James followed this tradition, taking on several responsibilities to ensure the continued welfare of his fellow citizens and his city.

From September 1817 to September 1818, James served his first of two terms as city alderman.[71] That same year, James served as manager for Savannah's Fourth of July Ball. Apparently planning for the event began early for the announcement appeared in the *Columbia Museum and Savannah Daily Gazette* on 28 February. James continued to be patriotic and served on the committee to celebrate the forty-sixth "Anniversary of American Liberty" in 1821.[72] The same paper reported after the event that Lieutenant Colonel J.S. Bulloch presented at toast at the Dinner of the Citizens for the Celebration of American Freedom. This toast came near the end of the evening's festivities after many, many others and was to "The Freedom of the People, called by Legitimates *Political Atheism*." Its meaning is unclear, as is the rank given to James. Although he had resigned from the militia in 1822 where he held the rank of major, James still served in the Chatham Artillery, and a 4 February 1826 article in the *Savannah Georgian* announced his election as first lieutenant. It must be assumed the title of *Lieutenant Colonel* was simply a mistake as James used the title "Major" for the remainder of his life. Other toasts during the evening included ones for President James Monroe, and future president Andrew Jackson, at that time the governor of Florida.

In 1822, James served a number of different groups in various positions. He was appointed secretary at a town meeting of the Savannah Poor House and Hospital Society. In early 1823, he served on Savannah's grand jury, was elected vice president of the Union Society, and ran for city alderman. James won the election, becoming one of Savannah's fourteen aldermen that year.[73] A newspaper notice in November of that same year, shows James serving on the Committee of Council's "Fx. Committee" and concerned with the leasing of the "Bar Room and upper Rooms of the Exchange."[74]

The next year James garnered the support of "the following gentlemen" for representative in the state legislature. The advertisement placed by "A Voter" in the *Savannah Daily Georgian* on 31 July 1824 did not include the list of "gentlemen." The *Georgian* again listed James as a candidate for alderman that same year; however, he declined being a candidate in late August, just before the election. Savannah's City Council appointed James as one of several Port Wardens in January of 1825. In May, the *Savannah Republican* reported James' appointment to the Board of Health for Washington Ward, where he resided. In October, James became Washington Ward's City Constable.[75]

This dedication to community service continued in the years to come with James serving again on the Board of Health in 1826 and 1827 and holding the polls that year. However, James was among five listed as defaulting on service to the grand jury on 30 March 1828. The *Savannah Daily Georgian* reported that "unless they file, with the Clerk, on or before the first day of the next term, good and sufficient cause of excuse on oath, they will be fined severely in the sum of forty dollars. . ." Newspapers failed to reveal the end of this story. James did serve on the grand jury in February of 1829.[76]

On 3 April 1829, Augusta, Georgia, suffered a massive fire that destroyed 800 to 850 homes in the main section of town. Lives were lost and businesses destroyed by a force that terrified most city dwellers of the period. Timber structures allowed the flames to spread quickly, and few municipal fire departments existed, especially in southern towns. Only ten days later, James accepted appointment as secretary of Savannah's town meeting to raise funds to help the Augusta citizens and victims of the last three fires in their own dear city. Two separate subscription lists were set up for the donation of funds to either city. On 16 April, the committee to raise funds for the fire victims reported amounts of $1,294.75 for Augusta and $1,695 for fire victims in Savannah.[77]

Following one additional unsuccessful campaign for city alderman in the fall of 1830, James all but disappears from the pages of the Savannah newspapers in regard to civic leadership, banking matters, and even his personal business ventures. Family matters had begun to take precedence in his life during the late 1820s. This pattern continued in the next two decades.

JSB - Temperance Leader

As early as the 1780s, some civic leaders recognized that alcohol abuse among sections of America's populace contributed greatly to poverty and violence, creating a major public health crisis. As urbanization advanced and ordinances related to alcohol sales and consumption relaxed, these problems increased dramatically. On the frontier, the conversion of grain into *ardent spirits* provided farmers with a more easily transported and stored product. Its inexpensive price led to increased consumption. Gin and whiskey soon took the place of beer.

Dr. Benjamin Rush, signer of the Declaration of Independence and one of America's leading medical professionals of the day, wrote, on 16 September 1810, to his close friend President John Adams about his "long-cherished hostility to ardent spirits." Rush did not desire to prohibit their importation and distilling but remained deeply committed to educating people about the hazards of distilled alcoholic beverages. His 1784 pamphlet "An Inquiry into the Effects of Ardent Spirits upon the Human Body and Mind" argued his case and was widely read, especially its later 1823 re-publication. Rush's concerns centered on alcohol's effects on the user's "industry, health, and morals." This pamphlet soon became a rallying point for the country's temperance movement.[78]

The temperance movement began early in our nation's history when a Connecticut community created a law to ban the making of whiskey in 1789. Temperance societies sprang up in many states during the early decades of the nineteenth century. Some were simply local temperance societies while others were statewide organizations. The American Temperance Society, formed in 1826 by a group of clergymen, grew to become a tremendous social movement. Many Protestant churches promoted temperance as a moral crusade.

As a moral and learned man, strong in his Christian values, James joined the temperance cause in June of 1829. At a meeting in the Baptist Church, attended by "numerous and respectable . . . citizens of both sexes," James became the president of Savannah's first temperance society. On 11 March 1830, the *Savannah Georgian* reported on a meeting of the society at the First Presbyterian Church, where the Reverend Mr. Hewit, an agent of the American Temperance Society (ATS) addressed the assembly. Hewit spoke about the ATS's accomplishments, and the prospects for the future benefits and blessings arising from temperance. Those in attendance then resolved that they were pleased with the actions and progress of the ATS and thanked

Rev. Hewit for his report. Seventy-five individuals became members and signed their name to the group's constitution.

James' involvement with the temperance movement continued for many years and later resulted in the formation of the Washington Total Abstinence Society in Roswell, his new home. [79] These members pledged:

> We whose names are hereunto annexed, desirous to forming a Society for our mutual benefit, and to guard against a pernicious practice which is injurious to our health, standing and families, do pledge ourselves as gentlemen, not to drink any Spirituous or Malt Liquors, Wine, or Cider.[80]

James kept the minutes of the society's meetings that began with hymns, prayers and thoughts on temperance. The society's members included white residents of the new "colony," as it was called, and several slaves, including *Daddy* Luke. The minutes reveal several "backsliders" who would confess to their sins related to alcohol and then retake the pledge of abstinence. In December of 1842, the Society modified the original pledge, excluding wine and cider.[81]

Chapter VI
The Marriages of JSB

In the complicated story of one's life, it is often impossible to relate the tale year by year. Instead, private and public personas might need to be presented somewhat separately. The story of James' two marriages *must be told* somewhat apart from his business ventures. For while one affected the other, his marriages seemed to most often rule his heart and direction. Additionally, the familial relationships need to be read and understood without any interference from business affairs and the world beyond.

A story has been and is often told of an early romance between James Stephens Bulloch and Martha Stewart. To date, no historical documentation for the story has been uncovered. As the *fable* goes, these two young individuals, raised together in the small, rural communities of Liberty County, knew each other from early childhood. According to the *fable*, James and Martha fell in love, and in 1817, James proposed to Martha who fashionably declined his request. No doubt, she believed another would be forthcoming from James, as this was also the fashion of the time. However, to her dismay, James instead proposed to Hester Elliott.

The above story appears to be nothing more than a *fable*. While James had no doubt known young Martha Stewart, he also had known Hester "Hetty" Elliott from a young age. They attended Sunbury Academy together. They worshipped at the same church. In an uncomplicated story, one more likely to be true, James *only* proposed to Hetty Elliott.

Two Weddings

In 1817, eighteen-year-old Martha Stewart, often called *Patsy*, received a proposal from 44-year-old John Elliott, widowed father of three living daughters, the second oldest of whom was Hester, destined to marry James S. Bulloch. The following letter from John to Martha provides some insight into this proposal.

Laurel View,
Saturday, 11th Oct., 1817

Your worthy father has no doubt divulged to you the secret wishes of my heart; and having obtained his kind permission, I can no longer resist the impulse which urges me to declare to you how much I love you. Yes, the heart and hand of my charming Martha have become necessary to my future happiness! And should I be so fortunate as to inspire her gentle bosom with a reciprocal passion, I shall ever cherish the blessing as a gift from heaven, designed to alleviate the remembrance of those afflictions through which I have passed, and to secure for my future life the most refined prospect of conjugal felicity.

From early life I have considered the matrimonial as the only happy life. And it is unquestionably so when entered into from proper motives, and by persons of similar tastes and correspondent dispositions of the heart. In you I think I perceive all that is necessary to the happiness of such a life. With a sound discretion and a knowledge of human nature too mature to lead you to expect perfection in the man of your choice, you possess those amiable qualities and disposition of the heart which will ever prompt you to overlook or paliate unavoidable errors. Cursed indeed, then, with a heart of ice must he be who could remain insensible to such worth; or ever cease to love an object so lovely. With sentiments of the matrimonial state thus exalted, and a passion for you so pure, sincere and ardent, may I not venture to indulge the pleasing anticipation of a favorable issue to my suit? The all important answer to my future happiness I hope to receive from your own dear lips on Monday evening next, when I propose to myself the gratification of a personal interview with you.

> I am, my sweet girl,
> Yours most devotedly,
> (sgd.)   J. Elliot[1]

John Elliott's plea met with success as Martha agreed to become his wife. Their difference in age, 26 years, while unusual even for this time was not completely uncommon. The community recognized John's need to provide a "mother" for his daughters and a wife for his own comfort and support.

A little over two months later, at the Midway Congregational Church, James and Hester Elliott married on 31 December 1817. The *Savannah Daily Republican* posted the following notice on 2 January 1818.

Married, on the 31st ultimo, in Liberty County, Mr. James S. Bulloch, merchant of this city, to Hetty A. Elliott, daughter of John Elliott, esquire of that county.

One week later, Martha married John Elliott, on 6 January 1818, also in the Midway Congregational Church. Dr. James Holmes wrote many years later of the Elliott wedding saying:

On another occasion it was the Honorable John Elliott and his second wife, Miss Patsy Stewart, the daughter of General Stewart - all of Liberty County. The appearance of the latter couple and some incidents of that occasion are fresh in my memory to this day. There were a number of Sunbury boys present, and I was among them. We were all tip-tow to witness the arrival of the splendid new carriage and bright blood bays with "Daddy Steven" in livery on the box and an out-rider. Also in livery, mounted on Pizarro, was Mr. Elliott who at time, was First Lieutenant of the Liberty Troop.

. . . A handsomer or more elegant gentleman or more beautiful lady are seldom seen. Nor did there seem any unfitness in the match, although Mr. Elliott had a daughter (by his earlier wife) older than his new wife. He still looked fresh, young, and only a trifle portly. There was yet another sight for us boys in seeing them leave after the service. We had been told that Mr. Elliott would ride Pizarro while a lady friend took his place in the carriage. Now a handsome man on a handsome horse, provided he is a graceful rider as Mr. Elliott was, a pretty picture. But he had undertaken too much, for after he galloped gaily alongside the carriage for a few miles, some young men (doubtless jealous of him) said he was thoroughly blown and had to pull up and take things more leisurely. He arrived at General Stewart's long after the ladies.[2]

Two Families Intertwined

Thus, began a much confusing story. A story built upon by time and familial relationships. For after the two weddings, the new couples began a close relationship, according to early historical records. Martha became James' step-mother-in-law, as Hetty was to her a stepdaughter. In addition, John Elliott and James Bulloch seemed to have formed a close bond based not only on family, but also of business. The two men often traveled together, resulting in this *Baltimore Patriot* article of 11 July 1818.

Savannah, July 2

An attempt was made on Tuesday night last on the Augusta road between Mr. Cuyler's plantation and the 16 mile house, to rob Messrs. John Elliott and James S. Bulloch, who left this city in the morning for the up country. —The villians [sp] had so far succeeded as to cut from the carriage the trunk of the former gentleman; but before they had secured their plunder, they were discovered in time to prevent them carrying it off. They retreated precipitately by taking to the woods.

James and Hetty resided in Savannah on Broughton Street (Washington Ward, lots 37 and 38) Hetty bore James at least two children of which only one lived to maturity, James Dunwody Bulloch (1823-1901). Their first son, named John Elliott for her father, died "very suddenly" at age two years and ten months in Burke

County (Waynesboro) in late September 1821.[3] John Elliott's family was related to the Elliott and Whitehead families of Burke County, thus explaining their presence in this area.

John Elliott's brother Daniel Roberts Elliott (12 December 1779) was a planter in Waynesborough, Burke County, before his death in 1810. He also owned property in Plymouth, Massachusetts. He left three-quarters of his property to his wife Betsy (1786-1871) and his two daughters Jane Amarinthea (or Amarinthia; 1805-1871) and Catherine Elizabeth (1807-1841) and a child his wife was expecting when the will was written on 17 February 1810. After Daniel's death on 12 May near Sunbury, the will was executed on 4 June, with John Elliott and Captain John Whitehead of Burke County, as executors. The child, a girl named Susan Louisa, was born in March in Waynesborough and died ten months later, on 16 January 1811 in Plymouth, where she was buried.[4]

In the next decade, Hetty became active in Savannah society and even served on the board of managers for the Savannah Female Asylum. The Asylum provided housing and food to widowed mothers with small children and other destitute women. Hetty and her sister-in-law, Jane Bulloch Dunwody, helped raise funds for the Asylum's support.[5]

Conversely, during the years from 1818 to 1827, Martha bore John Elliott several children, creating a large family that included four daughters by his first marriage. These were Caroline Matilda (age 22 in 1818, single), Hester Amarantha (age 21 in 1818, married), Jane Elizabeth (age 9 in 1818), and Corinne Louisa (age 5 in 1818). Martha's first child, John Whitehead, was born on 7 November 1818 and died in November 1820. Another son, Charles William, born in 1824, would survive a mere three years. Only three children from this union would live to maturity; Susan Ann (1820-1905), Georgia Amanda (1822-1848), and Daniel Stewart (1826-1862).[6]

From 1819 until 1825, during John's senatorial term, he and Martha spent much of each year in Washington, D.C. and Philadelphia. Martha was considered an elegant and charming member of society. As an extremely beautiful and very young wife, she called attention to herself by wearing stylish clothing and holding court at their home.[7] The remainder of the year was divided between John's Laurel View Plantation and their elegant State Street address in Savannah. Designed by Isaiah Davenport, this Federal period residence with a stucco facade embodied Savannah's most elegant homes (now demolished).

Both Martha and Hetty lived as wealthy, privileged wives. They ran their household and each directed slaves or servants to do the household chores. Both most likely had nurses or nannies and even wet nurses for their infants. They served their communities by sitting on social committees providing care for the sick, homeless, orphaned, and dying. During their confinements of pregnancy, they depended upon family for their entertainments.

Despite their ease of life, difficulties remained for each woman. Martha and Hetty mourned their first-born sons. Childhood death rates continued to be high throughout the antebellum period. Additionally, a woman's chance of death during childbirth remained a serious threat. The average woman bore six to seven children during this historical period, usually one every two years. However, common contagious illnesses such as measles, scarlet fever, and strep throat, along with outbreaks of yellow fever, dysentery, cholera, typhoid, and even the flu took many young lives. Very few women raised all their infants to adulthood. Martha had at least five pregnancies during this marriage. Like Martha, Hetty delivered her first son during her first year of marriage. Records indicate she did not carry another child to term until 25 June 1823.

A Letter from Washington, D.C.

Personal letters and newspapers provided a few details of each family's life in the subsquent years. We can trace with some accuracy when John and Martha were in Washington or at home at Laurel View. Yet, the following *Savannah Daily Republican* article fails to report if John was present at his plantation on 3 February 1820.

> We understand that a violent Tornado was experienced in Liberty county on Thursday last. It passed over the plantation of the honorable John Elliott: and destroyed almost everything in its way. It blew down the Cotton Gin house of Mr. E. in which there were thirty seven negroes, who were occupied in gining [sp] cotton. Killed one, and wounded severely, thirty—Many of them are so badly hurt that they will be unable to perform manual labor for some time to come. Such was the violence of the wind that it blew too [sp] bales of cotton across the river, a distance of many yards.

The tornado blew two bales of cotton, weighing between 200 and 450 pounds each, across the river. The article did not note if Martha, or the children, were present at the plantation when the tornado occurred.

Other articles noted John's travels. On 17 March 1821, John attended a meeting in Savannah and on the 25th of that month, his daughter Susan, born 6 August 1820, was baptized at the Midway Congregational Church. On 8 July 1823, John attended a meeting in Savannah and on the 22nd, "John Elliott, Lady, three children and servants" left on a ship for New York. The three children would have been Susan, Georgia Amanda (born 14 June 1822), and possibly one of John's daughters by his first marriage. On 4 April 1825, John arrived in Savannah on the Brig *Frances*.[8]

During his Senate tenure, John wrote of his family to an unidentified female friend, from Washington, D.C., saying:

Washington City.
Senate Chamber,
May 6th, 1820.
My dear friend:

My engagements here have been so constant and my duties so arduous as to compel me to neglect many of my friends, and it pains me to believe you may have supposed yourself among this number.

The session is now drawing to a close, and I cannot leave Washington without writing you a hasty scral [sp], the object of which will be to inform you of our continued good health and to renew to you the expression of unfeigned regard. Caroline's [Caroline Matilda Elliott] health has rather declined, but I hope it will improve again at the approach of summer. In a letter just received by Mrs. Efrom Lee, she speaks of her health as not materially altered, but W. Bulloch [William Bellinger Bulloch] thinks her more hoarse. Jane is at school in Philadelphia, and much pleased with her instruction; - Corinne with no other instruction than such as Mrs. Elliot could give her amidst the gaiety of this place has so improved as to read very correctly and spell promptly any words of five syllables. John has grown a fine boy and speaks very plainly. You may readily imagine our anxiety to set our faces homeward when you recollect how dear a part of our family are in Georgia, and how long it is since we left that State. We hope to leave Washington on Friday next for Philadelphia, from whence it is expected we shall sail for Savannah on the following Monday.

Two days since Mrs. Elliot and myself with a select party of about seventy-five persons revisited Mount Vernon. We were conveyed down the Potomac in a fine steam boat. The day being fine, thanks to the delicious notes of the Marine Band which was on board re-echoing from the banks of the river, now verdant with the fresh herbage of spring, and the graceful and airy footsteps of some half dozen sweet girls and obsequious youths lightly tripping through the changes of the cotillion under an ample awning tastefully spread over the quarter deck, presented to me such a contrast to the dull monotony of legislation, the crowded gallery, the discordant notes of ungraceful orators, that it seemed the work of enchantment, and I could hardly escape from the belief that we had invaded the unsubstantial dominions of Oberon. Having received an addition to our company at Alexandria, and touching at Fort Washington, which is reconstructing under the direction of a noble engineer, and which when finished will contain a battery of an hundred guns, some of which will fire from an elevation of an hundred and ten feet, we arrived at 11 o-clock in sight of Mount Vernon, which from its elevated position may be seen from a distance of several miles. The sight of this venerated spot, dear to the hearts of every American as the former residence and present repository of the ashes of the father of his country, suspended all amusements, while every eye was riveted and every faculty absorbed in contemplating the interesting objects which now rose to our view. When within a short distance of the landing, the music suddenly struck up and we landed with "Hail Columbia" in full band. The Judge and his lady being from home on a visit to Philadelphia, the family servants received us with a hearty welcome. The venerable mansion house and gardens were thrown open at our approach, and we had the satisfaction to see every apartment of the building and all the curiosities of the garden and grounds. What gave additional interest to every thing was the fact that it remained as left by the dear departed owner, except so far as it may have been altered in some degree by the very effort to preserve it. After everything else had been inspected, the whole party marched in a solemn procession to the vault. This too, is as it was when the body of the General was laid within its walls. Its summit is overgrown with cedars, from which every visitor by a simultaneous movement, plucked a sprig and placed it near the heart. While employed in this unconscious act of veneration and respect, the band played one of Pleyel's solemn hymns. The moment was solemn and the scene impressive. It awakened sensations which I love to cherish and which I trust I shall not easily forget. Among the visitors there were several French, Scotch, and English ladies and gentlemen. All national distinctions seemed lost here, and every tongue acknowledge the matchless worth of the departed Washington. I was peculiarly struck with the conduct of a Scotch lady of some literary merit, who is now traveling through the United States with the view of publishing her travels, and whose attachment for our free institutions, I trust, will insure from her pen more truth and impartiality than we have been accustomed to find in the works of other travelers in America. She called to her an old white headed servant of the General, and taking a seat by him on the grass near the vault, continued for some time in close conversation with him relative to the private life and family habits of the General; then she suddenly arose, shook him by the hand very cordially, and hastening to the vault picked off a green bunch of grass and deposited it in her bosom! - - Sure, thought I at this moment, how much more to be envied is <u>Washington in his tomb</u> than the proudest <u>living monarch on his throne</u>! How dear is the recollection of virtuous actions; how rich the reward of genuine patriotism!!

Remember us all with the tenderest affection to my dear nieces. Tell them to write to me after I shall have gotten home. Mr. B. [Bulloch] is directed to forward to you a bill for their use.

Mrs. Elliot unites in a friendly remembrance of your good parents, sister, aunt, uncle, and friends generally, - to all of whom be so kind as to present us most respectfully.

>In haste,
>>My dear Madam,
>I am,
>>Yours truly,
>>J. Elliot[9]

This letter indicates Caroline Matilda lived until at least 1820. A notice of the post office holding a letter for Carolina M. Elliott in the *Savannah Daily Georgian* on 5 March 1822 is the last reference to her found to date; however, Caroline must have died before her father's death in 1827, as she is not listed in the probate of his estate. This letter also indicates Caroline is not present in the north with her family but instead resides with Mrs. Efrom Lee, who has to date not been identified. Caroline's health appears to have been an issue of concern as early as 1820, and the idea of it improving upon the arrival of summer and warmer weather may indicate that she, like so many of the era, suffered from consumption, today known as tuberculosis. This letter also provides insight into John's concern for and pride in all his children and their accomplishments.

John's account of their journey to Mount Vernon reads like so many of the time. Upon, Martha Washington's death in 1802 the home passed to Bushrod Washington, an Associate Justice of the Supreme Court of the United States. As it had for many years, before and after Washington's death, Mount Vernon attracted many visitors who just wanted to see and touch something belonging to General Washington. After his death, his tomb drew visitors from far and wide, including those in government out for a holiday and sightseers from around the globe. John's description of their visit recollected the deep feelings all citizens of the newly formed republic held for the *father of our country*. As only thirty-seven years had passed since the end of the American Revolution, most of its citizenry knew many who had fought, remembered their sacrifice, and honored those who gave all. Martha Elliott's feeling during this visit are not expressed in John's letter; however, her memories must have turned many times to those relayed by her father, Revolutionary War hero, General Daniel Stewart.

A band accompanied the outing on the steamboat journey down the Potomac. As the party approached Washington's home, *Hail Columbia* was struck. The band later played a hymn by Pleyel as the party walked to the tomb. It is possible John Elliott was a Mason, as he recognized one of Pleyel's hymns, which were part of many Masonic rituals. Number 24 of 38 children, Ignatz Joseph Pleyel (1757-1831), an Austrian-born Frenchman, wrote many hymns used by Masonic lodges. His first hymn became quite popular in the United States, appearing in many shape note hymnals such as *The Sacred Harp*.[10]

Home to Georgia

In 1826, John's senate term ended, and he returned home, declining to accept a second term as Senator. Martha and the children had returned previously to Laurel View where she awaited the birth of her fifth child. Soon, John began negotiations to sell Laurel View to William Maxwell. He then accepted the directorship with the most prominent and prosperous bank in Savannah, the Planter's Bank of Georgia. John and Martha planned to take up full-time residence in Savannah.

During the intervening years, James Bulloch had established himself as a prominent businessman in Savannah. Hetty and James added another son to their family in 1823. The families had during this separation, remained close. With John and Martha's return the two families would meet often at social and civic events and church.

Only a year and a half later, John Elliott died on 9 August 1827 in Savannah of dysentery. His obituary in the *Augusta Chronicle* stated:

> On Thursday morning the 9th inst. the Honorable JOHN ELLIOTT, late a Senator in the Congress of the U. States from the State of Georgia.
>
> This estimable man had but recently determined to make this city [Savannah] his future home; his friends were about realizing the pleasures they had promised themselves from this agreeable society, when alas! he has been summoned hence, possessed of every thing calculated to attach him to the world, and the world to him.
>
> Mr. Elliott had received intelligence from his plantation situated about 40 miles from this place, of uncommon sickness and mortality among his negroes, by the prevalence of the Dysentery - he visited them to administer to their comforts and extend to them all the assistance which an enlightened and humane master could afford in their distress; but unfortunately, he remained there too long, and contracted the disease, of which he died, on his return to Savannah after an illness about ten days.
>
> Mr. Elliott had been repeatedly called to distinguished offices to the service of his country, the duties of which he ever discharged with fidelity and ability.
>
> As a public man, his loss is greatly to be deplored, with his family and in the circle of his associates and friends, he was amiable, instructive, and every thing that they could desire - endearing all to him by the suavity and urbanity of his manners and the flow of conversation, which was more than ordinarily intellectual.
>
> To be deprived of such a companion extracts from the bosom of friendship, its deepest regrets. Mr. E was 56 years of age, and died as he had lived a sincere Christian. *Savannah Georgian*.[11]

The *New York Times* published an obituary for John Elliott which was then reprinted in the *Savannah Georgian* on September 6th. It read:

> The New York Times is republishing the obituary notice of the late John Elliott, pay the following just tribute to his worth:—"Mr. Elliott was an alumnus of Yale College, and having passed through the ordinary term of four years, graduated with honor. He was not more distinguished as a proficient in elegant literature, than for his accomplishments as a gentleman—and by a rare union of whatever was calculated to claim respect and conciliate the affections of his fellow students and the faculty, his departure from New Haven, where he had attracted a numerous circle of friends, formed an era, which few students can lay claim to. As he was in youth, so he was in maturer years. In his domestic relations, he was every thing which could attract veneration and love,—As the head of a coloured [sp] population davolved [sp] upon him by inheritance, he was more their protector than their master. For many years, and probably to the time of his death, no white man held the rod over his slaves. His overseer, one of themselves, held more a patriarchal than a magisterial sway. Blessed with an elegant competency, he was one of those rare instances, where public office courted his acceptance, and to which he acceded more from considerations of duty than ambition. Were we to add any thing to the few remarks of our own, it would be that Mr. Elliott was in the habit of correspondence and possessed the affectionate esteem of the late President Dwight, down to the termination of his own invaluable life.

John Elliott's death left 28-year-old Martha with four small children from their union, including nine-month-old Daniel, and two stepdaughters, Jane Elizabeth, age eighteen, and Corinne Louisa, age fourteen, to raise. Compounding the family's grief was the death of three-year-old Charles William, one month later on 8 September 1827. The *Savannah Georgian* printed a notice of his death on 11 September 1827. The probate of John's estate listed a payment made on 21 January 1828 to George Farres "for coffins for John Elliott & child." An additional entry only a few days later stated "Pd J.S. Lamb bills part funerals expenses son Charles."[12] Both John and Charles were buried in the Elliott crypt at Midway Cemetery.

John Elliott's Estate

The death of John Elliott in August 1827 brought James, Hester, and Martha Elliott even closer together. John Elliott died *intestate*. At fifty-five and in robust health, John expected to live many more years. That first year, both families lived in "full mourning," especially Martha, now a widow, and Hetty, John Elliott's oldest surviving daughter and wife to James. Then for half a year, the families continued in half-mourning, attending only small social events and traveling little.

Martha had a choice in whom would be the executor of John's estate. Her stepson-in-law was an obvious choice. Asking a family member or personal friend to serve as executor was accepted practice. Additionally, James had extensive experience in such matters. Joseph Jones, William Ward, and Oliver Stephens also served in a legal capacity to prepare the inventory or probate listing of Elliott's estate. James Bulloch now became the executor. It fell to him to prepare all documents and deal with all legal affairs. Managing John's extensive plantations and other business holdings while the estate was inventoried and prepared for disbursement would occupy a tremendous amount of his time in the coming years.

> You, Joseph Jones, Wm. Ward & Oliver Stevens do swear, that you will make a just and true appraisement and inventory of all and singular the goods, chattel, and ___ of John Elliott, late of Liberty County deceased, or and shown to you by James S. Bulloch, administrator of said deceased, and that you will return the same, certified under your hands __ the said James S. Bulloch within the times prescribed by law:

Sworn before me this, eleventh day	Jos. Jones
of Dec. 1827	William Ward
John Dunwody, ___C.L.G.	Oliver Stephens[13]

On 10 December 1827, an application for Letters of Administration of John's estate appeared in the *Savannah Republican*.

> Georgia, Liberty county - By the hon. the Justices of the Inferior Court of Liberty county, sitting for ordinary purposes. To all whom it may concern. Whereas, Mrs. Martha Elliott and Major James S. Bulloch has applied to the honorable the court of Ordinary of Liberty county for letters of administration on the goods and chattels, rights and credits that were of John Elliott, late of said county deceased.
>
> These are therefore to cite and admonish all and singular, the kindred and creditors at the said deceased to file their objections (if any they have,) in my office in Riceborough on or before the 5th day of December next, otherwise letters of administration will be granted to the applicants. Witness, the Hon. John Dunwody, one of the Justices of the said court this 5th day of November, A.D. one thousand eight hundred and twenty-seven.
>
> Nov 10   E Riker[14]

The letters of administration, filed on that same date appoint James as the estate's executor, requiring him to:

> do make or cause to be made, a true & perfect inventory of all & singular the goods, chattel & credits, of the said deceased, which have or shall come to the hands, possession or knowledge, of the said James S. Bulloch or into the

possession of any other person for him, and the same so made do exhibited unto the said Court of Ordinary, when he shall be thereunto required, and such goods, chattels, & credits, do well & truly administer accordingly to Law, & make a just and true account of his actings and doings therein[15]

Five signatures identify those responsible for the probate of Elliott's estate. Along with James were his mother, Anne Irvine Bulloch Powell (second marriage to James Powell, Jr., widowed the second time in 1816), John B. Gaudry, John Bacon, and William Ward. Census records indicate that Gaudry resided in Old Franklin Ward, Savannah, while Bacon and Ward both owned numerous slaves in Liberty County, indicating they owned plantations.[16] The document's surety bond obligated the signees to pay the court $70,000 if administration of the estate was not carried out in a *true and perfect* account. Interestingly, the surety bond was provided by Anne Powell, indicating she now possessed a great deal of wealth.

The Elliott estate inventory, completed in early December 1827 and filed on 9 April 1828 with the Liberty County Probate Court, revealed both the goods and chattel of a wealthy Southern landowner.[17] (A complete transcription of the probate can be found in Appendix A.) Two hundred and nineteen slaves were listed on Elliott's Laurel View plantation, including three carpenters, Bob valued at $800, Vermont at $450, and Isaac at $600. Driver James was also valued at $600. The list appears to have grouped these enslaved Africans as families. For example, carpenter Isaac appears with wife Hannah ($400), and children Rose ($225), Mindy ($175), and Bob ($100) for a total of $1500. In terms of 2018 unskilled labor, this family alone equaled $462,000. The total value of the plantation's enslaved population was valued at $61,295 for a 2018 unskilled labor rate of $18,900,000![18]

The inventory also affords us with a glimpse of how enslaved persons were valued in 1827. For example, Ben, a tailor, was valued at $450 as was Stephens, the carriage driver, and Vermont, a carpenter. However, cooks like Kate and Miley were valued at $200 to $250. Ten slaves were listed as old or aged and valued from $10 to $300 for nine slaves, indicating that some, despite their age, still held value and probably continued to perform various tasks. The same holds true with those listed as diseased or invalid, including the shoemaker London ($300).

Six skills were noted among the enslaved population. The plantation's four drivers included James ($600), Tom ($300), Stephens, (carriage driver $450), and Nat (driver, aged, $350). The two cooks and one nurse (Phillis, old nurse $50) are the only skills associated with female slaves. Tailor Ben ($450) and shoemaker London (crippled, $300) probably supplied clothing to the enslaved population. The three carpenters, mentioned previously, were also highly valued.

Three notations in this inventory and appraisal are perplexing. Tom, valued at $300 has the notation *Congo*, after his name. This most likely denoted his land of origin, yet this designation was not made for any other slave. After "Tim, husband to Patience" there is a small notation, which is legible as "69 negroes." A very small illegible word proceeds 69. This may indicate that Tim was the father to 69 children. Finally, after the name Charlotte are the words "at Nabs" suggesting that Charlotte was "rented" out to another plantation.

Less than two years later, the 1830 U.S. Federal Census enumerated only 117 slaves on John Elliott's estate and listed Martha as the owner. These records showed no "white" inhabitants of the plantation. Incidentally, the earlier 1820 U.S. Federal Census showed 115 slaves on the plantation and six white residents which would have been John, Martha, Caroline Matilda, Jane, Corinne, and John based on age and sex designations. While the census was recorded on 7 August, it does not reflect the birth of Susan, recorded as 6 August of that year.[19]

The increase from 1820 to 1827 of more than 100 slaves seems to indicate a great increase in wealth and the purchase of additional slave labor by the Senator. This earlier 1820 census noted that fifteen of the male slaves were under the age of ten while twenty-one of the female slaves were in that age group. These numbers show that sixteen percent of the enslaved population were children, probably born on the plantation and not purchased. It appears very doubtful that the increase in 100 slaves during this seven-year period occurred simply by birth.

Along with the list of slaves, the estate inventory demonstrates the great wealth held by the family in material goods both at the plantation and at their Savannah residence. Included in the inventory for the plantation residence were a piano forte and stool, a backgammon box, and portable secretary. Many of the rooms had carpets including at least some of the bedrooms where walls were adorned with prints such as "the Annunciation," "two prints from Shakespeare," and two "Adam, Cain, & Able," as well as two entitled "Maternal Love." Books numbered over 210 *neatly bound* volumes along with "state papers" and 43 *Not. Ed. Review*. Elliott also owned six large maps.

Most Liberty county plantations owned some livestock for both subsistence and revenue, although never considered a main cash product. The plantation's inventory listed 159 head of cattle, forty-four sheep, and forty-two hogs, for a total value of $924. Also listed were horses named Buncombe, Burke, Charley, Rock, and Bachelor, and a pair of carriage horses for the plantation's four-wheel carriage. The male buck (possibly a small mule or donkey) probably pulled one of the four plantation wagons or the livery wagon.

Inventory and appraisement of the Elliott's Savannah residence indicated even more wealth and luxury. The gentlemen described much of the furniture as *Mahogany*. Carpets and rugs were numerous throughout the home. Sets of linens and bed linens occur along with fourteen quilts and eleven blankets. Dining wares include ivory knives and forks, a cordial stand with four bottles, new and old tea sets, both new and old dinner sets, and cut decanters along with dozens of wine, champagne, claret cordial, and other miscellaneous glassware. Silver items listed encompass a wide range from six dozen spoons of various sizes to a large silver ladle, a pair of gravy spoons, seven old spoons, and a teapot. Additionally, the family kept a cow and calf, probably for milk at this home, as well as another four-wheel carriage.

Looking just at the historic standard of living value (a way of measuring purchasing power of an income or wealth in its relative ability to purchase a bundle of goods or services) of the goods owned by John Elliott at the time of his death presents an timely and accurate view of his wealth. For example, the value of goods in his plantation home was estimated at $927.25, approximately $24,100 in today's money (All calculations compared to 2018). Additionally, the plantation inventory included $2024.00 in livestock, wagons, and carriages, for a value of $52,600.[1]

Considering the market value of the enslaved population, as opposed to the previously stated value of their labor, places their market value at just under $1.6 million. Not including the value of the plantation land, dwellings, and crops, John Elliott's family inherited approximately $1.7 million in Liberty County alone and another $111,000 in goods in the Savannah house based on 2018 values.[2]

John Elliott also owned bank notes and stocks and held bonds for approximately $6668 at the time of accounting in December of 1827. Today's value would be $173,000.[3] Even with seven heirs sharing this amount, each received more than two million dollars upon settlement of the estate. John Elliott's heirs included his wife Martha, his married daughter Hester Bulloch, along with his surviving unmarried children Jane, Corinne, Susan, Georgia, and Daniel Elliott.

The Years Passed

Life went on for the two Savannah families. In April 1828, James assigned his portion of John Elliott's estate to Joseph Cumming. "By virtue of his intermarriage with Hetty A." James was entitled to "one seventh part of the estate, real and personal" of the estate. Cumming paid James $10,000 for the portion. In today's money terms, this assignment would be valued at about $273,000 (real price) or $8,520,000 in income value.[4] Two years later, E. Baker, Clerk of Court, Liberty County, added the following to the document:

> Savannah, 13 June 1830. The object of the above assignment being accomplished, I, Joseph Cumming, for & in consideration of the sum of one dollar to me in hand paid, the receipt whereof is hereby acknowledged, have bargained, sold, released, and confirmed, and by these presents so bargain, sell, release, and confirm, unto the said James S. Bulloch, his heirs, and assigns, all the interest, right, property, and demand of the said James S. Bulloch in the estate of the said John Elliott deceased, which by the above deed is conveyed to me. In Witness, whereof I have hereunto set my hand and seal this day and year aforesaid. Jos. Cumming (Appendix A)

Why James and Joseph entered into such an agreement was not recorded, only that two years after receiving a large sum of money for his portion of the estate James purchased it back for only one dollar! The statement "the object of the above assignment being accomplished" leads to the belief that James as an heir of John Elliott, could not during this time it took to probate his estate hold and benefit from any portion of the estate. Therefore, Jos. Cumming purchased the portion and held it until the estate was settled.

James received a notice from the Court of Common Pleas in March of 1828 and failed to appear. A newspaper notice of a pending forty dollar fine was placed on 20 March.[5] Like so many stories gleaned from newspaper columns, it is unknown if James appeared or had to pay the fine.

On 7 April, a notice in the *Savannah Daily Georgian* invited "friends and acquaintances of the late Sarah Irvine, J. S. Bulloch, and [illegible] T. Stewart are requested to attend the funeral of the former, THIS AFTERNOON, at 5 o'clock." Sarah was the youngest sister (by twenty years) of James' mother Anne Irvine Bulloch Powell.

A Tragic Marriage

On 1 May 1828, Jane E. Elliott married John Stevens Law, a physician from Liberty County. Following her father's death by not quite nine months, while the family was still in mourning, Jane's marriage was rather unusual for the time. John was born 21 March 1800, at Ramoth Gilead Plantation in Liberty County, to Colonel Joseph and Elizabeth Stevens Law. Both Jane and John attended the Midway Congregational Church having been raised only miles apart on neighboring plantations. An 1822 graduate of Yale College, John served Liberty County as a "physician, druggist, and insurance agent" from 1825 to 1828. For the next ten years, he practiced in Savannah.[6]

As the oldest unmarried daughter, Jane would inherit property from her father's estate upon its final settlement. A marriage agreement (see Appendix A), with James Bulloch and John Dunwody, as her trustees provided a few additional details about this marriage. Jane was described as a "spinster," rather a harsh word applied to a young woman only nineteen or twenty years of age; however, this was the legal term used to describe her *never married* status. At this time, Georgia law prevented females from owning and managing property of their own. Therefore, Jane needed trustees to hold her inheritance in trust and an agreement of marriage in regard to her property (Appendix A). This agreement legally stated:

> To have and to hold, receive and take, the said undivided seventh part of all the estate both real and personal, of the said John Elliott deceased, unto the said James S. Bulloch and John Dunwody, and the survivor of them, and the executors and administrators of the survivor of them, in trust to and for the joint use, benefit, and advantage of the said John S. Law and Jane E.

Elliott, during their joint lives, and on the death of either of them, then for the use and benefit of the survivor during his or her natural life; and on the death of the survivor, to the issue of the marriage, if any, in case of no issue of the marriage, then to the sole use, benefit, and behoof of the survivor, his or her heirs and assigns forever.[7]

Sadly, Jane enjoyed only eleven months of marital bliss, for the *Savannah Georgian* on 18 April 1829, article carried the following related notices:

> Yet Another.—About eleven o'clock yesterday morning the stable of Capt. Wiltberger, on the lane in the rear of South Broad street near the Presbyterian Church, was discovered on fire, and was bursting into a blaze among many tenements of the most combustible description, when by prompt assistance it was extinguished, after being partly torn down. This stable is only two lots from those on which two attempts have been previously made, and as we have before stated, in the rear of Dr. Law's house and the lot next to it.—

On the present occasion there is no doubt the fire was designedly communicated in the rack. Perhaps in no part of the city could a better supply of water have been obtained, there being two private wells in the immediate neighborhood of the spot, and a public pump within one hundred yards; to which ready supply of water, with the active exertions of the Fire Companies and citizens, may be attributed the prompt extinguishment of the flames. Several individuals were arrested, and carried before the Mayor for examination, but we have not learned the result.

> We think proper here to repeat, what we mentioned a few days since that every tenement should be provided with buckets ready filled with water. Very frequently a single bucket properly applied, will extinguish a flame at the outset, which would otherwise involve a neighborhood or perhaps the city in wide-spread destruction.

> On the same day, the newspaper had the following notice:

A Card: Dr. Jno. S. Law tenders his warmest thanks to his friends and fellow citizens, for their unremitted exertions for his welfare during the fire of yesterday April 18.

On 30 April, the *Georgian* posted Jane's death notice.

> Died: On the morning of the 20th, Mrs. Jane E. Law, wife of Dr. John S. Law, in the 20th year of her age. Each passing breeze on times rapid wing sounds the knell of Man's mortality — the spring of life opens with all its freshness and beauty — the buds of love and innocence expand; but ere youth's short spirit is over, the verdure dies — those bowers of bliss cease to bloom. Thus bloomed and died the dear departed object whom we now lament. Blessed in tender infancy with the most competent of parents to mold each bursting

excellence, and soon exhibiting a mind of superior order, and a sweet and lovely temper, the bosom of each fond relative beat high with expectation. At an early period her anxious parent was willing to forego the sweets of her little society to place her under circumstances the most advantageous to her mental cultivation. Thus most of her life was spent distant from home. In due time the most sanguine expectations were realized. She now appeared under the paternal roof with all the attractions which youthful beauty, a highly improved mind, a modest demeanor, and an unaffected amiability could present. But she was not satisfied with their present attainments — she placed a just estimate upon them — and avoided the flatteries which her merits now called forth. That pride of life, which in the eye of folly swells into such importance, now sunk in her estimation into its native littleness— she grasped at] Heavenly wisdom — her soul became enamoured with the magnificence and splendor of eternal things. It now became her greatest pleasure to sit pensively at the feet of Jesus, and with delighted reverence to hear his words. Heaven called her to enter for a few short months in to the nearest relation of life. Ardently attached to her bosom companion, and as tenderly beloved by him that their tide of domestic happiness rolled on without a ripple. Bright were the prospects of long continued bliss to her bereaved partner, when suddenly "hope's young ray was quenched in earthly tears." What is his loss let his disconsolate soul answer. Her career was short but useful. She was a cheerful Christian; but I have heard the sigh steal from her bosom -- it was the sigh of a contrite heart. Her sigh was heard in Heaven, and methinks her Savior responded "let not your heart be troubled." Every day her character developed new charms. They continued to bloom in sickness -- have survived the desolation of the grave, and will brighten forever is those pure regions of light whither she had gone."

While the author of Jane's obituary remains unknown, its length and sentiments expressed great sorrow and sadness rarely displayed in newspaper obituaries of the era. Jane's death, occurring only three or four days after the fire, presumably at their home, causes one to speculate on the nature of her death.

Another Death in the Family

It seems Martha's period of mourning would never end, as one month after Jane's tragic death, on 27 May 1829, Martha's father General Daniel Stewart died at his Cedar Hill Plantation in Liberty County. Within a two-year period, Martha lost her husband and young son, her stepdaughter, and now her father. Daniel's obituary in the *Daily Georgian* read:

Obituary. General Daniel Stewart, a Patriot of 1776, died at his residence in Liberty County on the 27th ult. [*ultimo mense* – last month] aged 69 years. In the Revolutionary War, although but 16 years of age, such was his love of country and military ardour, increased by the aggressions of Great Britain, and the depredations of the tories in his neighborhood, he joined the standard of his country and was frequently in battle under Generals Sumpter, Marion, and Col. Wm. Harden, at Pocotaligo, was taken prisoner near Charleston, and put on board the English Prison Ship in that harbor: and probably no man suffered more or went through more perils and hardships during the whole war and the different Indian depredations afterwards, on the Georgia frontier. General Stewart enjoyed the confidence and esteem of his fellow citizens, to a great degree. He filled in his native county every public office in the gift of the people, and to his death was honored and respected by them, and from his retiring and unostentatious manners and love of the society of his family and friends, refused many offices tendered him. We have indeed few such men to spare!

The Legislature of the State, also conferred several appointments upon him unsolicited. He was an elector who voted for the venerable Madison to the Chief Magistracy of the Union and on raising a division of Cavalry, he was elected to Brigadier General.

It was in private life Gen. Stewart shone most conspicuously. In all the relations of Husband, Parent, Friend, Master, he was affectionate, kind, humane, and indulgent. The widow and the orphans will long remember his virtues and kindness, displayed towards them.

He was a Christian! and though all his titles here have now passed away like the shadow over the plain, he's now enjoying a nobler title, a more enduring inheritance in that world, where the righteous triumph and shine, as the stars in the firmament of Heaven.[8]

Unlike Martha's husband, Daniel Stewart left a will, dated 23 December 1828, only five months before his death. It read:

State of Georgia, Liberty County: I, Daniel Stewart, of the State and County aforesaid, planter, do make this my will & testament as follows; to wit, I give & bequeath to my dear wife, Sarah all the property which she brought me when married, except such as has been sold or died, with the increase of the former to her and her assigns forever. I also give her my household furniture during her life, at her death to be considered as my estate, except such part as she may give away. I also give my dear wife my four wheeled carriage, with the horse now belonging to the same, to her and her assigns forever. I give her the one half of my cattle & sheep, and all my plantation tools, waggon [sp], cart, ploughs & I also give her the one half of such monie [sp] as may come from the current crop, after all my just debts are finally paid. It is my intention and wish that the whole my landed estate remain for the use of my dear wife during her natural life and she is hereby authorized to occupy any part of the same annotated; but at her death to be my estate for the benefit of my children or grandchildren, as the case may be. I also give my dear wife my cooper fellow Bob, because I got him in an exchange for a fellow of Estate of Jesse Hines [his wife's father]. No part of corn [?] provisions is to be taken for the plantation, unless by consent of my wife.

I now give and bequeath to my dear children or grandchildren the whole of the remainder of my property in the manner following; that is to say, It is my intention and wish the same may be divided or put into four divisions, equal as possible. One division or fourth part I give and bequeath to my grandchildren, Daniel, Sarah, & Ripley, children of my deceased son John [son of Daniel and Sarah Oswald who died in 1823], to them and their heirs and assigns forever. Item. I give and bequeath to my grandchildren the children of Col. Josiah Wilson one division or fourth part, jointly to them, their heirs and assigns forever, provided nevertheless, my daughter Mary to have the use of this little pittance during her life. Item. I give and bequeath to my son Daniel M. Stewart one other division or fourth part of my estate together with my gold watch, to him, his heirs and assigns forever. Item. I give and bequeath unto my daughter Mrs. Martha Elliott one other division or fourth part of my estate for her own use, to her and her assigns forever. — My landed estate, with any other species of property which may hereafter become after the death of my wife, my estate, are to be distributed and divided in and among my children & grand children in an equal manner, by four dividends, as specified already.

I now nominate my dear wife Sarah as executrix, my friend Charlton Hines, my son in law Col. Josiah Wilson, & my son Daniel M. Stewart, executors to this my last will and testament. D. Stewart.

Signed, sealed, and acknowledged before us, subscribing witnesses, The twenty third day of December eighteen hundred and Twenty eight.[9]

Daniel Stewart's property appraisement [Appendix A] included a listing of 27 enslaved Negroes, valued at $6,685. Additionally, his furniture and other goods totaled $2,468. This property would be divided among his heirs later in the year. Although most of his property was left to the immediate use of his wife Sarah, she did not long survive the death of her husband. Mary Jones reported in letters to Charles Colcock Jones the death of Sarah Hines Lewis Stewart and of her sufferings at the end "being very great."[10] Sarah died on 7 November, her 55th birthday. Her will left four slaves to Martha and her three children by John Elliott. Her request read, "Sylvia and her three children I wish to be given to Mrs. Martha Elliott, her and her three children by Mr. John Elliott, with my particular request that she be ever treated with particular care and kindness." Based on names of identified Bulloch family slaves and the estate appraisement for Sarah Stewart, this author believes that two of Sylvia's children can be identified. Appraisements often value Negro children as well as adults. Children can often be identified by their low appraisement. A review provided two names Lavinia and Hagar that also appear among the Bulloch slaves in various documents. [Appendix A]

Daniel McLachlan Stewart, Martha's brother and executor of their father's will, was born in late 1791. He married twice, first on 7 October 1818, to Eliza Win Bacon (1791-1822). This marriage produced four children who all died before their mother. Daniel married, on 1 January 1824, Mary Eliza Eigelberger. This marriage produced eleven children.[11] The coming settlement of General Daniel Stewart's estate would greatly involve Martha and James over the coming years.

Changes in James' Life

On 9 March 1829, James offered his house and furnishing on Broughton Street (Washington Ward) for rent, with option to purchase, in the *Savannah Georgian* for $780 ground rent. This term meant that an individual could own a house, but someone else owned the actual property that the house sat upon. Therefore, the house owner had to pay the owner rent on the land. This kept initial home ownership costs lower, and the property could always be purchased later. The advertisement noted that "possession given at any time."

Taking the ship *Florian*, the Bulloch and Elliott families traveled north to New York on 30 June 1829, only one month after General Daniel Stewart's death. The party at that time included "JS Bulloch, Lady and Child . . . Mrs. Elliott, children and servant. . . Miss Elliott [Corinne], Miss Williams, Miss Bulloch . . . ."[12] Miss Bulloch perhaps was James' niece, Jane, the daughter of the late John Irvine Bulloch. The passenger list included a total of eight unmarried females. On 26 October 1829, James, Hetty, and their son along, with Mrs. Elliott, Miss Corinne Elliott, and three children (Susan, Georgia, and Daniel) arrived home from New York after five days ship passage.[13] In the early part of the nineteenth century, wealthy families often summered in the North to avoid the malarial summers of coastal Georgia. This extended summer vacation may have resulted from Hester's frail health. However, many families returned South only after the region's first heavy frost which would remove the "bad air" that they believed caused malaria.

During and after her period of mourning, Martha continued to live in the Elliott's Savannah home and eventually participated more actively in society. Newspaper notices provide us with some details of her life. She drew monies from shares of the Planter's Bank and the Central Rail Road. In 1830 and 1831, Martha and the children made several trips by steam packet to Charleston, South Carolina.[14] According to tuition payments in the probate records for John Elliott, Susan and Georgia both attended the Chatham Academy in 1829 and 1830. Daniel received lessons from G.B. Cummings. Corinne Elliott took piano lessons from P.P Morin, and the estate purchased a piano for $368.25 and a guitar for $25.[15] This expenditures listing from 1827 to 1834 provides a great deal of information about the family's activities, travels, and expenses.

The U.S. Federal Census for 1830 shows the Bulloch family residing in Warren Ward. The household included eight slaves: three men, four women, and one child. A *free, colored, female*, between the age of twenty-four and thirty-six, boarded with the family. An 1810 Georgia ordinance required that free blacks in Savannah have a white guardian of their choice and approved by the court. Passage of this ordinance was designed to discourage free blacks from settling in Georgia. White members of the family included James, his wife, one child and a white woman age sixty to seventy years. This unidentified woman could have been Ann Bulloch Powell or a woman who served as a nanny to young James Dunwody Bulloch, now seven years of age.

The eight slaves owned by the Bulloch's at their Savannah residence appear typical of the period. Upper class households of that time averaged between six and twelve household slaves. While the women carried out domestic chores such as cooking, cleaning, laundry, and care of the children, the enslaved males cared for the livestock and grounds, served as butlers, or drove the carriage. Additionally, a skilled male slave, such as a carpenter, cabinet maker, or blacksmith may have been hired out to provide a bit more income for the family.

Settlement with John Law

In 1830, some three years after the death of John Elliott and two years after the death of his wife, Jane, John Law brought suit against James over the Elliott estate. John Law was to have received one seventh of the estate as he inherited his wife's property upon her death. Perhaps John Law needed money and did not wish to wait for the final settlement of the estate. So, he asked for one seventh of Laurel View and one seventh part of second Tything Anson Ward and the improvements thereon in Savannah "by virtue of his martial rights as the husband of Jane." (See Appendix A) Basically, he asked James Bulloch to purchase as John Elliott's administrator the one seventh of each property that he now owned. The asking price was $2357.14, approximately $66,000 in 2018.[16]

The court agreement settled for John and he was paid one third of the amount immediately and the remaining amount upon sale of the properties.

James offered the Washington Ward house again for rent on 6 April 1830 (*Savannah Daily Georgian*). Finally, on 3 February 1831, less than a month before Hetty's death on 21 February 1831, S. Philbrick auctioned the household furnishings of this residence. The auction advertisement listed the following:

> . . . an assortment of Fashionable House hold and Kitchen Furniture, consisting in part Sideboard, Dining Tea do, Card do, bookcase, sofa, chairs, fenders, Andirons, shovels and tongs, Knives and forks, Cut Glass, china and Crockery ware, Wine coolers, Beds, Mattresses and Bed room furniture. Also - one superior English Piano 20 demijohns choice old Madeira and Juice of the Grape, warranted pure.

On this same date, the law partnership of James Bulloch and John Dunwody was dissolved "by mutual consent" (*Savannah Daily Georgian*). The advertisement indicated "James S. Bulloch . . . will settle the affairs of the current and continue to devote his time and best exertions for the interest of his customers."

Hetty died on 21 February 1831. Her obituary in the *Savannah Daily Georgian* read:

> Died, In this city on the 21st Mrs. Hetty A, wife of James S. Bulloch and daughter of the Late Hon. John Elliott, thirty-two years old. During a painful and protracted illness, she evidenced such patience, mildness of manners, complete resignation to the Divine will, as to prove that hers was a living faith in all sufficient Saviour. Whilst her afflicted relatives must grieve for one so much beloved and valued, they are comforted in the assurances that 'Altho' dead she still liveth—Lives in the memory of those who loved her—lives in the regions of bliss among the bright hosts of heaven— "Whose robes are washed in the blood of the lamb." "Blessed are the dead who die in the Lord."[17]

Hetty is believed to be buried in the Elliott family mausoleum in the Midway Congregational Church Cemetery, Liberty County, with her father.

It appears Martha may not have been present in Savannah when Hetty died, as the *Savannah Daily Georgian* noted Martha and her children's arrival from Charleston on the steam packet *John Stiney* on 28 March 1831. Martha and children returned to Charleston in April of 1831, arriving back in Savannah on 2 May.[18]

James meanwhile accepted the role of administrator of an estate, this time his wife's. In September of 1831, James, along with William B. Bulloch, his uncle, and John B. Gaudry, filed a petition and paid a surety bond of $2,600 for their role in completing Hetty A's "true and perfect inventory." The petition was filed in Chatham County, indicating this was their principal residence. James posted a newspaper notice of Washington Ward lots 37 and 38 "with the appurtenances" to be sold for the "benefit of the heirs and creditors of said estate." The estate was that of Hetty Elliott Bulloch.[19]

Newspaper notices from the time of Hetty's death in February 1831 until May 1832 appear to be the only historical record of James' first year as a widower. These notices show his business interests continuing as deliveries of cotton, rice, and other agricultural products arrived from Sunbury, Darien, and Riceboro, until July when

James closed his factorage and commission business. James remained active in the Savannah Temperance Society and his legal practice.[20]

As a widow, Martha invited her step son-in-law and his young son to join her family in their Savannah home. It is possible, James had moved his family to this home before Hetty's death. Perhaps even a year or more earlier when he first listed his home for lease. Such arrangements rarely upset polite society as James relationship to Martha was now considered to be "brother to sister" due to their earlier marriages. Additionally, this living arrangement provided young James Dunwody Bulloch a stable home with his step-grandmother and cousins. It provided Martha' three young children with a father figure.

On 12 January1832, Martha's stepdaughter Corinne Elliott married family friend Robert Hutchison. Scottish-born Robert (1802-1861) was a wealthy, educated Savannah merchant who had never married. Corinne was eighteen years old, but the match to thirty-one-year-old Robert was not much different than that of Martha's marriage to John Elliott.

Despite and because of these family relationships, the marriage of James and Martha on 8 May 1832, only one year and two months after Hetty's death, disrupted their *family* and set Savannah's society to talking. Savannah resident Mary Telfair wrote to Mary Few of Virginia that a good deal of buzzing was taking place over a match among members of the church and that one remarked that the church would weep over such a marriage. She wrote of this union:

> A very singular marriage is about to take place here in a few days. . . Mrs. John Elliott a woman I understand of exalted piety—she married in the first instance a man old enough to be her father and no doubt sacrificed feeling to ambition. She made a most exemplary wife & *(hardest of all duties)* an excellent Step Mother. For four years she has acted the part of *a dignified widow* which of all characters *(Step Mother excepted)* is the most difficult to support, and now she is about marrying her husband's daughter's husband — he has been living in the house with her ever since the death of his wife and I thought viewed by her with sisterly regard. I begin to think with Miss Edgeworth that propinquity is dangerous and beyond the relationship of Brother and Sister *mutual dependence* is apt to create sentiment more tender than *the platonic*. . . It does not strike me as a criminal connection, but one highly revolting to delicacy. . ."[21]

Mary Telfair went on to expound that the late Mr. Elliott's only surviving daughter's feelings "were very much enraged." This daughter, Corinne Louisa, once devotedly attached to her stepmother, now refused to have any intercourse with her brother-in-law.[22] Mary Telfair ended with "I feel sorry for Mrs. Elliott, she had in her first marriage to practice an Apprenticeship to self-denial, in order to conciliate the good will of daughters as old as herself — by a noble and disinterested course of conduct she received their confidence and affection and fulfilled her duties as a wife as faithfully as if she had married from Love."

Despite the talk, the wedding, held at the Elliott house in Savannah, was well attended. Eleven-year-old Jane Marion Dunwody (now Glen) and her father, John Dunwody stated in legal documents written years later, that they were in attendance. Along with Jane and John, one can assume James' sister Jane Bulloch Dunwody also attended the wedding along with their sons James, John, William, Henry, and Charles.[23]

Chapter VII: JSB's Life in Transition

Although James had closed his factoring concern, he continued to pursue other areas of investments. In 1832, the 1829 discovery of gold in north Georgia led James to place his name in the upcoming lottery drawing for those lands. In early April, just before his May wedding, James drew No. 260 District 11, Section 1.[1] The Gold Lottery of 1832 was the seventh lottery in the Georgia Land Lottery. The system was used by the State of Georgia from 1805 until 1832 to distribute land. The Seventh was authorized by the Georgia General Assembly on 24 December 1831, a few years after the start of the Georgia Gold Rush, near Dahlonega. The act specified that approximately one third of the 160-acre land districts would be designated as 40-acre gold districts and distributed in a separate lottery. This land currently belonged to the Cherokee people. Each successful person in the lottery had to pay a $10 per lot grant fee.

An 1832 Gold Lottery map shows James forty acres was located in what is now Lumpkin County. Two of James relatives also received land in the lottery, Archibald won a lot in the 4th Section, 12th District, while William B.'s lot was in the 2nd Section, 22nd District.

1832 Gold Lottery Map

On the first Tuesday in June of 1832, the Elliott home at No.6 First Tything, Anson Ward, with all improvements was sold "to make a division."[2] Almost five years after the passing of John Elliott, James still worked to settle the Elliott estate. The house had to be sold so that a division of the money could be made to Elliott's seven heirs; Martha, Susan, Georgia, Daniel, Corinne Elliott Hutchison, the estate of Jane Elliott Law, and James.

On 12 June 1832, in Chatham County, James and Martha signed the marriage settlement drawn up by her trustees. Daniel M. Stewart, her brother, and John Dunwody served as her trustees for her portion of the estates of her late husband and her late father. In the settlement, thirty-nine slaves are listed. [Appendix B] As with many marriage settlements of the time, the language of the settlement grants the following as to her worldly possessions:

> In trust, and to and for the joint use, benefit, and advantage of the said James S. Bulloch and Martha Elliott, during their joint lives, but to be in no event subject to any debts which the said James S. Bulloch may have heretofore contracted, or may hereafter contract, ...

Despite Mary Telfair's comments on the public outcry surrounding James' and Martha's wedding, the following August, James became embroiled in the banking controversy [see pages 79-81], and in September, ran for a seat as a Representative to the U.S. Congress.[3] His name continued to appear in Savannah's newspapers frequently throughout the year in connection with various enterprises and events. For example, on 27 September 1832, the *Savannah Daily Georgian* printed the following, "For Sale, A pair of Brown Bay Horses, 7 and 8 years old, and a neat Carriage. Apply James S. Bulloch."

On 2 October 1832, he received merchandise on the Sloop *John* from Charleston.[4] On 15 December, the *Savannah Daily Georgian* printed James' advertisement for the sale of a group of enslaved African Americans.

> Negroes: For sale, a small gang of prime Negroes at present working on the plantation of the late Mr. Elliott near Sunbury in Liberty County, from which they will be discharged on the first day of January 1833. An order to see the Negroes can be obtained from Mr. James S. Bulloch, residing at Cedar Hill Plantation near Riceboro in the same County and the terms of the sale may be obtained on application being made in Savannah to R. Hutchison.

This notice illustrates the close relationship James and Martha held with Robert Hutchison, their son-in-law, a prominent Savannah businessman. With James residing at Cedar Hill, Robert was representing him in business matters within the city. Robert and his wife, Corinne Elliott Hutchison now resided in the Elliott family home in Savannah, for Corinne's trust had purchased the home for her at the auction for $7025, approximately $218,000 in 2018 value.[5]

This advertisement also provided information about the family's current home, as it noted the family had taken up residence at Cedar Hill, Martha's deceased father's estate. It was there that Martha gave birth to Anna Louisa on 15 September 1833. Along with the new baby, Martha and James now raised his ten-year-old son James by Hetty, Martha's three children by John Elliott; Susan, age 13, Georgia, age 11, and Daniel not quite seven. This was Martha's sixth pregnancy.

Cedar Hill Plantation, near Riceboro. *Home and Flowers*, June 1902, Vol. XIL No.2 Floral Publishing Company, Springfield, Ohio

Death of His Brother and Mother

In 1827 at Cedar Hill Plantation, Liberty County, James' brother John Irvine Bulloch died leaving behind his wife Charlotte and two children William Gaston and Jane Dunwody Bulloch, ages 12 and 4. Executors for John then carried out all financial matters and settled his estate; to date none of those records have been found. In April of 1831, Anne Irvine Bulloch Powell, James and John's mother died. She left behind a will of which John Dunwody was executor. While a copy of the will has not been found, the record of her probate was found on Ancestry.com. [Appendix B]

Anne left an estate appraised at $19,072 including Cedar Hill Plantation valued at $4,500 and 58 slaves valued at $14,212. In 2018, the estate would equal $518,000.[6] While transcribing the inventory and appraisement, a series of lines and amounts within the two columns was analyzed. The answer came when the value for the slaves listed within two lines was realized as equal to the amount written between the columns. [This is easier to see and understand if viewed in Appendix B.] The inventory of slaves was made by family. For example, Old Jack is underlined. He has no family. Following Old Jack, Billy, Jenny, Ned and Lucy were listed before the next line. Each is given an individual value and as a family they equaled $1,500 in value. Not having a copy of Anne Powell's will leads to speculation that she specified that her *chattels* only be sold in family groups.

The U.S. Census of 1830 did provide a bit more information about these 58 people. The census recorded enslaved Negroes in categories by age and sex. Anne owned 12 male slaves under the age of 10, five males between 10 and 23, one male between 36 and 54, for a total of 22 male slaves. As for females, eight under age 10, seventeen between 10 and 23, three between 24 and 35, six between 36 and 54 and two between 55 and 99, for a total of 36.[7]

In 1833, James signed the following in front of witnesses in Liberty County:

> Know all men by these presents that I, James S. Bulloch of said State and County, Planter, am held and firmly bound with John Dunwody, trustee in the last will of Anne Powell deceased, for William Gaston Bulloch and Jane Bulloch, children of John Bulloch deceased and Charlotte Bulloch, in the full and just sum of nine thousand three hundred and sixty six dollars and fifty two cents.

Until William Gaston and Jane reached their maturity, James was responsible for their money, for giving them their biannual allotment of the interest and overseeing their finances. [Appendix B] Their mother Charlotte lived in Savannah and the children resided with her. After her death, believed to have been in 1840, the two children visited and lived with various family members.

Leaving Georgia for Connecticut

Several authors have speculated that eleven-year-old James D. Bulloch traveled north to Hartford, Connecticut, to attend the Hartford Academy in 1834. It is possible the family joined James in Hartford that summer and returned to Savannah for the winter. As was the common pattern of wealthy Southerners, the family once again traveled north in 1835, leaving Savannah on 1 June, aboard the *Celia* for New York City. Passengers included, Mrs. Hutchison, child and servant, Mrs. J.S. Bulloch, child and servant, Miss S. Elliott, Miss G.A. Elliott, J.S. Bulloch, Master Elliott (Daniel), and Jas. D. Bulloch. The Bulloch's took along Nancy Jackson, a slave and nursemaid.[8]

The family boarded at the Frederick and Mary Oakes Boarding House at 215 Main Street in Hartford. On 8 July 1835, just days after their arrival, Martha gave birth to her second daughter by James. They named her Martha and called her *Mittie*. Records indicate that James traveled to and fro from Hartford to Georgia at various times while Martha resided in that city.

The older girls attended the Hartford Female Seminary, while the boys may have attended the Hartford Academy or studied with tutors. Both institutions provided outstanding opportunities for their young students. The Hartford Female Seminary provided the girls with a well-rounded education while developing their moral character. The seminary's organizers had numerous Savannah and Liberty county connections, and the Seminary was widely recognized for its high standards.[9]

Records indicate James D. Bulloch began at Isaac Webb's Private Boarding School in 1837. The prestigious school located in Middletown, Connecticut, provided twenty students with a well-rounded education including French. Major J.S. Bulloch is listed in their 1839 catalog as a patron. Also listed in the catalog is Daniel S. Elliott, who followed his older half-brother to the school in 1838. Established in May 1833, the school's tuition was $250 per annum, about $7,800 per year in 2018. The boys had two one month vacations a year, May and October.[10]

Although absent from Savannah for long periods during the next two years, James remained active in business and personal matters within the city. In 1835, he continued his political aspirations by running for Representative to Congress on the Union Democratic Ticket.[11]

Guardianship of Free Negroes

Since at least 1828, James Bulloch had registered as guardian for several free Negroes. The law, enacted in 1819, required "persons of color to register with the clerk of the inferior court of the county in which they reside." Failure to register could result in the person being sold back into slavery (GL 1819 Vol 1 Page 41 Sequential # 025). In most cases, the free person could choose their own guardian. The Savannah Register of Free Persons of Color (1828-1864) contained references to both James and his uncle William Bellinger Bulloch as guardians of several free Negroes. Beginning in 1828, James was guardian for Joseph and Edward Beard, ages 38 and 30 respectively, born in Liberty County, who were employed as ship carpenters. Joseph stayed under James' guardianship until 1834, and Edward until 1838. Priscilla Boyd, a washerwoman, listed James as her guardian from 1828 to 1843. Sam Boyd was listed from 1832-1834 as under James' guardianship. These four free Negroes were found through preliminary searches of the register of free colored persons. Walter E. Wilson also carried out a search of these records and recorded several others under James' guardianship.[12]

James' guardianship of these free people of color reflected highly on his stature in the community and his standing within the "colored" population of Savannah. Each free person chose their own guardian. They would choose a person respected within their own community for fairness and respectful treatment of free Negroes. James' role was to make sure his *ward* registered each year, stayed out of legal trouble, and had employment. James would request any travel permits, obtain credit, and guarantee payment of debts.

Religious Education of those Enslaved

In early 1836, a newspaper listing demonstrated James continuing involvement with the Liberty County Association for the Religious Instruction of the Colored Population. According to the listing, James, both secretary and treasurer, acknowledged a five-dollar donation from a *Lady*.[13] Two years previous to this announcement of his involvement, the *Vermont Chronicle* posted a long article about the association's instruction of slaves. (Appendix B)

James joined the association at its initial meeting in March of 1831 in Riceboro.[14] Charles Colcock Jones, Jr. wrote of James as a "planter" in Liberty County. His brother-in-law, John Dunwody also joined the association that day. The planters agreed to "form themselves into a voluntary association and 'take the religious instruction of the coloured population into their own hand.'" It is not known how long James remained a member of this organization. Perhaps only as long as he held land in Liberty County.

Family Matters

In March of 1836, the United States Congress' Committee on Revolutionary Claims began an inquiry into providing pay to the heirs and legal representatives of Captain James Bulloch, deceased. Captain James died in 1807, some twenty-nine years earlier.[15] At this time, no determination of this claim has been uncovered.[16]

The following listing, also in the *Daily Georgian*, noted the arrival of James in Savannah from New York on 2 November 1836 on the ship *Milledgeville*, along with "Mr. Dunwody, Lady and five children; R. Hutchison, Lady and 2 children." James was traveling with his brother-in-law, John Dunwody and his step-son-in-law, Robert Hutchison, his wife Corinne and their two girls. James returned to Hartford at some point during the winter or spring. For in early May of 1837, he began preparations for the family's return to Savannah.

A Courtship

During the winter of 1836, a young man from Liberty County, visited the family in Hartford based on a letter from Martha Bulloch to John Jones, written 15 December. The letter, retained by John Jones, was annotated as having arrived in Philadelphia on 27 December and replied to on the 30th.[17] John (1815-1893), the son of Joseph and Sarah Jones, was studying to be a Presbyterian minister. Martha's letter described their joy at his visit, the family's current circumstances, and referred to a special friendship between John and Susan. Martha commented on Georgia and Matilda Bulloch[18] having consumption and their overall ill health. Matilda, who signed her name as *Till*, wrote a postscript chastising Jones for not writing to Susan and how heartbroken they both were. Till expressed her dismay due to Susan's heartache and because of the friendship she, herself, held for John. Although John Jones indicated he replied to Martha on 30 December that letter is not in the collection. In a letter dated 1 February 1837, he makes no reference to Susan or Matilda, only to Georgia's return to good health.[19] Till continued to write to John as did Martha. In a letter dated 4 August 1837, from Matilda A. Bulloch to John Jones, she writes:

> I suppose you long ago received Mr. Bulloch's unwelcomed letter and you are not of course quite unhappy, you must be if your feelings are still the same towards her, for since that communication you can have very little hope of gaining your long fond desire & cannot you yield & honorably bow in meek submission to this sore triad. . . . .S. seemed quite unhappy but said she could not help it- that she could not encourage you when her feelings for you were not stronger than those of true friendship- [20]

Nancy Jackson vs James Bulloch

Susan and Georgia had completed their studies at the Seminary, and with the boys enrolled at a boarding school, James decided to return the family to their southern home. However, a legal matter delayed their departure. Two years previously, in 1835, James had brought Nancy Jackson, a slave, to Hartford. During the intervening two years, Nancy expressed her desire not to return south with the family and had taken up residence with a free Black family. Nancy's situation came to the attention of abolitionist Edward R. Tyler, at a service of the Talcott Street Congregational Church on 20 May 1837. Tyler met with Nancy and urged her to file a legal case he would arrange. Tyler would also pay all expenses. Nancy agreed. A writ of habeas corpus was served on James on Wednesday, 30 May 1837.[21]

The Liberator, a weekly Boston abolitionist newspaper with widespread circulation, printed the two-column long article about the case on 7 July. In part it read:

> . . .Nancy Jackson claimed and held as property by Major James S. Bulloch, of Savannah, a Geo., a gentleman of fine mind, manners and character (slavery excepted,) an elder in the Presbyterian church, and author of a pamphlet defending slavery by a wrestling and blasphemy of the Bible for which he has examples for ministers of the gospel. . . . Before I took as single step in the case I knew it to be essential to ascertain beyond a doubt, that Nancy was really anxious to obtain her freedom, and so anxious,

that neither the threats of her master, nor the love of kindred and country, would shake her purpose, if a suit were once commenced at her request. I accordingly took every means in my power to discover her true state of mind. I was acquainted with some white persons, friends of Mr. Bulloch, who had frequently seen Nancy and who had the highest esteem for Mr. B. as a gentleman and a Christian; they told me Nancy was too much attached to him and his family to accept her freedom if it should be offered her. Knowing how much deception slaveholders practice on their northern friends, and how much slaves practice rather than excite the ill will of their masters, I placed much more reliance on the testimony of an intelligent colored person who told me that Nancy had frequently expressed a strong desire for freedom and the utmost dread of being carried back to Georgia. I was also told that she had once informed Mrs. Bulloch of her desire to be free, and this before she had a conversation with any other person on the subject; and that Mrs. B. replied that it was a foolish notion, that she could not support herself, or even earn her own clothes; in fine, that she must go back where she could be taken care of. . . .

The legal claim for Nancy's freedom cited the Nonimportation Act, a state law passed in 1774. The law stated that no slave could be "bought or imported" to be "disposed of, left or sold" within Connecticut. Once in court, much of Nancy's case hinged on the word "left." James claimed he was only in Hartford on a temporary basis and intended to return to Georgia with Jackson; therefore, Nancy had not been brought to Connecticut to be "left." Jackson's counsel pointed out she had lived in Connecticut for two years consecutively, while James traveled back and forth.[22]

On 13 July 1837, the *Savannah Daily Georgian* published the following:

Connecticut Abolition

Whenever the vile Incendiarium at the North, are able to interfere with the rights of Southern men, they spare nothing in the accomplishment of their nefarious designs.

We are astonished to find that a recent case in which Mr. James S. Bulloch was respondent that the highest Judicial tribunal of Connecticut has by a forced construction of one of their Statutes, deprived one of our citizens residing temporarily in that State, of his property, although guaranteed to him by the Constitution of the United States.

We have not seen the decision, but the subjoined extract from the Hartford Times will give some idea of the grounds on which the decision turned.

We are pleased to find that the decision is generally unsatisfactory to the community where the same was rendered.

Mr. B. owes it to himself and the South to carry the case to the Supreme

Court of the United States, where a dispassionate and unprejudiced decision may be rendered. If the decision should be against him, which we cannot believe, the Constitution should be amended, we think, as to protect our citizens from the legislation of the Northern States.

If the soil of Connecticut were similar to that of Georgia, her citizens would doubtless gladly discriminate between the colors of the human family. As her soil is, however, we learn that Slavery has not been abolished there from the dictates of philanthropy, but from its injurious effects upon a deserving class of her population.

In her bill of rights, we are informed the following occurs - "Whereas the increase of slave in this state is injurious to the poor, and inconvenient.

A Statute of Connecticut (posted in 1784) enacts - "That no Indian, negro, or mulatto, shall at any time hereafter be brought or imported into this State by sea or land from any place or places whatsoever to be disposed of, left or sold within this State.

How, even under this Statute, can a Southern man be deprived of his property, until he, at least exhibits a disposition to sell, dispose of or leave (i.e. abandon) his property within the limits of Connecticut. We have referred to this case (as we have done to others) because we view it as a duty to appraise our Fellow Citizens, of the South, what they are to expect, when adjourning to Connecticut, but while we do so, we trust that any action will be had, whereby to settle on a more secure basis on of our dear _____ rights.

The case of Nancy Jackson was widely publicized in northern and southern papers. James' response to the case first appeared in the *Savannah Georgian* on 19 August.

The following from Mr. James S. Bulloch, the gentleman who was judicially robbed of his property in Connecticut, we give to the public. We are glad Mr. B has determined to maintain his rights by presenting them to the tribunal in the last resort. We are happy to perceive that the feelings of the community where this violation of the law and the rights of property took place, are in favor of sustaining our Constitutional rights.

Hartford, 7th August 1837

To the Editor of the Georgian:

Sir:—I have noticed your remarks upon the decision of my Slave Case before the Court of Appeals in Connecticut; and you are right in saying it is a duty I owe to the South to carry it up to the highest Judicial Tribunal. It has been forced upon me, and I will do all that is proper to be done.

I do not believe a gentleman in this city had any hand in enticing my servant to leave me. It was some of the colored people, with a Mr. E. B. Tyler, an agent of the N.Y. Anti-Slavery Society. Had I been surrounded by friends in Savannah, I could not have experienced more good feelings towards me, and indignation expressed at the whole course of the procedure, that was manifested by the citizens here—the most respectable and influential of *all parties*.

It would be improper to mention names, (I shall never forget them,) but many of the citizens of influence and property tendered me their names as surety if required, and any *other service!* In truth, nothing but a sense of what is due to good order and law prevented the leaders being furnished with a coat of tar and feathers!—Suffice it to say, in proof of the good feeling here and opposition to those Abolitionists. E. B. Tyler in giving his account of the result of the case in their paper, "The Emancipator," printed in New York, animadverts [to speak out against] freely upon the citizens for their conduct displayed toward me. I have the best legal advisers in the State, both *employed* of counsel and *volunteers*. Connecticut is by no means an Abolition State at this time, the views of her leading men are adverse to those of the Anti-Slavery Society, and say it is a matter left altogether to the slave States to regulate. All her members of Congress are Anti-Abolitionists; her Governor as much so as the Governor of any Southern State, and he makes no secret of his opinions; and if I mistake not, some of her judicious, talented and gospel men, (and she has not a few,) will soon come out and take a stand against and arrest the movements of the reckless immediate Emancipationists. Connecticut has, on more than one occasion, thrown herself in the breach on great and perilous occasions, and I have no doubt on this exciting and difficult subject, will signalize herself again.

Some of our laws relating to this subject should be repealed and amended, and I shall endeavor the ensuing Legislature to have the subject brought up. It may not be improper in this place, to expose some of the vilest of these immediate Emancipators, these would be Philanthropists of the colored race—these men, who from their speeches and letters published, seem to wish to die Martyrs, and thereby to get a name to live! One, who now resides in Troy, N.Y., who fattened and grew rich in Georgia, and who sold the slaves he owned and put the money in his pocket, is now declaiming on this subject. Another in Pennsylvania, a merchant in a country town, whose father sold out his slave property in Liberty county, to my family—a portion of which I inherited, and he from his father a portion of the proceeds, and from which he is now supporting *his* family, has such humane and brotherly love for these poor, ignorant people, that he said he looked upon me as a sinner, and that I ought immediately to liberate them. He did not propose to refund the money. How clean these hands! How pure these hearts? Judge ye!

The seasons have been very propitious in this region. The grain and grass crops abundant. Many of the operatives in the Factories were discharged in time to go on Farms and the county will be maintained by an abundance of the staff of life.

Notwithstanding the pressures of the times, the inhabitants of this city have raised by subscription upwards of $1,000.00 for the foreign Missionary cause. I send you herewith the last annual report of the Deaf and Dumb asylum. Those from our State are educated here.

James S. Bulloch

The Connecticut Supreme Court ruled out two possible extreme interpretations of the act and its wording, discarding the notion that the slave must be left permanently in the state in order to meet the law's intent. The court also rejected the idea that a slave might claim freedom during a temporary stopover in a free state. In a three-to-two decision, the court found for Nancy and set her free. Only one year later, Connecticut's legislature increased the rights of African Americans identified as fugitives. The state did not abolish slavery until 1848 when only about six slaves remained in the state.[23]

Other Matters in the Summer of 1837

Despite their legal troubles and delay in returning to Georgia, James continued his correspondence on personal matters. This letter to Robert Hutchison reveals much about the family's situation.

Hartford 7th July 1837

My dear Hutchison,

As you did not come in the [Northman] stage last evening I suppose we shall not have the pleasure of seeing you & hearing from your own lips about Corrine & the dear little children and I the satisfaction of an hours talk on business matters, Savannah etc etc-This is a second disappointment both Sue & Georgia were quite sick- Sue had the fever July night & took an emetic which made her very sick and both of them were all day anticipating seeing you.

Georgia is not at all benefitted by steam boat travelling I will take her to you by land to Saratoga or send her with Mr Smith & the 2 Dunwody's who will arrive next monday week & put up at the Union Hall you can go down or send for her. I am at a loss to account for Mr Cooper & the Kings' conduct. If I do not hear satisfactorily from them I will have to go to [N.Y.] & take the steam boat next week for Savannah! I must have money- Your letter appraising me of your fortunate escape from the dreadful pressure of the times relieved my mind very much for I felt greatly for you & now hope

you will ride through the failures around you [&] it will give such a lesson that will benefit you during life. I wrote you from West Point but presume you did not get the letter about our cotton I advised its shipment to L'pool & that I could procure an endorser & we could sell. I was sold bills at 15 per ct [i.e.&] and upwards on [Esg] which would bring up the prices- Did the P.B.R [Planter's Bank?} & Rail road give dividends before you left- I left an order with you for Mrs Bulloch's & Montgomery's. Let me hear from you about the cotton- I like the situation of Judge Davis' House very much from the rent however I should say I Savh. felt none of the disturbing times! The rent is as high, as the prosperous times of '16 & '17- It has a fine office attached to it which will be very convenient for me. I shall get a good fair office, if I can, in the month of Oct for congress will do some thing to have commissioners or cashiers appointed for all the principal sea Ports. When is the House considered as in my possession? I wrote Judge Wayne a few days ago about his house as I understand his family remains next winter in Washington & Baltimore- I have rec'd letters from Indiantown, Cedar Hill & Laurel view this week- crops looking up- If a stop is put to this dreadful & shameful mania of speculation in everything and overtrading & we shall have peaceable & profitable times again- I have a letter from [Rus?] of the [20/26 June]. The heat for 4 days & nights, was almost insufferable- James is now in the room studying his Spanish lesson & sends love to you & Aunt Conie & says Aunt Conie must kiss Corre & Caroline for him. He is now prepared for college but as he is just 14 yrs I have him at home with an excellent French & Spanish teacher until 1 Oct. He also goes to singing school. Daniel is at a Clergyman's in North Hampton Mass: Well and doing well when we last heard-
Our United love-
Yrs affectionately
J.S. Bulloch

I am quite disappointed my very dear Corinne that you could not come to Hartford. I long to see you all particularly my dear little Corinne & Caroline. Susan and Georgia can scarcely bear the separation, which is now to be protracted through another summer It is really tantalizing to have you in New York and not be able to see you- I hope you may spend a pleasant summer at New Port, and better health than you did the last. I am quite well but as you will see in Mr Bulloch's letter both the girls and Matilda are very unwell. Susan's is only a slight bilious attack, but Matilda and Georgia are poor puny things. Georgia will meet you at the Spring if her heart does not fail her, but she does not appear very willing to leave me. If she does, dear Corinne, do not permit her to sleep alone, as she has paroxysms [sp]

of suffocation sometimes which might be fatal if she was not attended at all times. She looks pretty well, and I am in hopes that when she ceases to grow so fast she will recover. It is quite uncertain tho' as she has at times considerable pain in her chest and side. If she goes to Saratoga beg her try the waters, and if it does not agree with her you can make her leave it off- Little Anna and Mittie are quite well Anna has commenced the steep ascent of the "Hill of Learning" and Mittie will be two years old tomorrow. Mittie is an arbitary little thing- takes all of Anna's play things from her constantly. you see Nancy has left us. Take care of Sarah, there are abolitionists in N. Port as well as Hartford. I am quite pleased with the prospect of our next winter's location. Dr. [dear] Cona] I hope if it is the will of Providence we may all meet again and reside near each other- Give my love and the girls to Mr Hutchison and a kiss to each of the precious little ones- I have much to say to you but must offer it until I see you. I long to have a long conversation with you- My cup of blessings has overflowed since I saw you dear Corinne. The Lord has dealt very mercifully with me for which I desire to be truly grateful- Good bye- I never forget you and your dear family my poor prayers.
Yours with heartfelt affection
M Bulloch[24]

So much is learned from personal letters. James was still heavily invested in business matters and dealing with three plantations, Indiantown, Cedar Hill and Laurel. Obviously, he left overseers at each to attend to daily affairs during his absence. Hutchison served as his manager/factor in Savannah. The letter also touches on James's position as a member of the U.S. Military Academy's Distinguished Board of Visitors. After an invitation by the Secretary of War posted in the *Savannah Georgian*, 13 May 1837, James visited and inspected West Point that summer.[25] At this point, young James D. Bulloch would have been looking at career options. Further education at West Point and an officer's posting was possible due to his father's connections.

James also touched on the nation's financial situation during the Panic of 1837 and his own financial situation. After the 1833 transferring of federal funds to the state banks by President Andrew Jackson, the United States economy fell into disarray and resulted in total panic four years later. This financial panic led to a major recession that would last until the mid-1840s. In 1837, prices and wages rose. Speculation and pessimism were rampant. Unemployment rose. In the South, the failure of the New Orleans cotton brokerage firm, Herman Briggs & Company in March created a different type of panic, as plantation owners worried over the ability to sell their cotton at a profit.[26] James' answer to Hutchison was to ship the cotton to Liverpool for sale directly to the English cotton mills. As for James' claim of needing money, James most likely needed cash to pay bills and provide for their daily needs. The situation with the nation's banks made it even more difficult to transfer funds as there was little or no stable currency for exchange. Notes issued by various banks were difficult to transfer to proper currency as many of the local and state bank notes were worthless.

In the letter, James and Martha both mentioned the illnesses of Susan and Georgia. In particular, Martha decried Georgia Amanda's serious breathing episodes. The ending of this letter once again confirmed the loving and close relationship between Corinne and Martha.

Residence in Savannah

Finally, in November 1837, the family returned via New York on the Ship *Moctetumn*. Listed are James, Martha, and two children (Anna and Mittie), and servant (not Nancy Jackson). The listing also included Robert and Corinne Hutchison and their two girls, Miss S. Elliott and Miss G. Elliott, indicating the boys James and Daniel, had indeed remained at their boarding schools in Connecticut.[27]

While there is no information concerning their residence directly upon their return, a newspaper listing from March 1838 showed the family residing at a house fronting on Savannah's Chippewa Square.[28] The house was leased and may well be the house of either Judge Davis or Judge Wayne mentioned in the Hutchison letter.

Upon the family's return in the fall 1837, James resumed his busy professional life. In January 1838, James was elected as a director of the Branch Bank of Darien along with Roswell King, W. Woodbridge, H.J. Douglas, and R.A. Lewis. The Bank of Darien had a branch in Savannah. Roswell King was re-elected to the post of president. Likewise, Martha continued her charitable work and was elected to the board of managers of the Widow's Society on 16 January.[29]

On 7 May, the Milledgeville Convention of the Union Party of Georgia met in that city to nominate a congressional ticket. James served as a Chatham County delegate.[30] On the 14th, the *Macon Telegraph* reported James was appointed to the committee to fill any vacancies appointed by the convention.

The spring of 1838, proved a prosperous one for Martha. Various newspaper announcements showed her owning twelve shares in the Planter's Bank worth $960. She also received a dividend payment of $375 from her ten shares of the Central Rail Road and Banking Company of Georgia in late May and another $575 in June.[31] Newspaper notices of dividends paid over the coming years include Martha in 1839 and 1840. In 1839 James is shown owning sixteen shares of Central Rail Road stock at 37.5 per share for a value of $1,400, approximately $39,000 relative value in 2018. In 1840, their shares' value had risen to $1,000 for Martha and $1,600 for James.[32]

CHAPTER VIII:
LEGAL MATTERS

Beginning with John Elliott's death and continuing into the mid-1840s, James dealt with several estates and probates, along with his own business affairs. His business life became complicated and full of legal wrangling, dealing, buying, selling, recording, and whatnot. Combining this information, into the already busy flow of James' personal life with family and friends, overwhelmed and disrupted the narrative of his life's story, both in reality and in this retelling. Yet, these events often affected his personal life; therefore, they cannot be absent from his story. This chapter relates some of these legal matters, transfers of property, settlements, and agreements. Transcriptions of these documents are presented in Appendix C.[1]

Property Records

Statements found in various books and documents about which family owned which plantations created a research dilemma until a serious study of these families showed the interrelationships and intermarriages. Also, death and estates interrupted and changed ownership frequently. On the following page a table presents some of the legal transfers, deals, and settlements of James and Martha beginning in 1832.

With the death of Daniel Stewart and his wife Sarah, both Tranquil and Cedar Hill plantations went on the auction block for a division of inheritance. These were the plantations of Martha's childhood, her family homes. On 20 March 1833, James and Martha each bought a portion of Tranquil Plantation from Daniel M. Stewart, executor. These deeds were not recorded until one year later in March of 1834. In December of that year, James sold 845 acres of Tranquil to Samuel Spencer for $1,100. The sale arranged for Spencer to pay James installments of $200 on 1 January 1837, $100 on 1 January 1838, $400 on 1 January 1839, and the final amount of $400 on 1 January 1840. This deed was recorded 27 days later.

James and Martha had purchased 924 3/10 acres of Tranquil Plantation for $2,030. They sold 845 acres for $1,100, leaving them with 79+ acres. While they purchased the land for approximately $2.20 per acre, they sold it for $1.30 per acre. In neither deed are any structures such as homes or slave dwellings mentioned. When James and Martha sold the remaining acres is unknown at this time.

In May of 1835, James took out a security deed for Cedar Hill Plantation with Andrew Low and Company in partnership with Robert Hutchison. The security deed itself explains why James needed to do so, for this deed states:

> ...above mentioned all of which, said land and negroes are under mortgage executed by the said James S. Bulloch to one Charles W. Rizing having date the 12th of May 1831 & recorded in Book 22 folio 316 of the clerks office of the Superior Court of Chatham County...

James had purchased Cedar Hill Plantation in May of 1831 and owed Rizing $15,900. Without a copy of this initial deed, speculation leads one to believe that Rizing held the mortgage on Cedar Hill. One month later, James took out a mortgage on 16 slaves, and their issue, for $15,900! A sum of approximately $993 per slave! He promised to repay the money within five years with interest. This was the exact amount of money owned to Rizing. This transaction explained why James made this mortgage of slaves and security deed on Cedar Hill.

Therefore, by 1833 or 1834, James and Martha owned a portion of Tranquil Plantation, perhaps the portion containing the home, and Cedar Hill Plantation.

John Elliott's Estate Settlement

From 1827 until 1834 James handled all of the monetary affairs associated with John Elliott's estate. When the estate was settled these files became part of John's probate and were registered in Liberty County. While some snippets of this information are presented in Chapter 7, there are other pieces of information of particular interest. For example, John Elliott was responsible for the monetary affairs of his niece Mrs. Catharine Russells, and regularly received dividends due her from her State Bank stock holdings. In December 1827, she held 50 shares and received $175.00. Coffins for John and son Charles cost $85.00. In May 1828, James paid one dollar to record the marriage settlement for Jane Elizabeth Elliott which cost $15 to be drawn up. In the early part of 1828, James paid $43 for Corinne's clothing, and $100 for clothing for the minor Elliott children.[2]

Large amounts are recorded for the sale of cotton and $368.62 for a carriage sold in New York, both in 1828. That same year, he recorded the sale of a bedstead, knives and forks, a dining table, and a mahogany table. In February of 1829, James received a physician's bill for Daniel Elliott, who was ill and required a physician from the 14th to the 19th of September 1828. Another personal item was for travel on the Ship *Hamilton* and expenses while traveling at the North, including clothing for the winter, for Susan, Georgia, Daniel, and servant in 1829. This totaled $584.02.

Property	Date	Purchaser	Seller	Acreage / # of Slaves	Price
Tranquil	20 March 1833	James Bulloch	Daniel M. Stewart	855 acres	$1500
Tranquil	20 March 1833	Martha Bulloch	Daniel M. Stewart	69 3/10	$530
Tranquil	1 Dec. 1834	Samuel Spencer	James Bulloch	845 acres	$1100*
Mortgage on Slaves	25 June 1835	James Bulloch	A. Low & Co.		$15,9000
Security Deed Cedar Hill	19 May 1835	James Bulloch	A. Low & Co. & Rob. Hutchison	955 acres/43 slaves**	
Purchase of 9 Slaves	7 March 1837	Augustus Bacon	James Bulloch	9 Slaves	$4500
Purchase of Cedar Hill	4 April 1837	James Bulloch	T. Quarterman	6/7 acres	$200
Security Deed Cedar Hill & Clifton***	1 Jan. 1838	James Bulloch	Daniel M. Stewart	965 acres/81 slaves	$13339.28
Warranty Deed on Cedar Hill	17 Jan. 1839	William LeConte	Daniel M. Stewart	951 acres	$10250

*To be paid in installments

** also 1/6 John Elliott estate and 52 negroes of the estate of Jane Irvine Bulloch Powell

*** and 6 acres containing slave settlement

Corinne was also traveling in the North and her expenses came to $427.98. On 16 November, Susan and Georgia returned home. Daniel's passage home was not noted.[3]

On the final pages of the 1829 expenditure accounting, James' cost for administration of the estate came to $3295.11. This amount would equal $92,600 in 2018. This amount had increased by the time the last entry was made on 1 January 1834.

Selling Land

More dealings associated with Cedar Hill occurred in April of 1837 when James purchased six to seven acres of land adjacent to Cedar Hill. This tract contained a house and slave settlement. The purchase price was $4500, the exact amount of the May of 1831 appraisement of Cedar Hill Plantation listed in his mother's estate.

In January of 1838, Daniel M. Stewart set up a security deed for Cedar Hill, buying the plantation from James Bulloch. He promised to pay off the note by 1845. This sale occurred some six months before James and his family moved north to Roswell. James needed cash money to buy the land near Roswell which he named Clifton Farm and to invest in the Roswell Manufacturing Company. This sale seems to indicate that the family intended to make Roswell their permanent home. One final deed relating to Cedar Hill was dated 17 January 1839. Daniel M. Stewart sold the plantations to William LeConte. The bottom of this deed notes:

> You will please enter satisfaction in full on mortgage of record, Daniel M. Stewart to James S. Bulloch of Cedar Hill tract of Land.
>
> Your Obt Servant
>
> James S. Bulloch

Recorded this 23rd March 1839   E Way Clerk

> The tract of land referred to in the above release (D. M. Stewart to Jas S. Bulloch) mortgage of Cedar Hill Plantation you will refer back to folio 16 & 17 of this book.
>
> E. Way   Clerk

This indicated James received all of his money from Cedar Hill in March of 1839.

James had purchased both Tranquil and Cedar Hill plantations in the early 1830s. By 1839, it appears he no longer owned any land in Liberty County, or at least only a small portion of Tranquil Plantation. This was sold by 1849 for Tranquil Plantation was not listed in James' probate records. Or the portion of Tranquil Plantation that the family retained was deeded in Martha's name.

Division of John Elliott's Slaves

Not until 1844 did the final division of John Elliott's slaves take place. Three lots of 34 or 35 slaves each were created, equaling approximately $14,275 each (Appendix C). These three lots of slaves were assigned to Susan, Georgia, and Daniel. Each would inherit approximately $494,000 in 2018 value from the sale of these enslaved people.[4] While no record of their actual sale has been found, none of these three children owned a plantation or owned a property where these individuals could be cared for and utilized.

Susan and Georgia received their final share of their father's estate on 16 December 1845. Susan was twenty-five, and Georgia was twenty-three. Daniel reached maturity and received his inheritance on 17 November 1847, three days before his twenty-first birthday. Finally, a little over ten years after John Elliott's death, James had completed his management of John's estate and was no longer responsible for his children's monetary affairs.[5]

Bulloch Hall
Historic American Building Survey,
Photographer Branan Sanders, March 1934

Chapter IX:
The Roswell Decade

Still engrossed in business affairs throughout the beginning of 1838, James planned yet another venture for his family. Instead of Connecticut or upstate New York, the family would spend the summer in what was considered the wilds of north Georgia. So, in the late spring or early summer of 1838, Martha, James, and four of their children (Susan, Georgia, Anna, and Mittie) left Savannah for the "colony" at Roswell, Georgia. Fifteen-year-old James Dunwoody Bulloch and eleven-year-old Daniel did not make the trip with the rest of the family, as both still attended boarding school in Connecticut. The family would be one of the first Roswell Manufacturing Company investors to reach Roswell as a family.

Almost no historical references to this move have been found, leaving several questions unanswered. When did James and Martha decide to make this move? Did James visit Roswell before the family's move? Did they plan to make this a permanent relocation? Had they sold off all their land in Liberty County? Did the family's health concerns relating to Georgia and Susan influence their decision?

Facts that are in evidence through historical documents are few. James Bulloch had invested in the Roswell Manufacturing Company, newly established in the town, and had received ten acres for a home as part of the deal. Located in Georgia's Piedmont region, Roswell sprang into being due to the efforts of Roswell King and his son Barrington. In the early 1830s, Roswell King initiated a plan to build a cotton mill on Vickery Creek (now called Big Creek) on what was then Cherokee land. He and his son purchased land lots, started recruiting investors, and began building the mill and other business concerns. James Bulloch possibly invested in the company early in its conception.

Atlanta, settled in 1837, at the terminus of the Western & Atlantic rail line was only a small camp of railroad men and such. Marietta was still a small town, only about twelve miles from Roswell, situated along the proposed path of the Western & Atlantic rail line. The discovery of gold in north Georgia had brought investors and speculators to the region. Along the Etowah and other rivers, cotton plantations were being established. Yet, north Georgia was still inhabited by many of its Cherokee settlers. Most would leave in 1838 on the Trail of Tears.

It is believed that six slaves joined James and Martha on the journey. These were most likely *Daddy* Luke Monroe, the butler and handyman, and his wife *Maum* Charlotte, the housekeeper, along with *Daddy* Stephen, the coachman, *Maum* Rose, the cook, *Daddy* William, and *Maum* Grace, the nursemaid. Taking along oxcarts of belongings, the family traveled first by sloop or steamship to Augusta, and then by coach across eastern Georgia to the Chattahoochee River, and finally on to Roswell.[1]

The family lived in a cabin, formerly inhabited by a Cherokee family, on a large farm, not adjoining their town home plot, which they called *Clifton Farm*—for a plantation they had recently owned in Liberty County—while their new town home was under construction.[2] Clifton lay approximately four to five miles east of what would become their town home, now named Bulloch Hall. James had most likely purchased the land on an earlier visit to the newly proposed village. He continued to farm his Clifton Farm plantation throughout his residence in Roswell.

Having invested in the Roswell Manufacturing Company, some others of James and Martha's social circle had already arrived or arrived soon after. Henry Merrell, in his autobiography, wrote of his arrival in Roswell in May of 1839.

> Arrived in Roswell at Cobb County Georgia in the month of May 1839. I met a cordial reception literally at the hands of Mr. King and as many of the future colonists as were already on the grounds; for they shook hands not only at introductions, but upon meeting in the road every day and as many times a day as they happened to see each other. I had been accustomed to the flying recognition, a nod, or a jerk of the hand on the street to gentleman, & a touch or lifting of the hat to ladies, which is all the time a busy population at the North could afford to bestow upon politeness every day; and the elaborate manners of Southern gentleman seemed very stupid to me until I at last became satisfied that to me at least they were as kind and cordial as they seemed.[3]

Merrell also described the setting of the small village and the initial residences of the "gentlemen" and their families.

> I found the Roswell colonists living in the woods & in such rude buildings as they found already upon the lands they had purchased from the original settlers. Major Bulloch was at a farm five miles distant on the Lawrenceville road. John Dunwody had his temporary residence one mile nearer on the hill beyond Howell's mill. Arch. Smith at his farm on the Altoona Road, and Barrington King with his numerous family of children marooned at the place afterwards called the "Labyrinth" because of successive additions. At that time it consisted of a double log cabin & a few outhouses only.[4]

Greek Revival

In the early nineteenth century, Greek Revival became the architectural symbol of America's democratic ideas and its figurative link to the republic of ancient Greece. This movement began as the result of America's philosophical connection with the Greek War of Independence (1822-1828) and the Enlightenment's yearning to return to its simple and pure forms. During this period, James' hometown, the city of Savannah, developed quickly as a dignified and busy seaport, Georgia's population expanded rapidly and spread west and north across the landscape. From Savannah to Macon to Columbus to Roswell and beyond, Greek Revival public buildings and homes began to decorate the ever-expanding frontier.

Either Roswell King, a Connecticut native, or his son Barrington arranged for Willis Ball, a Connecticut skilled-builder, to come to Roswell and oversee construction work in the town. Little is known about Ball except that the 1840 U.S. census shows his household contained six men between 15 and 40; two boys, ages five and nine, an infant girl; and a woman in her twenties, along with seventeen slaves. Historic preservation architects agree Ball based his work on the widely used Asher Benjamin books such as *The Architect, or Practical House Carpenter* and *The American Builder's Companion*.

Willis Ball may have first constructed the log schoolhouse, some of the original mill buildings, and nearby worker's housing. However, King's ledgers show that he was quickly put to work designing and building homes for several of the founding families. King brought additional slaves to the area to assist in the new construction. A sawmill in Roswell, established by the King family, and one in nearby Marietta probably provided much of the lumber for the new homes.[5] In 1839, Ball completed the first of the formal homes, Primrose Cottage, for Eliza Hand, widowed daughter of Roswell King.

Primrose Cottage is a two-story plank structure with a hip roof; it has a one-story Classic portico with each of the four columns being flanked by a matching pilaster. A local Roswell historian suggested this portico once ran completely across the east face of the structure; however, this may have been a modification to the original plan.[6] A farmhouse elevation in Lafever's *Young Builder's General Instructor* shows the same portico.[7] The interior has a four-square central hall plan with kitchen and dining room in the lower back. Roswell King's records mention the large brick, in-wall oven, built by slaves employed for this specific task.[8] This same feature is present in most of the original Roswell homes. While little about Primrose Cottage is of the Greek Revival tradition, the next homes completed in Roswell by Willis Ball demonstrate his ability in this style.

It is unknown as to why James and Martha chose to build a Greek Revival home. No doubt they were aware of the style's immense popularity. Additionally, style books such as those mentioned earlier were readily available. Perhaps, James even owned copies. Soon, with each new structure throughout the village, including buildings at the mill, Greek Revival was *the* style in Roswell.

Within the next two years, Willis Ball completed Bulloch Hall, Phoenix Hall (now called Mimosa), and the Roswell Presbyterian Church all based on the colossal or full temple form. Both homes are massive structures based on a four square, central hall plan. Nichols, in *The Early Architecture of Georgia*, wrote that these along with Barrington Hall "are all superb examples of the temple house with full pediment, the ultimate of the whole movement."[9]

Ball built all three houses of heart pine with maple and oak interior accents on brick foundations. The bricks were made in Roswell by slave labor.[10] Bulloch Hall's temple front east elevation has four Tuscan—non-fluted Doric—columns flanked by matching pilasters. The clapboard siding is laid flat on the east elevation only. The pediment contains matching windows on the east and west elevations. Bulloch Hall also has two additional rooms on the first floor in a one-story extension, original to the home; below these two rooms are the kitchen and what was originally a storage area. The central hall contains a columned arch and an elaborate staircase with cut leather and wood trim in a closed string below the subrail. Eleven fireplaces, one in each room, provided heat for the home. Like Phoenix and Barrington, a second stair provided access to the rear of the house by way of a single ramp to the landing of the main stair. At Bulloch, the stairs to the ground floor kitchen are located under the back or second stairs.

John and Jane Dunwody's original home was almost identical to Bulloch Hall; however, it burned on the night of its housewarming. Dunwody was so fond of his home that he had it rebuilt in its original style five years later (completed in 1847), except this time he built it of scored, stuccoed brick, hence its name Phoenix Hall. The brick walls are said to be 18 inches thick.[11]

Barrington Hall is the largest of the three homes known to have been designed by Willis Ball. It is surrounded on three sites by a Tuscan-columned portico. Nichols wrote of Barrington Hall that it "demonstrates the dilemma of the designer who was concerned primarily with form . . . it was wider than it was deep and, when the portico was run across the front of the house, the monumental pediments came at the end of the house . . . the pediments do not emphasize the entrance." The entry hall and stairs are almost identical to the ones at Bulloch Hall.[12]

Barrington King's Ledger from 1835 to 1864 listed a number of entries for Willis Ball. Mostly King is paying Willis Ball's expenses and occasionally labor. On the journal's initial page, Willis Ball is listed as "carpenter Connecticut." The following is a listing of these expenditures.[13]

March 1836*	sundries** $22.75
March 1836*	$5.00, $17.75
April 1836*	$9.50 from Bank of Darien
June 1838	paying for sundries, wheat and wagon, $10.16 and $0.60 sundries, $23.29

July 1838	sundries, $41.95
	96lb bacon $15.84
August 1838	sundries, $35.33
September 1838	amount of tuition for his child's education, total of $15.00
	John Dunwody of Liberty County paid Ball $7.50
October 1838	for ____ *** in Factory and sundries $249.74 (included "Error 31 July 4.37")
December 1838	Roswell Factory Co. For 1 hog from Willis Ball 218 lbs $14.17
January 1839	Roswell Factory for amount paid Willis Ball on 15th on work $200.00
	E.B. Hand to build kitchen $200.00
	Roswell Factory Co. . . . for work $250.00
March 1839	On order Bills Receivable to Dr. To N. Dangger for ____ Willis Ball balance, at settlement $14.32
	Roswell Factory direct to Profit and Loss, for the hire of Fanny 1 year to Willis Ball $50.00, also cash direct to Wagon for the amount charged to W. Ball in Factory books hauling lumber $5.06
April 1839	Bacon to W. Ball 58 ½ at ____ $7.90
March 1840	Sundries DR to A.H. Hand - paid tuition to the school or the following, his 7 children, E.B. Hand - 3 children, S.G.P. Portell (?) - 1 child. Roswell Factory paid for J.S. Bulloch - 2 children, Dunwody - 4 children, A. Smith - 1 child, W. Ball - 2 children, W. Frazer - 2 children. Also paid directly for the son of William King (McLeod) - a total of $212.50
September 1840	Presbyterian Church, King Sawmill for 267 quartered board ____ feet delivered to Willis Ball for the church, 3461 feet $10_____ $34.61 ____ for the mill
December 1840	Paid A.H. Hand salary $212.50, with the balanced paid by King,
December 1841	To King sawmill $26.36 (Another page list this lumber as "for his workshop")
February 1842	sundries to Farm W. Ball for $1.20 - $6.00
	sundries $24.32
March 1842	To Willis Ball by Roswell Factory $24.32
April 1842	sundries $21.45
July 1842	sundries ____ $1089.22
	"By Building" $31.95

September 1842   W. Ball for paid him 3 September $15.00
                 sundries ____ $30.50
October 1842   sundries _____ $13.59
December 1842   "To Bal: [balance] dft R.F." $1000.47
                 "To Ros: Factory . . ." $147.75
                 "Bill - payable. . . ." $1255.62
                 "To Ros: Factory $221.91
                                  $2625.75
November 1843   paid ___ $55.19

Two additional entries with illegible dates:
1835-1838   list of expenditures for Willis Ball, includes sugar, sundries,
            and expenses in the amount of $220.74
1838-1842   list of expenditures paid to Ball for work at King sawmill,
            and for the factory

* South Hampton Plantation records, indicating Ball worked for the family in South Georgia before moving to Roswell.
** Sundries include household and personal items such as cloth, whiskey, combs, cinnamon, tobacco, buttons, thread, curry combs, harness, etc. . . .
*** _____ denotes illegible item/entry

Ball, obviously, had worked previously for the Barrington King family on their South Hampton Plantation in Liberty County. King sold the plantation to his brother Roswell about the time of the family's move to north Georgia in 1838.[14]

Noted in King's Ledger are items such as payments to the King sawmill for wood for Willis Ball to be used on "B. King for new house" and 649 board feet lumber taken from yard for N.A. Pratt's study, and "184 feet for doors for BK's." King's Ledger suggests that Ball may have been directly employed by King and hired out to various residents as needed.

There is no clear record of all the buildings in Roswell where Ball contributed either actual work or expertise. Architectural historians have questioned whether Ball participated in the building of the Marietta Presbyterian Church and one home in that same town. Yet, by 1848, Ball had moved south and was employed in Savannah and at various plantations along the coast.[15]

Family Matters

About the time of the family's move to Roswell, tragedy struck again. In June of 1838, headed north from Savannah for the summer, Robert Hutchison, his wife, and their two small daughters boarded the Steamship *Pulaski* in Savannah. Some ten miles off the North Carolina coast, during the night, the *Pulaski's* boiler exploded, killing Corinne and their youngest daughter immediately. Robert survived the explosion, clinging to debris with others for several days. His oldest daughter also survived for a period of time; yet, she was swept from his arms into the ocean during a storm not long before their rescue, near Palmetto Bluff, South Carolina. Robert, along with fifty-eight others, lived. Approximately 100 men, women, and children perished.[16] How and when the Bulloch family learned of this tragedy is unknown. Despite the loss of his wife, Martha's stepdaughter, Robert continued his familial relationship with the Bulloch/Elliott family.

In late 1838 or early 1839, James and Martha's family expanded with the birth of Charles Irvine. Little Charles was baptized by the visiting Reverend Nathaniel A. Pratt during his first trip to the colony on 20 October 1839, the same day the Roswell Presbyterian Church was organized.[17]

Years passed, their children grew, and life in Roswell for the Bulloch family was filled with social events, church, school, and trips south to Savannah. James and Martha traveled to Savannah frequently. In late April of 1839 in Savannah, they anxiously awaited the return of James, age fifteen, and Daniel, age twelve, from boarding school. The boys traveled alone on the SS *North Carolina* into Savannah. Soon, young James made the decision to go into naval service and was appointed an acting midshipman in the U.S. Navy. James wrote his letter of acceptance on 25 June, his sixteenth birthday.[18] Considering a long tour of Europe with Robert Hutchison, a passport application for James entered by Robert, described the fifteen year old as 5 feet, 8 inches with a low broad forehead, small chin and thin lips, large nose on a round face. He had brown eyes and dark brown hair.[19]

James and members of the family were still in Savannah in June 1839. Their presence in the city provided James with the opportunity to meet the Honorable Charles J. McDonald, Union-Democratic candidate for Governor of Georgia.[20] McDonald had served as a brigadier general in the Georgia Militia from 1823 to 1825 and was from Hancock County. In September of 1839, James ran an advertisement in the *Savannah Daily Georgia* related to his campaign for state representative. This advertisement was printed several times from about the nineteenth of the month and continued throughout. James was not elected.

This interlude in Savannah must have been a welcome change for the family; however, they did return to the little cabin near Roswell at some time before the Spring of 1840. On 19 April of that year, Jane Marion Dunwody, James' niece, married the Rev. Stanhope W. Erwin at her father's farmhouse near Roswell. The Bullochs hosted a party for the young couple several days later at their Clifton Farm house.[21]

Probably in the late Spring or early Summer of 1840, the family moved into their stylish new home. Here, they once again lived in the style and manner to which they had all been accustomed. Beside the house stood two or three small slave cabins, which served to house the family servants. Others of the Bulloch's enslaved Negroes remained at Clifton Farm.[22]

In 1841, Charles Irvine Bulloch, age two years, died during an outbreak of scarlet fever. The family buried their beloved boy in Roswell's original cemetery, on a hill crest near the factory.[23]

Gravestone of Charles Irvine Bulloch, Aged 3 years and 9 months, Founders' Cemetery, Roswell

A Visit by Northern Cousins

Jane Amarinthia Elliott Sever and her daughters Catherine, age fourteen, and Jennie, age 10, came for an extended visit in the fall of 1841. Jane was Martha's niece from her first marriage to John Elliott. The Sever family resided in Plymouth, Massachusetts, and Jane was recently widowed. Jane traveled south, alone, with her two daughters. Catherine, called *Kate*, would many years later write of their adventures traveling to Roswell and their life in the new village, for they remained the entire winter and into spring.[24]

Kate wrote that the "town then consisted of six houses, only one being a regular frame house. This was the house where we were, a large two story house with piazza. There was a little white church, a school house built of logs … There was also a small factory." Kate went on to describe the family's life, their enslaved servants, and even a slave child's funeral, writing "at night with pine torches. They looked so weird, winding through the trees in the distance."[25]

Kate, her mother, and sister enjoyed the winter festivities, only returning home in the Spring. Susan Elliott continued to correspond with her for years.[26]

Roswell, September 26, 1843

On looking over my unanswered letters today dear Kate I found one from you dated <u>March</u> to which I think it is high time to reply. I still bear you in affectionate remembrance dear cos although I have proved so punctual a correspondent. <u>Why</u> I have not written before I cannot say for my thoughts have frequently been with you, and your name is often on my lips. Indeed dear Kate, you are associate with the objects by which I am surrounded that I <u>would</u> not forget you if I <u>could.</u> Your room so near our own, the entry in which we have not often walked hand in hand, the nursery where we have spent so many pleasant hours together, the parlour fireside, all, all, breathe of you and "when the bright fire shineth, sad looks your place." Flowers always recall you to my mind, you were so fond of them, and for long time after you left Roswell whenever the children would find a beautiful flower they would wish that Kate could see it, or wonder if Kate had such at her home. We spend our time very much in the same way as when you were here with us. I do not know if you could recognize mother she looks so differently from what she did when you were here. She is so much more cheerful. And there is one other to whom I suppose you would have to have an introduction. The "itty boy" as we call him. He is a very young gentleman of very <u>low</u> at present. Very bright, very mischievous, very amusing, and very much of a pet. Annie and Mitty have grown astonishingly are well advanced in their studies and quite expert with the needle. Daniel is almost out of sight, so tall. Indeed all of the boys have grown much. Your old friend William King is a tall slim handsome youth, he has resumed his studies with the new teacher with whom he is much pleased. William is retiring in his manners reserved before strangers. I much do him the justice to say he has a very good <u>memory</u> where young ladies are in question. "Have you heard from Kate lately" has been asked me more than once.

Henry Dunwody has entered college at Athens. <u>Dan</u> [Daniel Stewart Elliott] I believe you know goes to Princeton. James Bulloch is not at home as you supposed and we know not when to expect him. When we last heard of him he was in Italy. It is nearly four years since we parted and it seems a much longer time. I need not say we look forward with impatience to his return.

Janey Bulloch [daughter of John Irvine Bulloch] is still in Savannah and I regret to add in very bad health. Her friends feel quite anxious about her. The pain in her side has returned with a harsh distressing cough. She in anxious to return to Roswell, but we think it is better for her to remain where she can obtain good medical advice and where the climate is not so variable.

There is another Janey here now, a Miss H_____. Very agreeable, very amiable and very pretty. She is the sister of the gentleman who teaches.

We miss Mrs. Hands family much. They are quite pleased with Hartford and with the Seminary which Elise and Julia both attend. They board at the same house that we did, and with the same family. I believe too they have our rooms.

Fanny Pratt's departure has made a chasm in our circle which cannot easily be filled. I feel her loss particularly. She was very companionable to me, and I feel untied to her by the strong bond of <u>sympathy.</u> I do not wish her back, however, she is so happy at home surrounded by those she loves best. How inexpressibly delightful it must be to return to the comforts and endearments of "home sweet home" after so <u>long</u> an absence. By the last mail we heard from cousin James and Leelah [Dunwody] who have arrived in New York. Both in excellent health, and most impatient to reach Roswell. They are not expected home however until December. This I believe dear Kate is all the news of Roswell. We tread on the even tenor of our way just as when you were here. We have little change or excitement, but we possess peace and happiness. We live almost as one family. "Acknowledge God in all our ways "and trusting in him to "direct our paths." The bible is our chart to our Father's house in heaven where we hope to meet and spend eternity together. May that glorious "house made not with hands" receive us all. He washed from me sins and saved all through the mercy of Jesus Christ.

I feel much interested in you dear cousin. May light the "lamp of Light" ever illuminate your path till it terminate in Heaven. May the Savior guide and bless you ever more. As a Christian you know dear Kate that I profess to have the glory of God as the first object of my life, of course then it is natural for me to dwell sometimes upon subjects connected with religion. Out of the overflow of the heart I have written. Forget if I have wearied.

I suppose you hear frequently from home. I intend inviting your dear mother very soon. We received a very interesting letter not long since from your Uncle James, how he must enjoy home after much moving. All send much love to dear Kate—the servants too to be remembered.

Affectionately yours

S. Elliot

The "itty boy" Susan wrote of was Irvine Stephens Bulloch born on 25 June 1842. Martha delivered her ninth and last child when she was just shy of her forty-third birthday (15 August). She had five children by John Elliott and four by James Bulloch. Two boys, both named Charles, one by each husband, died as toddlers.

James' fourth son, Irvine, arrived on the same day, some nineteen years after James Dunwoody Bulloch. The lives of these two men would coincide more closely than could be imagined giving their difference in age.

The family worshiped at the Presbyterian Church, only a short walk on Mimosa Boulevard, then called Main Street, from their home. They socialized with the colony's other prominent founders, all relocated from southern Georgia. These included the Barrington King family, the Archibald Smith family, the Reverend Nathaniel A. Pratt family, and their cousins, the family of John Dunwody. The Dunwodys raised five sons and one daughter and occupied Phoenix Hall directly adjoining the Bulloch property.[27] The Bulloch family frequently traveled to the coast to visit friends and relatives and for various reasons to the North. The Bullochs were wealthy, well educated, and well traveled.

The Academy

In late March 1840, Barrington King paid A.H. Hand tuition fees for several of Roswell's families, including two for James Bulloch.[28] Given that Mittie was only four, these two students would have been Anna, age 6, and Daniel, age 12. The Academy, originally a log structure, sat just north of the Roswell Presbyterian Church on land donated by the Kings. It was organized and administered by the Reverend Nathaniel Pratt. A. H. Hand, of Augusta, was the first teacher. He served for several years.[29] One of the visiting Sever girls also attended the school during their visit to Roswell. Many years later, Kate wrote:

> Every day we went to school, the house was divided into two rooms, one occupied by a northern lady for the younger children, the other was taught for a time by a college student of the older ones. There was only one girl beside myself. My only study was Virgil, which I read with the older boys.

How strange was the room with its logs filled in with mud and its mud chimney with its brilliant fire of pine knots. Soon our teacher, a young minister, a graduate of a northern collect, left us to be married, and that was the end of school.[30]

After A. H. Hand's departure, a Mr. Hunt was briefly the instructor, followed by Charles D. Dodd. After Dodd's departure, Mrs. Ardelia Hamilton was the teacher.[31]

In time, Anna, Mittie, and Irvine would also be educated at the Academy. After their father's death, the two girls would attend boarding school in South Carolina, and Irvine would attend school in Philadelphia.[32]

Expenses

While the little village of Roswell grew quickly, the first occupants often found themselves traveling on the road to the Lebanon community to visit the Howell Brothers store. The store was established in the mid-1830s and continued in business until 1844 when they sold out to the Roswell Manufacturing Company for company stock.[33] As the store housed the post office during those early years, everyone visited the establishment to retrieve their mail. In 1841, entries for James in the store's ledger included many recorded at the adjoining blacksmith shop. These fees included the laying and sharpening of plows, shoeing horses, repairing harnesses, and repairing wagons and carriages. At the post office, James regularly purchased postage. Sometimes the note included information relating to postage for S. [Susan] Elliott or Miss Wilson [unidentifed]. There was at the store an account for Jane Dunwody Bulloch, James' niece, whose account listed nothing more than postage from March to June of 1842.

Roswell Manufacturing Company

James' decision to move to Roswell had a great deal to do with his investment in the Roswell Manufacturing Company. Roswell King and his son Barrington had begun the venture several years earlier and had offered investors several incentives, including ten-acre plots within the new village. This allowed the major stockholders to reside in the somewhat cooler upcountry during the summer months and avoid the heat and disease of a Savannah summer without going to the North. Most came and stayed throughout the year, finding the winters of the upcountry to be mostly mild and enjoyable.

Among the early investors were John Dunwody, Archibald Smith, Ralph King, Henry Atwood, and the heirs of Bayard E. Hand. Few of the records of the early years of the company exist; however, the following notes were taken from the Stockholder's Minutes. The factory building was completed in November 1839, and the company chartered in December.[34] On 6 October 1840, the stockholder's meeting minutes showed that James was called to the chair and Ralph King appointed secretary. Ralph was Barrington King's brother. In April 1841, John Dunwody chaired the meeting, however, the 5 October meeting that year was postponed due to lack of participation—James was present—and rescheduled for 18 October where James was once again appointed to the chair and John Dunwody to secretary. In April 1842, the minutes show the price of a share was $600. There is no record of their initial price or how many were owned by any one individual. Six hundred dollars equaled about $19,100.00 in 2018 value.[35]

The Roswell Manufacturing Company employed white mill workers and hired enslaved labor from local owners. The mill also owned slaves that labored at various strenuous tasks. On 29 April 1842, the Company purchased nine Negroes, all one family, from Archibald Smith for $2,450 and gave him one share of stock worth $600. The receipt was signed by James.[36]

At the October 1842 meeting, James was present, and the stockholders were paid ten percent of the capital. These dividends continued throughout 1843 in various percentages. In April 1844, the minutes showed a balance in the company of $13,015.26, net profit. This amounted to approximately $451,000 in 2018, a tremendous amount for a small mill company in rural Georgia. No dividend was designated at this meeting, instead the stockholders agreed to spend $5,797.31 on machinery.[37]

At this same meeting, James introduced a motion which was passed.

> On motion of Major Bulloch resolved a non-resident stock holder pay five dollars per share annually for the benefit of the Society connected with the Roswell Factory.[38]

The reason for this fee is unknown. It was rescinded in October of 1845, but could be paid "from time to time, if so desired."

James was not present at either meeting in 1844. John Dunwody held his proxy at the October meeting. The price per share was now $850.59, a forty-one percent increase in two years! Interestingly, the 1845 meeting minutes do not list James as present. The April 1846 meeting was the last time James Bulloch is mentioned in the minutes. John Dunwody holds his proxy. At this meeting, the Company paid a ten percent dividend.[39] James Bulloch's name disappeared from the minutes after this time. It is likely James sold his shares and invested in other ventures.

Henry Merrell, serving as Barrington King's Assistant Agent at the Roswell Manufacturing Company, usually attended the stockholder's meetings. In April of 1844, the stockholders allowed Henry to purchase one share of stock at $750, approximately $26,000 in 2018 terms.[40] This was a significant sum for a working man.

Other Business Matters

Barrington King's Ledger provided some interesting information about James' connections and use of slaves for profit. In 1842, Dr. William Gaston Bulloch, James' nephew, who resided in Savannah, hired out Primus to the Roswell Factory for unknown work. The total cost for his labor was $94.00 on 30 June, $79.00 on 30 September, and $67.25 for sundries on 30 November for a total of $240.25. James himself hired out his enslaved man and carpenter Isaac Elliott to King for work at the factory. A carpenter, named Isaac, appeared on John Elliott's estate appraisement. [Appendix A] Either James or Martha could have inherited him from John's estate. It was not unusual for slaves to take the surname of their master as their own. The first charge in August 1839 for $30.00 paid James for Isaac's work in July. James received $45.00 for Isaac's labor on 31 October 1839. King then hired out Isaac to work for B.E. Hand for $8.00. Another charge for Isaac's labor was $10.38 on 30 November 1839. King also hired a Bulloch or Elliott slave named June at a much lower rate during these same months. June worked at the King farm, the factory, and for others such as Hand. His or her monthly rate was $7.00. Hand's expenses were handled by Barrington King due to his father's death in 1838. Eliza's son was only eight years of age at the time of his father's death. He had two older sisters who became great friends of the Bulloch girls.[41]

James continued to handle estate cases such as serving as the administrator for William H. Coe of Lebanon, Cobb County, Georgia in 1841. A previous letter, dated 12 [?] February 1839, from James to the Judges of the Inferior Court, Chatham County, shed some light on this administration.[42]

> I have been served with notice to make my returns as Admin. On Est. Hester A. Bulloch (my late wife) & Wm H. Coe. To the first Estate I have nothing to render. It was closed the day I took out the Papers: being merely a matter of form I being the only Heir & no will.
>
> The latter my clerk who owed me a balance of 263 12/100.
>
> He gave me before his death the Platt & _____ of Land 185 of 4th Carroll county. I cannot obtain over one hundred dollars for it and the present _____ it is best to hold on. When I find I can sell will advertise according to Law and then make my return.
>
> James S. Bulloch

The Coe matter had not been resolved by March of 1841 when James advertised the land for sale on the 5th day of April at the Court House in Franklin, Heard County. At that time, James was selling 202.5 acres to benefit the heirs and creators of the estate.[43]

James, must have wanted the matter of Hetty's estate settled as he failed to report in this letter the sale of her two lots and their home in Savannah. Also, there was an additional heir – James Dunwody Bulloch. No record of a will for Hetty has been found.

The *Federal Union* listed the stockholders for the Central Rail Road Company of Georgia for 1841, 1842, and 1843. In each year James owned 16 shares and Martha owned 10.[44]

There are several references to James investing in and prospecting for gold. Henry Merrell's autobiography never discussed this directly; however, Henry drew a pencil sketch entitled "Digging Major Bulloch's gold 'On Sheers.'"[45] James had obtained a forty-acre lot in the Gold Lottery of 1832. It was perhaps this land where James had men panning or digging for gold.

In June and July 1842, two letters to the *Savannah Daily Georgian* shed additional light on James investments and interest in mineral speculation in north Georgia. The first, a letter written by James, was dated 27 June 1842.

> Dear Sir, — I take this public method of informing the numerous correspondents that have addressed me, to ascertain the value of their lots of land of the Cherokee country, that it is Impossible for me to do so with correctness, and my advice is to all, *not to sell* at this time. Mining is now being carried on to more profit than formerly, and there is no telling the value of land. From what is [...] doing and what I have seen and heard, I am within bounds, in stating that half a million will be the product of mining this year, and if our Legislators would appoint a geologist of known qualifications or if the lot holders would (and it would be in their interest to have an meeting and do so) gold, lead, and iron would to an astonishing amount would be exported from this region. The iron ore of Cass county is of the very best and said by those qualified to judge sufficient to supply the whole United States for every purpose. I have recently been through many counties, and have never seen more promising crops. Provisions will be abundant and cheap. Providence seems to be smiling upon the labors of the *Agriculturists,* and with [...] prudence and perseverance, we [...] extricate ourselves from present embarrassments. All the iron for the State Rail Road, authorized to be laid down, has been purchased and [...] to the Eastern terminus at the road in DeKalb county. The State Agent and Chief Engineer are efficient and seem determined to unite this beautiful, salubrious and valuable section of our country with the seaboard. . . .

The second letter was printed 28 July 1842 but written on 11 July.

> Sir — Major Bulloch has requested me to send you some particulars concerning the mineral resources of this section of the country. My attention was first attracted by the abundance of iron ore I . . . found in Cass county, and to this my remarks will now be confined.

The Allatoona Hills mark the boundary between the primary veins (?) of the gold formation and the great lime ___ formation to the North West. The situation therefore of this range of hills bordering on granite and cal___ rocks shows at ___ different ___ within the range of the gold veins running north ___ south west

The furnace now in ___ cannot supply the demand for iron. Much is brought in wagons from the furnaces North Carolina, and sold at a price which would afford great profits to the smelter in Georgia.

I have given you a rough sketch of the advantages of this country ___ for carrying on the manufacture of iron ore on a large scale and so well am I convinced of the importance that I have determined on that account to remain some time in this country to aid in developing these resources. The details I have ___ of most advantageous I ___ at some future time communicate to ___ of the Scientific Journal for publication, or make known to individual able and willing to embark in the business. In such a communication an account of the various other beds and veins such ___ the little vein of ___ (lead ore), the immense beds of Sulphate ___ & e. will find a more proper place than in the pages of a daily paper.

With respect I am yours, _____

Mr.(?) James T. Hodge

James T. Hodge was a geologist from Plymouth, Massachusetts, who reported earlier on the gold deposits of the Carolinas in *Reports of the First, Second, and Third Meetings of the Association of American Geologists and Naturalists*. These meetings were held in Philadelphia and Boston in 1840, 1841, and 1842.[46] Why Hodge was in north Georgia and who hired him is unknown.

James did manage to find gold! There is no record of how much, but on 3 August 1847 he sold or paid for his order at the Lebanon store with "three grams gold @ 95 9.62" and on February 14 traded eight grams of gold.[47]

In October of 1842, James served as foreman of the Grand Jury of Cobb County and reported on the theft of funds by the county attorney, the need for permanent schools, funds for improvements, and the need for the collection of unpaid taxes. He additionally gave his support to Judge Ezzard.[48]

On 10 November 1842, an article printed in the *Charleston Courier* referred interested parties of the sale of a Savannah River plantation and slaves to James S. Bulloch, Savannah. It seems James still operated at least some type of office in his hometown. The plantation was part of the estate of Hugh Rose, esquire.

Politics

James retained his interest and stayed active in politics after his defeat in 1839.

His activities appear to be widespread, for in September 1840, he attended a meeting of the Modern Democracy of Cobb County for the purpose of appointing delegates to the Indian Spring Meeting. James addressed the meeting, where the paper reported "a few abusive disconnected remarks against General Harrison and his supporters; and then taking his seat in some evidence of confusion his having done nay good he was followed by Col. George D. Anderson."[49]

The Whig Party had nominated General William Henry Harrison for President and to balance the nomination, they ran former Senator John Tyler from Virginia for Vice President. Even though he had been born on a Virginia plantation, many Southerners considered Harrison a Northerner as he resided in Ohio. The ticket defeated the incumbent Van Buren in the 1840th presidential election. James appears to have opposed Harrison.

In June 1842, Major James S. Bulloch was appointed and attended as a delegate to the Democratic State Convention from Cobb County.[50] James continued his alliance with the Democratic Party, also called the Democratic-Republican Party, the party of Thomas Jefferson.

In early 1847, the *Cherokee Advocate* reported on a "Meeting of the Citizens of Cobb county, Georgia," at Marietta to "express their view on important national measures, among which the war against Mexico, and the proscription of the press by the Senate of the United States." James was called by those attending to be chairman and "briefly but ably explained the object of the meeting." The meeting resulted in several resolutions, including granting their support to President Polk, and expressing their dismay at Congress' lack of action regarding supplies for the conflict in Mexico. The article presented the following statement in regards to the veto of supplies for the conflict, "Incredible as it may seem, propositions have been made in the Congress of the United States, and disgracefully advocated by a senator and resentative [sp] of the State of Georgia, that this government should offer or accept terms of peace, without demanding indemnity for the expenses of the war, and thus throw on our people the ultimate costs of Mexican outrage."[51]

James' outrage, no doubt, was partially influenced by his son James D. Bulloch's service on the continent's west coast during this conflict.

Agricultural Fair

An *Augusta Chronicle* article, printed on 24 November 1845, noted the reelection of James to the post of vice president of the Cobb County Agricultural Society. The Society meeting discussed creating a lending library for agricultural periodicals and information on successful crop practices provided by members. They also advised members to subscribe to such publications as *Southern Cultivator* and *The Cultivator*. After the meetings on the 14th and 15th, prizes and recognition were awarded in several categories at the Society's Agricultural Fair. Categories included

Domestic Manufacture, Agricultural & Horticultural Products, Stock, and Agricultural Implements. This last group highly recommended a turning plow imported by R. M. Goodman and a turning and subsoil plow invented and built by James Lemon that sold for $5.

Religious Instruction of Enslaved Population

Within the Bulloch household lived enslaved people. Some worked in the big house, some at Clifton Farm, some taking care of Bulloch Hall's grounds, and some just lived there. This last group was the very elderly and the very young.

As James had done in Liberty County, he allowed his slaves to share in religious education. Some attended the Roswell Presbyterian Church with his family. There they positioned themselves in the balcony to hear the gospel being taught and preached.

The church had organized under the direction of the Reverend Nathaniel Alpheus Pratt after he received an invitation in April 1839 from the new community. Pratt was married to Barrington King's sister Catherine and at that time headed the Darien Presbyterian Church. At the 20 October 1839 meeting, Pratt agreed to become their minister and promised to take over the church in May of the following year. Included in the list of initial members were most of the village's prominent families, including John and Jane Dunwody, their daughter Jane, and James and Martha Bulloch, along with Susan Elliott. On the same day, Rev. Pratt baptized Charles Irvine Bulloch and John Bayard Hand, the only son of Rev. A.H. Hand. In addition, seventeen slaves became members before the church was even built and attended the meetings in Primrose Cottage's parlor. The Roswell Presbyterian Church history enumerated its communicants in 1857 as fifty-nine whites and forty-four colored.[52]

Other enslaved members attended the Lebanon Baptist Church according to the Minutes of that organization from 1836 to 1853.[53] These minutes help to identify these enslaved people who so often are forgotten in the written record. On the fourth Sunday in September 1839, Susan became a new member. She is listed as "a servant of James D. Bulloch, James' oldest son. On the Saturday before the fourth Sunday in May 1840, "John Maxwell was received by Experience and George was recd. by letter," both are listed as servants of Major Bulloch. The following describes a service held on Saturday before the fourth Sunday in July 1840.

> By leave of the church a door was opened at night after feet washing, and Nelly a colored woman belonging to Howell and Paul a colored man belonging to Jas. S. Bulloch were recd. by experience & Mariah, a Colored woman belonging to Arch. Smith was recd. by letter.

On the fourth Sunday in October 1841, a man named George, belonging to Martha

Bulloch was received by experience and Fanna by letter. It is unclear if Fanna also belonged to Martha. In August of 1842, Rose, who belonged to James was received by experience. Three months later Stephen, property of J.S. Bulloch joined in the fellowship of the church by experience, followed one month later by Sandy, who also belonged to James. This was the last entry related to Bulloch family slaves.

James' oldest son and step-children

James Dunwoody Bulloch

Life in Roswell for the Bulloch family was filled with social events, church, school, and trips south to Savannah. After years of boarding school, James Dunwoody Bulloch entered the U. S. Navy as an acting midshipman in 21 June 1839. At age 16, four days shy of his 17th birthday, James was assigned to the USS *United States*.[54]

In 1844, James's oldest son, James visited the family in Roswell while on leave from the USS *Delaware*. He arrived in early April and remained throughout his leave. James departed just before Mittie's birthday in early July and reported to the USS *Pennsylvania* at Norfolk, Virginia. Desiring to pass the exam for midshipmen, James requested additional training and traveled to Philadelphia in August for the Naval School's eight-month curriculum. Stepsister Susan and cousin William E. Dunwody visited James during his term of study.[55]

In late 1846 or early 1847, James no doubt glowed with pride and boasted all over Roswell about his son's heroic actions upon the sinking of the USS *Shark* off the continent's west coast at the mouth of the Columbia River. On 10 September 1846, while attempting to leave the Columbia and enter the Pacific Ocean, the *Shark,* upon which James served as acting master, had been driven aground on the Clatsop Spit. Lt. Neil M. Howison wrote to James of his son's actions which included offering to stay aboard the ship in place of a married officer and ultimately saving the lives of seventeen seamen who had been stranded aboard all night after the initial actions of abandoning the ship.[56]

Howison and the crew stayed nearby and for the first part of the winter attempted to salvage their vessel before abandoning the effort and taking refuge on a leased, fur-trading vessel bound for San Francisco. Now, once again a midshipman, Bulloch soon found himself back on the USS *Erie*, which sailed for Mazatlan and participated in the naval brigade's occupation there on 11 November 1847.[57]

Daniel Stewart Elliott

Daniel Elliott, after returning from boarding school in 1839, spent only a small portion of his time in Roswell. In 1843, Daniel followed in his father's footsteps by going to college; however, he chose to attend Princeton University rather than Yale. Also, he did not study law, but instead was listed as a "litterateur" a person interested in literature. The college files show he was originally a member of the class of 1846 but became a non-graduate member of the Class of 1847. A listing for Daniel in the Zeta Chapter of Delta Kappa Epsilon provided the information about his area of study. Interestingly, Daniel enrolled as a resident of "Laurel View, Georgia." According to a letter from Henry B. Munn, written in 1886, Daniel left school in his junior year after a close friend, R. S. Boudinot, committed suicide, probably in 1845 or 1846.[58] In November of 1845, Daniel was in Roswell and wrote a short invitation to George Hull Camp, stating:

> I give a feed tomorrow at 4 P.M. in honor of my birthday. Be sure you come along. You'll find all "us youth" there. I count on you.[59]

The next few years of Daniel's life appear absent from the historical record. Letters written in 1853 by Mittie Bulloch indicate Daniel had been in Europe for an extended period of time. Daniel's will, written on 29 August 1853 showed him to be in Liverpool, England, on that date.[60]

Daniel was a talented musician and writer. He played the flute and wrote illustrated stories for his younger half-sisters. Yet, during the intervening years, Daniel fought a duel with a close friend, Thomas Daniels, near Savannah. Daniel Elliott attempted several times to make amends with Daniels, yet in the end, the duel commenced, and he killed his opponent. This event seemed to change Daniel's life for he married, had children, and gave up alcohol.[61]

Daniel's duel came some 25 years after his stepfather joined the Savannah Anti-Dueling Association at its initial meeting on 28 December 1827. The Association was established with this goal:

> The sole object of this association shall be the restraining, and if possible, the suppressing by all lawful and honorable means, the practice of dueling.

James continued his membership for several years, according to the attendance rolls. The Association met once a year in various churches, and attendance was open to both men and women. The last meeting of the Association was on 8 January 1838.[62]

Susan Ann and Georgia Amanda Elliott

James, Susan, and Georgia returned on 16 September 1846 into New York harbor from Le Havre France aboard the *Iowa*. The American clipper/passenger ship of the day made between 14 and 17 knots, so the trip from Le Havre to New York lasted some 9 to 12 days. Walter E. Wilson in *The Bulloch Belles* states that James and the two girls left Charleston on the *Versailles* on the morning of 4 May 1846 for Le Havre, France. There they visited with Dr. William G. Bulloch, son of James' late brother John. William, a graduate of Yale, had obtained his medical degree from the University of Pennsylvania and had recently completed additional studies in Le Havre.[63] Allowing for travel times on each end, James and the girls would have enjoyed the sites on a grand tour of Europe for approximately three months. Unfortunately, no record of their European travels has been found.

Soon, Susan Elliott's (1820-1905) first serious romance began. While history has failed to reveal their first meeting, at some point before September 1847, Susan had met Hilborne West (1818-1907), a member of the wealthy West family of Philadelphia. Hilborne West was the son of James (1785-1867) and Rebecca Coe West (1791-1882). The city's 1830 directory listed James as a "Gentleman."[64] James' family had owned wharves and ships in Philadelphia for at least three generations back to James West (1658-1701), a shipwright, who had emigrated from England before 1683.[65] The term *gentleman* denoted a level of financial independence and status. Hilborne's father was listed with this designation for most of his adult life. He took up residence at 366 Walnut Street as early as 1849 and resided at 1316 Walnut Street from 1859 until his death in 1867.[66]

In 1847, Hilborne was employed at the Sayles Company Mill, in Daysville [now Dayville] Connecticut, a woolen mill about 50 miles east-north-east of Hartford near the New Jersey border. The mill was built by John Day, a wealthy farmer, in 1846.

After Susan and Hilborne's initial meeting, Hilborne wrote to his friend and brother-in-law Silas Weir Roosevelt (1823-1870) and to Silas's younger brother James "Jim" (1825-1898) about his new infatuation. The following is Silas' response.

New York, Sept 16, 1847

Dear Hilborne,

You began a sneer, at my pictures, which you attempted to scratch out and left unfinished probably being frightened when you recollected what you were doing. And it is very well for you that you did get frightened in good time. Beethoven used to play such dry discords and when his friends complained of his sinning against the rules of music he answered "I make the rule". All I have to say is that, if there should be no machinery in a mill fit for my purpose, I make the machinery; if you have entirely overlooked the arts of design in constructing the factory it is not my fault. Make a cigarette of that and smoke it. However I sympathize deeply in your present frame of mind, which I suppose to be terribly out of order from the fact of your having written two letters in succession to Mary [Mary West Roosevelt (1823-1877] and several simultaneous, to Jim. Jim being an excellent confidant, regularly, with every letter that comes from you, affects a mystery and keeps what you tell him profoundly secret until he hears what you have written to Mary when he indignantly denounces and exposes you. From motives of delicacy I have refrained from reading your epistles and have contented myself with having them read to me by Mary. In this way I judge that you are effervescing with happiness and want sympathy. And you have a remarkably good right to be happy unless my view of the young lady's character is altogether mistaken. To be sure our acquaintance was short but it is improbable for me, as you know, to be ten minutes in the company of a stranger without coming to a conclusion about him. In the first place her great beauty impressed me - the lustrous eye, the hair and the peculiar brow which gives a strange and very noble cast to the whole countenance. Then her lips are very feminine and you know the mouth only, of all the features, is, at ordinary times, the key to the habitual mood of a person's mind. The charm of her presence, as far as you can separate it from the halo of personal attractions, is the atmosphere of purity which surrounds her, and the impression one has that he is with a lady (in the higher sense of the word) and still has a woman to deal with. I wish there were more of the sex who gave the impression; society would be a different thing. As it is there is a continual exhibition of female weakness, on one side, and a feverish struggle to be the first to take advantages of it, on the other, which produces the effect, to a person who sees below the surface, of a dew drop in a microscope. Glittering and pure it is outside - but within alive with all uncleanness - a perfect riot of ugly and devilish shapes. But I grow excited and begin to commit myself although my eyes are open to the fact of your sneering disposition. If you let me off this time I wont do it again

Your's
SWR[67]

From Liverpool, England, in August 1848, Robert Hutchison wrote to his wife Mary Caskie in Richmond, Virginia:

Susan [illegible] to me the information of her engagement in the following terms which I quote to you as an amusing, but rather pretty, specimen of the manner in which a lady may make such an avowal. 'Our visitor Mr. West leaves us next week, and I wear a ring, his gift, upon the first finger of my left hand.'

She says nothing of the probable time of her marriage, but Mr. Bulloch tells me that it will not be earlier than January. I have urged her not to delay, but to bestow her hand on Mr. West as soon after 10 Nov. as she can, so that we may be present at the ceremonial before settling down for the winter in our own dwelling.[68]

In 1848, Susan visited Philadelphia and told tales of her family's home and of the beauty of her half-sister Mittie Bulloch to those in attendance, which included many of the Roosevelt family. Later, Susan and Hilborne invited all to their upcoming wedding.

Another letter from Robert Hutchison to Mary Caskie, on 12 October 1848, told of more depressing family news:

> . . . received two communications one from Mrs. Bulloch, and the other from Mrs. Ervin. . .My dear favorite sister Georgia than whom a more innocent lovely girl never lived is no more. Released at last from protracted and most distressing suffering and gone to her angel sisters above.

On 29 September 1848, Georgia Amanda Elliott died of consumption, known today as tuberculosis. Although her will has not been found, Hutchison referred to the copy he was sent in a letter to Mary Caskie from New York, dated 18 October 1848.

> . . . Yesterday when I went down to the Post office I found a letter from Mr. Bulloch of the 12th acquainting me with the welfare of our friends in Roswell and enclosing to me a copy of dear Daisy's [family nickname for Georgia Amanda] will, which I am named coexecutor with himself. It was made out by herself in her own handwriting & phraseology & without allusion to it to any one just one week before she died. She bequeathed her little property (about $13,000) one half to Susan & one fourth each to her mother & brother Daniel all simply & clearly expressed in very concise terms and the divisions are which way both natural & proper.
>
> This unlooked for access into Susan's means will make her worth $20,000. So ample a provision that even if Mr. West's circumstances prove next to 'Nihil' I shall advise her to conclude her marriage without any further delay thus will be respectful to Georgia's memory and leave scenes which must be full of gloom to her for the cheerful ones of the north.[69]

According to the appraisement, Georgia left her slaves to her sister Susan, her brother Daniel, and her mother Martha. Interestingly, Susan and Georgia owned nine slaves jointly. The appraisal of these enslaved people in September of 1848, listed their worth as $4,250, approximately $140,000 in 2018. For the division, first the nine slaves were divided into two lots based on value. Then lot two was divided between the three heirs. Susan received three slaves worth $1,000 total, whereas Martha received two individuals worth $550, and Daniel received George worth $600. To make the totals equal, various amounts of cash had to be paid. (Appendix D).

Hutchison and her family urged Susan to proceed with her wedding despite her sister's death. Hilborne and Susan married on 29 January 1849, in a quiet ceremony at the family's home, officiated by the Rev. N. A. Pratt.[70] Susan, now worth over $20,000, was well prepared for marriage and at twenty-eight years of age, no doubt, felt the need to proceed with her life. Her $20,000 equaled in 2018 an income value of $11,200,000. Susan was a wealthy woman. Although a copy has not been found, there was most likely a marriage settlement.

For the time being, Susan and Hilborne stayed in Roswell but planned a trip to Philadelphia in the spring. Winter travel was difficult and treacherous.

On left: Georgia Elliott's gravestone.

Below: On left, Charles Bulloch's gravestone. On right, Georgia Elliott's crypt. Dunwoody plot can be seen in rear.

CHAPTER X: THE DEATH OF JSB

On Sunday, 18 February 1849, James left home, headed for the Roswell Presbyterian Church, to first teach Sunday school and later to attend the morning service. James had left earlier than other members of his family and died before the beginning of the Sunday school session. He was 56 years old.[1] Florida Bayard walked with Irvine Bulloch that morning toward the church and wrote that Mittie was "just at the head of the avenue by, I don't remember who, & was told of her fathers death, she having started before Anna that morning. Having a late breakfast that morning, each hurried off to S. school, as they got ready. Anna so regretted that she had not given her father his usual morning kiss, the first omitted in months."[2] In 1849, Florida was approximately fifteen years of age, and Irvine only six.

One of those already in attendance at the church was Barrington King, who later wrote of hearing James' final words. Barrington advised John Dunwody of James' death, then these two men, already grieving for the life of their close personal friend, transported James body home, to Bulloch Hall and placed it in the home's library. James body may have lain in a wicker basket shaped like a coffin while his box was prepared, as this was the custom of the time. John Dunwody wrote about staying all night in attendance of James' corpse at Bulloch Hall.[3]

The house soon stood dressed in black, windows covered, black crepe draped over mirrors, and a mourning wreath hung on the door to symbolize the grief felt by its inhabitants. Already dressed in mourning after the death of Georgia the previous September, the family donned their darkest black once again. Even their slaves wore black arm bands.

The prominent members of Roswell society attended James' funeral and his burial at Roswell's first cemetery, now called Founders'. James was interred next to his stepdaughter Georgia Elliott and beside his young son Charles. It is likely members of his enslaved population also walked to the cemetery, especially *Daddy* Luke, a man completely dedicated to the man he had served for years. Absent at his funeral was his oldest son, James D. Bulloch.

His stone reads "James S. Bulloch Died in Roswell February 18th in the 56th year of his age. There are no partings in Heaven."

News spread quickly across Georgia of James' death. Probably the first obituary was in the *Marietta Advocate*; however, few copies of this paper exist today.

Due to severe damage, James S. Bulloch's original gravestone
has been removed to Bulloch Hall.
His grave in Founders' Cemetery is now marked with a replica of this stone.

This version of that obituary was printed in the *Savannah Georgian* on 22 February 1849.

> The Marietta Advocate of the 20th inst. says—It is with feelings of deep regret that we announce the decrease [sp] at Roswell, of Maj. James S. Bulloch. He died very suddenly on Sunday, the 18th inst. His Christian character, his many manly virtues, his kindness of heart, and his public spirit, render his loss an irreparable one to his family, a large circle of friends, and to the community in which he lived.

The *Savannah Republican* printed the following obituary on 21 February 1849.

> It is with unfeigned sorrow that we have to record the death at Roswell, on Sunday last, of James S. Bulloch, Esq. He died (as we learned through a telegraphic dispatch received in this city yesterday,) very suddenly while attending divine service in Church. His disease was one of the heart, from which he had been an occasional sufferer, though his general health, sustained and invigorated by the pursuits of a temperate and active life, was otherwise excellent.
>
> The deceased has left a most interesting family, and troupe of sincere friends, to lament his sudden exit from a scene where he had acted well his part. He has been summoned away thus suddenly, from the social fireside, from the genial sunshine of the warm hearts and bright faces to whose comfort and happiness he so largely contributed, to take his place among the pale retinue that throng that other and invisible stage of being. No more will he be present to gladden the domestic circle by his cheerful philosophy, or to encourage desponding friends by the suggestions of a hopeful resignation. His light is extinguished, and thick darkness now broods over the spot where so lately all was brightness. But Time will bring healing to wounded spirits, and many a pleasant and sweet memory will assuage the sorrow of those who are called to mourn his sudden departure.

Two New York newspapers carried James' obituary. On Monday, 26 February, the *Commercial Advertiser* printed the following:

> It is with unfeigned sorrow that we have to record the death at Roswell, on Sunday last, of James S. Bulloch, Esq. He died (as we learn through a telegraphic despatch [sp] received in this city yesterday,) very suddenly, while attending divine services in Church.—*Savannah Georgian*, Feb. 21.

Obituaries also appeared in the *Charleston Courier* on 24 February and on page one of the *New York Spectator* on 1 March.

James' Estate

James may have had a will. If so, no copy has been found. Considering the Cobb County Courthouse was burned by Federal troops in 1864, this is not unusual. At that time, Marietta residents were able to save only a portion of the courthouse records. With or without a will, James' estate had to be probated and heirs provided for. Five men were appointed by the Cobb County Inferior Court to prepare the appraisal of James' estate. These five were John Dunwody, Nicholas J. Bayard, Barrington King, Archibald Smith, and William Fuller, Justice of the Peace. Robert Hutchison was appointed executor and along with John Dunwody and Barrington King provided a bond of $12,000 that they would carry out a "true and perfect inventory of all and singular, the goods, chattels, and credits, both real and personal" of James S. Bulloch. This was completed and recorded on 20 June 1849. All documents related to James' estate are presented in Appendix D.

James inventory of household goods was extensive. Besides the usual list of household items James owned one yoke of steers, 16 head of cattle, 48 hogs and 12 sheep. Three horses are listed along with four mules, one only a colt. The total was $1,672.50. This appraisal does not include Bulloch Hall, Clifton Farm, or James' slaves.

James did not leave a large estate for his family; however, he owned valuable property. Just after his death Hutchison wrote to his wife Mary Caskie on 11 May 1849. Robert stated he had just returned from Roswell and continued with these details:

> Mr. Bulloch's estate will pay all his debts and leave a trifle to his widow if properly managed.
>
> In of her own right Mrs. Bulloch has a trust $25000 and I suggested to Susan the propriety of buying out her mothers contingent claim on her one half of Georgia['s] property. she immediately _____ and on my naming $2000 as a fair compensation to be given to her mother for the relinquishment of this right she & Mr. West agreed to it with most commendable kindness and even offered to allow more but we would not ~~allow~~ name it. so this possible cause of discontent between mother and child is disposed of to their mutual entire satisfaction and Mrs. B's property increased to $27000 on the interest of which in Cobb County she can support herself and her children in great comfort.
>
> It is arranged that Marion & Mr. & Mrs. West shall accompany me on the Tennessee to [Nenza Ranch] 23 inst. the former will stay with a cousin in Brooklyn till you come on & Mr. & Mrs West will stay with the former's parents till August when probably they will join us at Newport.[4]

Martha's $27,000 equaled an income value of $15,300,000 in 2018. Hutchison was no doubt comparing Martha's income/wealth with his own. Hutchison was an extremely wealthy man. James' appraisement listed no stocks, bonds, or investments. His appraisement listed no slaves, yet the Bulloch family owned a farm managed with slave labor. Martha had inherited 39 slaves from various relatives and her first husband. It is possible James did not own a single slave at this time.

Robert Hutchison served as executor for James' estate. Robert did not handle the everyday affairs of James' monetary estate while the probate was in effect, but simply settled James' debts.

In February of 1851, Hutchison turned over $1,509.36 to William Gaston Bulloch when they transferred James' role as Jane Bulloch's trustee to her brother William. From 1849 to April 1852, Robert collected and paid James' outstanding debts. For example, in July of 1849, Robert paid H. E. McGinty $9.00 for 600 bricks and labor "to repair on chimney." In January 1850, Robert paid for "one head & ____ of stone $16.00" and an additional $1.92 to cut 48 letters on same. This may be the stone for Georgia, as she is buried in a crypt. On 7 February, Hutchison paid sixty-five cents for the signing of two deeds in the presence of William Fuller, Justice of the Peace.[5]

An outstanding bill from 5 August 1848 provided some additional information of purchases the family made at Northcutt's Dry Goods Store on the west side of the Marietta square.

Marietta August 5 1848

Jas. S. Bullock [sp] ____ to J. J. Northcutt

			$	¢
Aug. 6th	Per Order		15.00	
Nov. 6th	41 1/4 yds of kersey at 17 1/2c		7.21 3/4	
"	29 yds of	kersey @ 20	5.80	
"	3	knives .62 ½	1.87 ½	
"	1 pair of shoes	1.00	1.00	
Nov. 12th	1 Congress knife		1.50	
"	28 yds of kersey @ 25		7.00	
	28 ½ yrds of Kersey @ 22		6.27	
"	flax thread		0.20	
"	Black buttons		0.18 3/4	
" 27th	24 yds of Ga plains @ 17 ½		4.25	

Dec 6th	Balance on Shoes	0.20
Jan 23rd	1 box of mustard [?]	0.15
"	1 bottle sweet oil	0.25
		50.90
Dec 6	Apples	3.73 3/4
" 22nd	Sundries	2.90
[illegible]		57.43 3/4

Named for Kersey, England, where it originated, kersey was a coarse, ribbed woolen cloth used for hose and work clothes. Given the large amount of cloth James purchased, this was most likely meant to be made into winter clothing for his slaves. For 18 cents, James purchased a large number of buttons. Buttons were extremely cheap. He also purchased 24 yards of Georgia plain fabric. A Congress knife is a folding knife with a blade or blades at each end.

On 14 February 1850, George Hull Camp wrote to Jane Margaret Atwood stating:

> A few days since, the property belonging to the estate of Bulloch was disposed of. Mrs. B. secured the house and most of the furniture, and Mrs. West (Susan) purchased the farm, so that now we are sure of Mrs. B. remaining in Roswell and have the promise of West residing in the place…[6]

Hutchison sold Bulloch Hall on 7 December 1850, to Alexander Howell for $3,350, approximately $111,000 in 2018. Former part owner of the Howell Brothers Store, Archibald Howell had in 1849 just completed construction of a new large Greek Revival home on Kennesaw Avenue in Marietta.[7] Why Howell purchased the home is unknown, but Martha and the children continued to occupy it. When the laws about women owning property changed in the mid-1850s the deed reverted to Martha. On 7 February 1850, Robert Hutchison, trustee for Susan West, purchased from John Dunwody, trustee for Martha, land lots in the first district, second section of Milton County. These land lots were Clifton Farm. Susan purchased the Farm for $3000, approximately $99,800 in 2018.[8]

Conclusion

James Stephens Bulloch lived the life of a moderately wealthy Southern aristocrat. Unlike the gentlemen of England during this period who were not employed in or even active in trade, James was an AMERICAN gentleman. He created his own wealth through hard work, speculation, and contacts within a wide circle of friends, family, and acquaintances. He ventured into various investments, some successful and some risky ones that failed. He educated himself on a variety of subjects. James served his city, county, state and country as an officer in the state militia and his community by being active in various social organizations, charities, civic affairs, and politics.

JSB believed in slavery and owned slaves. It was a reality of his time that many men and women owned other individuals. Records indicate he treated his enslaved African Americans kindly and educated them in his Christian faith. As far as records show, he believed in and followed the practice of selling slaves in family groups. Even during the Nancy Jackson case, many men of the North lauded him as a Christian gentleman of strong principles.

Beginning with the first James Bulloch, a Scottish immigrant, the Bulloch men lived as upstanding, educated, and Christian citizens of their new country. Three served the Patriot cause - James, Archibald, and Captain James. Major James Bulloch never faced battle, yet he prepared himself for service and was called Major for his entire life. Many in Georgia recognized James Stephens Bulloch to be a leader of men, as was his grandfather. Throughout his life, in his political, business, and social activities, James was elected and/or appointed to roles of leadership. Respected as an authority, he was asked for and readily gave his opinion on various topics in his business ventures such as banking and investing.

James was active in his religious life, attending church, helping to establish the Roswell Presbyterian Church, and teaching Sunday school. As previously mentioned, James believed in educating the enslaved in his Christian faith. He allowed them the freedom to attend the church of their choice on Sundays and for evening meetings.

James married twice. He fathered six children, mourned two, and raised four to be upstanding citizens. He served as stepfather to his second wife's three children from her first marriage to his close friend John Elliott. James educated each child to the best of his ability, sending the boys to northern schools and the girls to the finest finishing academies. While historical records leave much unknown about a person's character, this author believes you can observe it in their children.

It is obvious James was endowed with a sense of adventure. He tried new occupations such as mining for gold. He once uprooted his family from the ease of Savannah's genteel life, moving them to a small log cabin in the north Georgia wilderness. What an adventure they must have all had, living in close quarters, without the luxuries they had always held as their birthright! Later in life, with his two stepdaughters, James traveled to Europe, spending a summer to do the "grand tour."

James S. Bulloch was mourned deeply by his friends and family. He left behind three young men who would, several years later, fight for their beliefs, and three young women who served their Christian faith and supported those of their beloved South during the War Between the States. Few men can claim legacy of such a life.

Believing we are a product of our ancestral heritage, that we inherit our ancestors' traits, and in many cases, their character, it is understandable that President Theodore Roosevelt, James' grandson, and Eleanor Roosevelt, his great granddaughter, exhibited such exuberant personalities and strength of character. Through the Bulloch line, both Theodore and Eleanor were endowed with an intense fortitude, a desire to learn, a lust for life, and a deep love of family and country from the men and women who came before them.

Endnotes

Chapter 1:
1. J. G. B. Bulloch, *A History and Genealogy of the Families of Bulloch and Stobo and of Irvine of Cults* (Salem, MA: Higginson Book Company, 1990), 12-14.
2. Ibid.
3. Henry A. M. Smith, "Charleston and Charleston Neck: The Original Grantees and the Settlements along the Ashley and Cooper Rivers," *The South Carolina Historical and Genealogical Magazine*, Vol. 19:1 (1918), 62.
4. "Original Rules and Members of the Charleston Library Society," *The South Carolina Historical and Genealogical Magazine*, Vol. 23:4 (1922), 163-170.
5. *Georgia Gazette*, 30 August 1769.
6. Elizabeth Austin Ford, "The Bullochs of Georgia," *The Georgia Review*, Volume VI:3 (1952), 321-322.
7. *Georgia Gazette*, 13 July 1768.
8. Ibid.
9. Ibid., 30 August 1769.
10. Ibid., 20 April 1868.
11. Records on Ancestry.com indicate Josiah Perry (1727-1773) and Jean Bulloch (1730-1771) married and had one son Isaac in 1757 and possibly another James M. born in 1769. No references were given. Christina married Henry Yonge in 1774, in Georgia. They had one son William Yonge, 1753-1845.
12. Ford, 321.
13. *Georgia Gazette*, 3 January 1770.
14. William H. Bragg, "Wormsloe Plantation," New Georgia Encyclopedia, Found Online (https://www.georgiaencyclopedia.org/articles/history-archaeology/wormsloe-plantation, [last update, 25 September 2014]).
15. Ford, 321-322.

Chapter II:
1. Ford, 322.
2. Ford, 323.

3.   Ibid.; J. G. B. Bulloch, *A Biographical Sketch of Archibald Bulloch, President of Georgia 1776-77* (Privately Published, 1907) 7-8.

4.   Charles C. Jones Jr., *Biographical Sketches of the Delegates from Georgia to the Continental Congress* (Spartanburg, SC: Reprint Co., 1972), 15-27; William Bacon Stevens, *A History of Georgia, from Its First Discovery by Europeans to the Adoption of the Present Constitution in MDCCXCVIII* (Original Publication1847; reprint, Savannah, GA.: Beehive Press, 1972); Bulloch, *A Biographical Sketch,* 7-8.

5.   Ibid.

6.   Gordon Burns Smith, *History of the Georgia Militia, 1783-1861.* Volume 4 (Milledgeville, GA: Boyd Publishing, 2000), 127.

7.   Bulloch, A Biographical Sketch of Archibald Bulloch, 8.

8.   Pete Force (complier), *American Archives: Consisting of A Collection of Authentik Records, State Papers, Debates, and Letters and Other Notices of Public Affairs, The Whole Document Forming a Documentary History of the Origin and Progress of the North American Colonies; of the Causes and Accomplishments of the American Revolution; and of the Constitution of Government for the United States, to the Final Ratification Thereof* (Washington, D.C., Clerk's Office of the District Court of the District of Columbia, 1843), 1137.

9.   William Bacon Stevens, *History of Georgia, From its First Discovery by Europeans to the Adoption of the Present Constitution in MDCCXCVIII*, Volume II (Philadelphia: E.H. Butler, 1859), 295-296.

10.   "To John Adams from Archibald Bulloch, 1 May 1776," National Archives, Found Online (http://founders.archives.gov/documents/Adams/06-04-02-0065 [last update: 2015-12-30]), Source listed as: Robert J. Taylor (ed.), *The Adams Papers, Papers of John Adams, Vol. 4, February–August 1776* (Cambridge, MA: Harvard University Press, 1979), 158–159.

11.   Hezekiah Niles (ed.), *Principles and Acts of the Revolution in America.* (Baltimore, MD: W.O. Niles, 1822), 159-160.

12.   "From John Adams to Archibald Bulloch, 1 July 1776," National Archives, Found Online (http://founders.archives.gov/documents/Adams/06-04-02-0141 [last update: 2015-12-30]). Source: *The Adams Papers, Papers of John Adams, Vol. 4, February–August 1776*, Robert J. Taylor (editor), (Cambridge, MA: Harvard University Press, 1979), 352–353; On 23 June 1999, the *Atlanta Journal Constitution* reported the sale of this letter for $635,000 at Sotheby's auction house in New York City. The letter had previously been in a private collection. The buyer was not identified.

13.   L.H. Butterfield, Leonard C. Faber, and Wendell D. Garrett (editors), *Diary and Autobiography of John Adams,* Volume 2. (Boston: Harvard University Press, 1990) 204.

14.   Randall M. Miller (editor), *"A Warm & Zealous Spirit": John J. Zubly*

and the American Revolution, Selection of His Writings (Macon, GA: Mercer University Press, 1982); William E. Pauley, "Tragic Hero: Loyalist John J. Zubly," *Journal of Presbyterian History* 54 (1976): 61-81.
15. *Harper's New Monthly Magazine*, Volume 85:506 (July 1892): 186-187.
16. Ibid.
17. Lucian Lamar Knight, *Reminiscences of Famous Georgians*, Vol.II (Atlanta: Franklin-Turner Company, 1908), 26.
18. Georgia Historical Society, Archibald Bulloch Papers (1769-1777) MS 0103.
19. William Harden, *A History of Savannah and South Georgia*, Vol. I (Chicago: Lewis Publishing Company, 1913), 178 and 200-201.
20. Bulloch, A Biographical Sketch of Archibald Bulloch, 5.
21. Ford, p. 322-324.
22. Ibid.

Chapter III:
1. Mary Granger (editor), *Savannah River Plantations* (Savannah: Georgia Historical Society, 1947), 296-297.
2. Ford, 325.
3. Caroline Price Wilson, *Annals of Georgia: Important Early Records of the State Abstracted and Compiled. Volume I, Liberty County Records and A State Revolutionary Pay Roll.* (New York: Grafton Press Publishers, 1928), 133; Measuringworth.com
4. Gordon Burns Smith, *History of the Georgia Militia, 1783-1861.* Vol. 4 (Milledgeville, GA: Boyd Publishing, 2000), 127.
5. Ibid, p. 325.; No record of this James Bulloch attending any college or university has been found. It was common practice during those years for a young man to "read the law" in the office of a relative or friend while serving as a clerk.
6. Measuringworth.com
7. Ford, 325.
8. David Starr Jordan, "The Inbred Descendants of Charlemagne: A Glance at the Scientific Side of Genealogy," *The Scientific Monthly* Vol.13:6 (1921), 481-492.
9. Both mother and daughter's names are alternatively spelled *Ann* or *Anne* in various historical documents.
10. Jordan, 481-492.
11. *Georgia Gazette*, 13 November 1788.
12. Virginia Fraser Evans, *Liberty County, Georgia: A Pictorial History* (Statesville, NC: Brady Printing Company 1979), 27-29; "Catalog of the

Scholars of the Sunbury Academy, July 30th 1807," Papers of Charles C. Jones, Jr. Collection, Duke University Manuscript Department, Durham, N.C. as found in John McKay Shefthall, *Sunbury on the Medway: A Selective History of the Town, Inhabitants and Fortifications* (Norcross, GA: National Society Daughters of the American Colonists, Georgia State Society, 1995), 168.

13. John McKay Sheftall, *Sunbury on the Medway: A Selective History of the Town, Inhabitants, and Fortifications* (Atlanta: Georgia Natural Resources, 1977), 61-62.

14. Evans, 28-29.

15. Measuringworth.com, Amount shown is based on the Consumer Price Index for 2018.

16. Sheftall, 137, 213.

17. James Stacy, *History of the Midway Congregational Church, Liberty County, Georgia* (Newnan, GA: S.W. Murray, Printer, 1899), 30-32.

18. Evans, 3-9.

19. *Columbia Museum and Savannah Advertiser,* 12 December 1796

20. Ibid., 23 May 1797.

21. Adelaide Wilson and Georgia Weymouth, *Historic and Picturesque Savannah,* The Boston Photogravure Company, 1889:229

22. Measuringworth.com

23. *Columbia Museum and Savannah Advertiser,* 23 June 1804 and 26 December 1804.

24. Smith, Vol. 4:128.

25. *Register of Deaths in Savannah, Georgia: Volume II, 1807-July 1811.* Compiled by the Genealogical Committee Georgia Historical Society, Publication made possible by a grant from the R.J. Taylor, Jr. Foundation, 1984:2. Volume viewed at the Georgia Historical Society, Savannah, Georgia; The Chatham County Health Department Death Card (MS 1712 Georgia Historical Society) gives the same information
with the addition of his occupation "Clerk of Superior & Inferior Courts.

26. *Patriot* (Savannah), 19 February 1807.

27. *Columbia Museum and Savannah Advertiser,* 23 October 1807.

28. Georgia, Wills & Probate Records, 1742-1992 found at Ancestry.com

29. J. G. B. Bulloch, *A History and Genealogy of the Families of Bulloch...* (p. 18) states only that Ann is d. s. p. or without issue. The remainder of this paragraph contains information from United State Census records and other official state records obtained through Ancestry.com.

30. Ancestry.com, Found Online (https://www.ancestry.com/mediaui-viewer/tree/3452545/person/-1730999434/media/b5797267-fcc6-4c1f-a33c-9499a4443fdd?_phsrc=SUE353&_phstart=successSource.)

31. Death Index, Chatham County, Georgia, May 1818. Found at the Georgia Historical Society, Savannah.

32. Will of Mary DeVeaux Bulloch, dated 18 May 1818. Copy on file at Bulloch Hall, Roswell, GA; Deed, A.S. Bulloch to William B. Bulloch, Deed Book 2B, p.424. Chatham County Superior Court Record Room.
33. Will of Mary DeVeaux Bulloch, dated 18 May 1818; The two references to her granddaughter Ann D. Bulloch seem to indicate James sister still lived; however, Mary may have been referring to Ann Louisa Bulloch, daughter of her son William Bellinger Bulloch.

Chapter IV:
1. Historical documents indicate the family originally spelled their name as *Dunwody*; therefore, it is spelled as such in this document.
2. Snoby, Paulette. *Georgia's Colony of Roswell: One Man's Dream and the People who Lived It.* (Roswell, GA: Interpreting Time's Past, 2015), 67-71.
3. Stacy, 201, 208.
4. Clarke, Erskine, *Dwelling Place: A Plantation Epic.* (New Haven: Yale University Press, 2005), 132.
5. Clarke, 238.
6. Helmers, Lois (editor), *Early Records of Liberty County, Georgia.* (Winchester OH: Badgley Publishing Company, 2013),143.
7. Groover, Robert Long, *Sweet Land of Liberty: A History of Liberty County, Georgia* (Roswell, GA: W.H. Wolfe Associates, 1987), 4-8; Stacy,18-30.
8. *Gazette of the State of Georgia* (Savannah), 30 January 1783.
9. Stacy, 55.
10. Helmers, 3.
11. Coleman, Kenneth and Charles Stephen Gurr (editors). *Dictionary of Georgia Biography.* Volume One:288-289. 1983. University of Georgia Press, Athens.
12. Helmers, 265.
13. Ibid., 257; Measuringworth.com
14. Ibid.
15. Helmers, 278.
16. Midway Congregation Church Records, Liberty, County. Found Online (https://www.ancestry.com/search/collections/midway1/).
17. Coleman and Gurr, 289.
18. *Columbia Museum and Savannah Daily Gazette*, 12 December 1811.
19. Coleman and Gurr, 289.
20. Stacy, 18-19, 55, 76, 89, 93.
21. Daniel Stewart (1761-1829). New Georgia Encyclopedia. Found Online (https://www.georgiaencyclopedia.org/articles/government-politics/daniel-stewart-1761-1829).

22.   Stewart, Daniel (1761-1829). Liberty County Historical Society. Found Online (https://libertyhistory.org/history/people/people-all/stewart-daniel-1761-1829).
23.   Bulloch, Joseph Gaston, *History and Geanology [sp] of the Stewart, Elliott and Dunwody Families* (Savannah: Robinson Printing House, 1895), 1-10; Note: Bulloch also listed Susannah (1794-1804), Sophia (1793-1794), and Joseph Oswald (1798-1798).
24.   Helmers, 201, 209, 217, 231; Northen, William J. and John Temple Graves, *Men of Mark* (Atlanta: A.B. Caldwell Publisher, 1907), 302-304; Colquitt, Neyle, *An Historiette of Midway* (Midway, GA: 1915), 29-33; Stacy, 93-94.
25.   Clarke, 56. Note: Clarke "out of the Midway congregation alone, with no more than 340 whites, 39 died in four months."
26.   Letters of Charles Colcock Jones, Jr., Hargrett Manuscripts, University of Georgia, Box 1, Folder 18.
27.   Bulloch, 18-19.
28.   Jan Flores in apaper for Atlantic State University found on file at Bulloch Hall, Roswell, Georgia; Fold3.com, citing NARA M602, RG: 94, Roll: M602_0029; Braynard, Frank O., *S.S. Savannah: The Elegant Steam Ship* (New York: Dover Publications, Inc., 1988), 28-34.
29.   "William Bellinger Bulloch," Biographical Directory of the United States Congress, http://bioguide.congress.gov.

Chapter V:
1.   "Embargo Act of 1807." Found Online, Research Subjects: Government & Politics, The Napoleon Series, (www.napoleon-series.org/research/government/us/c_embargo.html, [July, 2002. 21 July 2018]).
2.   "Embargo Act of 1807." Found Online, The Jefferson Monticello, (www.monticello.org/site/research-and-collections/embargo-1807).
3.   Harden, William, *A History of Savannah and South Georgia*. Volume 1. (Chicago and New York: The Lewis Publishing Company, 1913), 272-276.
4.   Ibid.
5.   *Savannah Republican*, 20 June 1812.
6.   Ibid., 276-277.
7.   Ibid., 280.
8.   "James S. Bulloch Pension/Land Bounty Papers." Fold3.com, Found Online, (//www.fold3.com/browse/247/h5iT6dgqRwM3YLOCSkutf_uaui8TATc4G6_dkY8pX).
9.   Smith, Gordon Burns, *History of the Georgia Militia, 1783-1861*, Volume 4: The Companies. (Milledgeville, GA: Boyd Publishing, 2002), 33.

10. Ibid.; "Military Records of the War of 1812, Muster Rolls," Found Online (www.fold3.com/search?full-name~=James+S.+Bulloch&military.conflict=War+of+1812).
11. "Replies," *Magazine of American History*, VII:1 (July 1881), 299.
12. Smith, 19.; *Savannah Georgian* 3 August 1824, Article about the Timothy Tugmutton Affair.
13. See numerous references to James being in Savannah during these years in subsequent text.
14. *Savannah Republican,* 7 June 1818.
15. "Savannah Tax Digest, 1816," Found Online (//search.ancestry.com/cgi-bin/sse.dll?indiv=1&dbid=2428&h=517254&tid=&pid=&usePUB=true&_phsrc=SUE294&_phstart=successSource).
16. Ford, 326; *Savannah Daily Republican*, 3 January 1818; *Savannah Daily Georgian*, 2 December 1818.
17. "Savannah Tax Digest, 1817" Found Online (//search.ancestry.com/cgi-bin/sse.dll?indiv=1&dbid=2428&h=518692&tid=&pid=&usePUB=true&_phsrc=SUE296&_phstart=successSource).
18. Phalen, William J., *The Consequences of Cotton in Antebellum America* (Jefferson NC: McFarland Publishers, 2014), 98.
19. Ibid, 99.
20. A tierce is an antiquated measure of liquid and equal to one third of a pipe or 42 gallons.
21. Granger, 35.
22. Scott Derks and Tony Smith, *The Value of a Dollar: Colonial Era to the Civil War, 1600-1865* (Millerton, NY: Grey House Publishing, 2005); "Seven Ways to Compute the Relative Value of a U.S. Dollar Amount - 1790 to Present" Measuring Worth.com. Found Online (//www.measuringworth.com/calculators/uscompare/). Hereafter, listed as Measuringworth.com.
23. Derks and Smith, 320.
24. Measuringworth.com.
25. Savannah Tax Digest, entries for James S. Bulloch at Ancestry.com. Found Online (www.ancestry.com/search/?name=James+S._Bulloch&event=_savannah-chatham-georgia-usa_18029&birth=1793).
26. Ford, 326; Braynard, Frank O., *S.S. Savannah: The Elegant Steam Ship* (New York: Dover Publications, Inc., 1988), 28-31.
27. Braynard, 27.
28. Ibid., 102-104; This home is now known as the William Scarbrough House and houses Savannah's Ships of the Sea Maritime Museum.
29. Letter from William Scarbrough to his wife, Julia, dated May 6, 1819. Georgia Department of Archives and History: William Scarbrough collection, MS 1400.
30. Measuringworth.com

31. Braynard, 28-29.
32. Ibid.
33. *Mount Pleasant (NY) Westchester Herald*, 26 May 1818.
34. Braynard, 29-31.
35. Measuringworth.com
36. *Columbus Museum and Savannah Gazette*, 1 March 1819.
37. Thorp, Willard Long and Hildegarde E. Thorpe, *Business Annals: The Annals of the United States of American* (Washington, D.C.: National Bureau of Economic Research, 1926), 113-123.
38. *Savannah Georgian*, 7 April 1819.
39. Bell, Malcolm, Jr., *Savannah, Ahoy! The Steamship and the Town in the Gala Year of 1819* (Savannah: The Pigeonhole Press, 1959), 27-28.
40. Ibid, 31.
41. Spratt, H. Philip, *The Birth of the Steamboat* (London: Charles Griffin & Company Limited, 1958), 107-110.
42. Measuringworth.com.
43. *Savannah Daily Georgian*, 20 April 1819, Note: Author of letter is unknown.
44. Braynard, 97-98, 103.
45. Ibid., 102-103.
46. Ibid.
47. *Columbian Museum and Savannah Daily Gazette*, 10 May 1819.
48. Braynard, 104-105.
49. *New York Gazette*, 21 May 1819.
50. Braynard, 192-194.
51. Ibid., 199-201.
52. Lawton, Alexander R., "An Address by Alexander R. Lawton: Delivered in the City Hall, Savannah, Georgia, April 21 1919." *The Georgia Historical Quarterly* Volume 3:2 (June 1919), 45-60.
53. *Savannah Republican*, 3 November 1825.
54. *Savannah Daily Georgian* and *Savannah Republican* both contain numerous entries for the firm of Bulloch & Dunwody from 1820 until 1831.
55. *Savannah Daily Georgian*, 23 March 1822.
56. Ingrisano, Jr., Michael N., "The First Officers of the United States Customs Service: Appointed by President George Washington in 1789." (Washington, D.C.: United States Customs Publication 578, 1987), PDF Found Online (//www.cbp.gov/sites/default/files/documents/First%20 Officers%20of%20the%20U%20S%20Customs%20Service%20-%201987.pdf).
57. Sieffert, Justin L., "*United States v. Klintock:* Reconsideration of *United States v. Palmer* as to General Piracy as Defined by the Law of Nations through the Applicable Standards of Political Action of Acknowledgement

and Recognition and the Status of Statelessness." University of Maryland Francis King Carey School of Law 2016:2. 8 August 2018. Found Online (https://digitalcommons.law.umaryland.edu/cgi/viewcontent.cgi?article=1069&context=mlh_pubs).
58. Ibid., 10.
59. United States v. Klintock, 18 U.S. 144 (1820); Appellate Case File, RG 267.3.2, M214, Roll 53, *United States v. Klintock*, Case No. 1029.
60. Sieffert, 49; *Savannah Daily Republican* 28 January 1819.
61. Sieffert, 26.
62.. Ibid., 27.
63. *Savannah Georgian,* 14 December 1821, 7 December 1822.
64. *Milledgeville [GA] Reflector*, 16 June 1818; *Savannah Republican*, 14 December 1818.
65. "NOV 16, 2009 1833 Andrew Jackson shuts down Second Bank of the U.S." This Day in History. Found Online (//www.history.com/this-day-in-history/andrew-jackson-shuts-down-second-bank-of-the-u-s); McCutcheon, Robert, "Andrew Jackson and the Bank War" History Now. Found Online (//www.gilderlehrman.org/content/andrew-jackson-and-bank-war).
66. "Panic of 1837," Armstrong Economics. Found Online (https://www.armstrongeconomics.com/panic-of-1837/).
67. *Savannah Daily Georgian*, 11 August 1832.
68. Ibid, 12 January 1839.
69. Sullivan, Billy, *The Darien Bank: A Celebration of 100 Years 1889-1989* (Darien, Georgia: The Bank, 1989).
70. "A List of Mayors and Aldermen of the City of Savannah, Georgia, 1790-2012." Savannah Document Center. Found Online (//www.savannahga.gov/DocumentCenter/View/1971/List-of-Mayors-and-Aldermen?bidId=).
71. *Savannah Daily Georgian,* 31 May 1821.
72. "A List of Mayors and Aldermen of the City of Savannah, Georgia, 1790-2012." Savannah Document Center. Found Online (//www.savannahga.gov/DocumentCenter/View/1971/List-of-Mayors-and-Aldermen?bidId=).
73. *Savannah Daily Georgian*, 13 April and 23 April 1822; 35 May 1823; and various notices from 12 July to 4 September 1823 regarding his election as city alderman, and 12 November 1823.
74. *Savannah Georgian*, 31 July, 24 August, and 31 August 1825, 3 January, 14 May, and 15, October 1825.
75. *Savannah Georgian*, 12 May 1826, 16 March and 1 May 1827, 20 March 1828, and 5 February 1829.
76. *Savannah Daily Georgian*, 13 April and 16 April 1829.
77. Katcher, Brian S., "Benjamin Rush's Educational Campaign against Hard Drinking." *American Journal of Public Health*. 83(2), (February 1993), 273–281.

78. *Savannah Daily Georgian*, 17 June 1829; Walsh, Darlene M., *Roswell A Pictorial History*. Second Edition. (Roswell, GA: Roswell Historical Society, 1994), 39.
79. Walsh, *Roswell* 39; Temperance document is stored in the History Room of the Roswell Presbyterian Church.
80. Ibid.

Chapter VI:
1. Letter found in Theodore Roosevelt Collection, Houghton Library, Harvard University.
2. Holmes, James, *"Dr. Bullie's" Notes: Reminiscences of Early Georgia and of Philadelphia and New Haven in the 1800s* (Atlanta: Cherokee Publishing Company, 1976), 173-174.
3. *Darien* (Georgia) *Gazette,* 22 September 1821; John Elliott to James Smith, Oct 6, 1821, MS1065, Reverend John Jones Family Papers, Hargrett Rare Book and Manuscript Library, University of Georgia Libraries.
4. Totten, John Reynolds, *Thacher-Thatcher Genealogy*, (New York: New York Genealogical and Biographical Society,1910), 462; Jane Amaranthea married Charles Sever on 31 December 1826. They had four children, Catherine Elliott, John Elliott, Jane Elliott, and Charles William.
5. Walter E. Wilson, *Bulloch Belles* 17.
6. Midway Church Records; Susan Ann Elliott, born 6 August 1820; Georgia Amanda Elliott, born 14 June 1822, and Daniel Stewart 20 November 1826.
7. Hickey, Lu, "Women in History of Scots Descent: Martha "Mittie" Bulloch Roosevelt," Found Online (http://www.electricscotland.com/history/women/wh50.htm.
8. *Savannah Daily Republican*, 17 March 1821, 22 July 1823, 8 July 1823, 4 April 1825.
9. Typed copy found in Theodore Roosevelt Collection, Houghton Library, Harvard University.
10. "Ignace Joseph Pleyel" All Music. Found Online (https://www.allmusic.com/artist/ignace-joseph-pleyel-mn0001276239/biography).
11. Augusta *Chronicle*, 15 August 1827.
12. *Savannah Georgian*, 11 September 1827; Obituary reads in part "On the 8th inst. Charles Williams, son of the late John Elliott, age three."
13. John Elliott Probate File, Probate Court, Liberty County Courthouse, Hinesville, Georgia.
14. Probate File of John Elliott, Probate Court, Liberty County Courthouse, Hinesville, Georgia. Transcription of entire document presented in Appendix A.

15. Ibid.
16. U.S. Census Records, 1830; William Ward owned 57 slaves while John Bacon owned 38.
17. Probate File of John Elliott, Probate Court, Liberty County Courthouse, Hinesville, Georgia.
18. Measuringworth.com.
19. U.S. Census Records, 1820 and 1830.
20. Measuringworth.com.
21. Ibid.
22. Ibid.
23. Deed Book K, Liberty County Courthouse, Hinesville, Georgia: Measuringworth.com.
24. *Savannah Daily Georgian*, 20 March 1828.
25. Myers, Robert Manson (editor). *Children of Pride: A True Story of Georgia and the Civil War*. (New Haven: Yale University Press, 1972), 1590-1591.
26. Marriage Settlement for Jane E. Elliott. James S. Bulloch and John Dunwody, trustees, Liberty County Deed Book I, page 299, Liberty County Courthouse, Hinesville, Georgia.
27. *Savannah Daily Georgian*, 3 June 1829.
28. Will and Appraisement of Daniel Stewart's Estate (Liberty County, Georgia, Court of Ordinary, Wills and Appraisements). As transcribed in *Historical & Genealogical Collections of the Martha Stewart Bulloch Chapter*: Volume 592:2001.
29. Clarke, 85.
30. J. G. B. Bulloch, *History and Geanology of the Stewart, Elliott and Dunwody Families* (Savannah: Robinson Printing House, 1895), 2-7.
31. *Savannah Daily Georgian*, 6 June 1829.
32. *Savannah Daily Georgian*, 26 October 1829.
33. *Savannah Daily Georgian*, 3 May and 2 June 1828.
34, Probate File, John Elliott, Probate Court Liberty Count Courthouse, Hinesville, Georgia, 3 March 1829, 5 November 1829, 4 & 10 May 1830; Transcription presented in Appendix A.
35. Measuringworth.com.
36. *Savannah Daily Georgian*, 26 February 1831.
37. *Savannah Daily Georgian,* 28 March 1828, 2 May 1831.
38. *Savannah Republican*, 8 September 1831.
39. *Savannah Daily Georgian*, 1 March 1831, 12, March 1831, 26 March 1831, 6 April 1831, 9 April 1831, 22 April 1831, 26 April 1831, 10 May 1831, 13 May 1831, 16 May 1831, 25 May 1831, 6 June 1831, 15 June 1831.

40. Johnson, Jr., Charles J. Mary Telfair: *The Life and Legacy of a Nineteenth-Century Woman* (Savannah: Frederic C. Beil Publisher, 2002), 93-94.
41. Wood, Betty, *Mary Telfair to Mary Few: Selected Letters 1802-1844* (Athens: The University of Georgia Press, 2007).
42. "James S. Bulloch Pension/Land Bounty Papers." Fold3.com, Found Online, (//www.fold3.com/browse/247/h5iT6dgqRwM3YLOCSkutf_uaui8TATc4G6_dkY8pX).

Chapter VII:
1. *Savannah Daily Georgian*, 8 April 1832.
2. Ibid., 5 April 1832.
3. *Milledgeville* (Georgia) *Journal*, 6 September 1832.
4. *Savannah Daily Georgian*, 2 October 1832.
5. Chatham County Deed Book 2-R, p. 127, Office of Clerk of Superior Court, Chatham County Courthouse, 133 Montgomery Street, Savannah, Georgia; Measuringworth.com.
6. "Inventory and Appraisement for Anne Powell" Ancestry.com Found Online (https://search.ancestry.com/cgi-bin/sse.dll?indiv=1&dbid=8635&h=564969&tid=&pid=&usePUB=true&_phsrc=SUE517&_phstart=successSource); Measuringworth.com.
7. U.S. Census, 1830.
8. Kinnaman, Stephen Chapin, *Captain Bulloch: The Life of James Dunwoody Bulloch Naval Agent of the Confederacy* (Indianapolis: Dog Ear Publishing, 2013), 55-56.
9. Clark, Erskine, *Dwelling Place: A Plantation Epic* (New Haven: Yale University Press, 2005), 82-83; Wilson, Walter E. *Bulloch Belles* 26-28; Wilson and McKay, 10.
10. "Catalogue of the Pupils of Isaac Webb, esq. Private Boarding School, Middletown, Connecticut." Ancestry.com Found Online (https://search.ancestry.com/cgi-bin/sse.dll?indiv=1&dbid=2395&h=513412&tid=&pid=&usePUB=true&_phsrc=SUE447&_phstart=successSource); Measuringworth.com
11. *Savannah Daily Georgian*, 25 June 1835.
12. "Savannah, Georgia, Register of Free Persons of Color 1817-1864" Ancestry.com, Found Online (https://search.ancestry.com/cgi-bin/sse.dll?indiv=1&dbid=8969&h=10653&tid=&pid=&usePUB=true&_phsrc=SUE464&_phstart=successSource); Wilson, 25, 203-204n47.
13. *Savannah Daily Georgian*, 8 January 1836
14. Clarke, 101.
15. *Savannah Daily Georgian*, 12 March 1836.

16. Settlement for this claim might be found at National Archives in Guide to House Records: Chapter 6: Revolutionary Claims 1825-1873: Chapter 6. Records of the Claims Committees in Washington, D.C.
17. Reverend John Jones Collection, University of Georgia, Hargrett Rare Book and Manuscript Library, MS1065.
18. The identity of Matilda Bulloch has not been determined.
19. Reverend John Jones Collection, University of Georgia, Hargrett Rare Book and Manuscript Library, MS1065.
20. Ibid.
21. Piascik, Andy, "Jackson v. Bulloch and the End of Slavery in Connecticut." ConnecticutHistory.org Found Online (https://connecticuthistory.org/jackson-v-bulloch-and-the-end-of-slavery-in-connecticut/).
22. Ibid.
23. Ibid.
24. Robert Hutchison papers, MS411. Georgia Historical Society Research Center, Savannah Georgia.
25. James was one of 24 men invited by the Secretary of War and the only one from Georgia.; Wilson, Walter E. *Bulloch Belles* 46.
26. "Panic of 1837," Armstrong Economics. Found Online (https://www.armstrongeconomics.com/panic-of-1837/).
27. *Savannah Daily Georgian,* 2 November 1837.
28. *Savannah Daily Georgian,* 17 March 1838.
29. *Savannah Daily Georgian*, 15 January 1838, 16 January 1838.
30. *Savannah Daily Georgian*, 7 May 1838.
31. *Savannah Daily Georgian*, 25 May 1838, 2 June 1838.
32. *Savannah Daily Georgian*, 3 June 1840; Measuringworth.com.

Chapter VIII:
1. This author conducted or compensated others to conduct searches of historic records in both Liberty and Chatham counties. The narrative here presents only information found during those research sessions. There are no doubt other documents that related to James Bulloch that have not been found, so this is not a comprehensive account.
2. Probate Records of the Estate of John Elliott, Liberty County Courthouse, Hinesville, Georgia; Copy on file, with transcription by author, at Bulloch Hall, Roswell, GA.
3. Measuringworth.com estimates that $100 during this time frame equals about $2,730 in 2018.
4. Measuringworth.com.
5. Deed Book M, page 300, Receipt for Shares for Susan A. and Georgia A. Elliott from the estate of John Elliott, Liberty County, Hinesville, Georgia;

Deed Book n, page 59, Receipt for Share for Daniel S. Elliott from the estate of John Elliott, Liberty County, Hinesville, Georgia.

Chapter IX:
1.   Information taken from Clarece Martin's *A Glimpse of the Past: The History of Bulloch Hall and Roswell Georgia, (Roswell: Lake Publications 1987)*. Martin failed to cite references for any of this information.
2.   Hitt, Michael, personal communication; Skinner, James L. III (editor), *The Autobiography of Henry Merrell: Industrial Missionary to the South.* (Athens: University of Georgia Press, 1991), 140.
3.   Skinner, James L. III (editor), *The Autobiography of Henry Merrell: Industrial Missionary to the South* (Athens: University of Georgia Press, 1991), 140.
4.   Ibid., 141.
5.   Carithers, Julie, Self-Sufficiency in the Antebellum South: A Study of Greek Revival Architecture in North Georgia and Its' Relationship to Local Industry. *The Atlanta Historical Journal* Vol. 34(3), 31.
6.   Walsh, Darlene (editor), *Natalie Heath Merrill's Narrative History of Roswell, Georgia.* (Roswell, 1996), 14.
7.   Hamlin, Talbot, *Greek Revival Architecture in America* (New York: Dover Publications, 1944), XXXVIII.
8.   Walsh, *Natalie Heath Merrill*, 1996, 13.
9.   Nichols, Frederick Doveton, *The Early Architecture of Georgia* (Chapel Hill: University of North Carolina Press, 1957), 132.
10. Walsh, *Roswell, A Pictorial History*, 39.
11. Walsh, *Natalie Heath Merrill*, 22-23.
12. Nichols 1957, 132.
13. Barrington King's Ledger 1835-1838 and Barrington King's Journal 1837-1840, Roswell Historical Society/City of Roswell Research Library and Archives, Roswell, Georgia.
14. Clarke, 490.
15. Hoffman, Charles and Tess Hoffman. *North By South: The Two Lives of Richard James Arnold.* (Athens: University of Georgia Press, 1988), 35.
16. White, George, Reverend, Historical Collections of Georgia. (New York: Pudney & Russell, 1855), 353-364; McLeod, Rebecca, "The Loss of the Steamer Pulaski," Georgia Historical Quarterly 3:2 (1919):88; Underwater explorers discovered the wreck of the *Pulaski* in 2018 off the coast of North Carolina. The wreck had long been believed to be off the coast of South Carolina.
17. Walsh, *Natalie Heath Merrill*, 16.
18. Wilson Walter E., *Bulloch Belles* 45-46.
19. Wilson and McKay, 11, 302n34.

20. *Macon Weekly Telegraph*, 2 July 1839.
21. Skinner, 184; *Charlotte (North Carolina) Journal* Marriage Notices 23 April 1840.
22. Several historic documents indicate two cabins; however, a Bulloch family letter, from the 1850s, indicated a slave dwelling closer to the house. Archaeological investigations carried out by this author and other archaeologists confirmed a dwelling just to the right of the home. It may not have been erected at the time of the main house's construction.
23. This cemetery is now known as Founders' Cemetery.
24. Sever, Catherine Elliott, "A Memory of the South, with Introduction by Monroe F. Cockrell" *The Atlanta Historical Bulletin*, Volume 14:1; Research by Walter E. Wilson in the Sever Papers, Kingston Massachusetts Library, revealed a letter dated 6 December 1841, addressed to Kate in "Lebanon, Cobb County, Georgia, Care of Major Bullock." This letter details newspaper reports of the Sever family's carriage being overturned on the road out of Savannah, mentioned in the previously listed article. Additionally, Wilson uncovered *a New York Evening Post* listing dated 1 June 1842 announcing the arrival "In the brig. Sterling, from Savannah-Mrs. Sever, Miss C. Sever, Miss J. Sever. . ." Personal email Walter E. Wilson to Gwendolyn I. Koehler, Bulloch Hall.
25. Sever, 17-19.
26. Theodore Roosevelt Collection, Houghton Library, Harvard.
27. Mimosa Hall currently is owned by the City of Roswell.
28. Barrington King's Ledger 1835-1838 and Barrington King's Journal 1837-1840, Roswell Historical Society/City of Archives Library and Archives, Roswell, Georgia.
29. Walsh, *Natalie Heath Merrill*, 23.
30. Sever, 21.
31. Cox and Walsh, 631n664 and 589n212; Both notes cite: Walsh, Darlene, M., "*Natalie Heath Merrill's Narrative History of Roswell, Georgia.*"
32. Huddleston and Koehler, 11; Koehler and Huddleston, 161.
33. Walsh, *Roswell, A Pictorial History*, 61.
34. "Minutes of the Roswell Manufacturing Company," Roswell Historical Society/City of Roswell Research Library and Archives; Skinner, 130.
35. "Minutes of the Roswell Manufacturing Company"; Measuringworth.com.
36. "Minutes of the Roswell Manufacturing Company," Roswell Historical Society/City of Roswell Research Library and Archives.
37. Ibid; Measuringworth.com.
38. "Minutes of the Roswell Manufacturing Company," Roswell Historical Society/City of Roswell Research Library and Archives.
39. Ibid.

40. Skinner, 131; Measuringworth.com.
41. Barrington King's Ledger 1835-1838 and Barrington King's Journal 1837-1840, Roswell Historical Society/City of Archives Research Library and Archives, Roswell, Georgia.
42. Cobb County Records, Georgia Department of Archives and History.
43. *Milledgeville (Georgia) Standard of Union*, 12 March 1841.
44. *Milledgeville (Georgia) Federal Union*, 2 May 1841; 3 May 1842; 23 May 1843.
45. Skinner, 177.
46. *Reports of the First, Second, and Third Meetings of the Association of American Geologists and Naturalists, at Philadelphia, in 1840, and 1841, and at Boston in 1842.* (Boston: Gould, Kendall, & Lincoln, 1843).
47. Roswell Historical Society/City of Roswell Research Library and Archives.
48. *Milledgeville (Georgia) Recorder,* 18 October 1842.
49. *Milledgeville (Georgia) Southern Recorder*, 8 September 1840.
50. *Macon Weekly Telegraph*, 21 June 1842.
51. *Daily Union* (Washington, D.C.), 15 March 1847.
52. Martin, Clarece, *A History of the Roswell Presbyterian Church.* (Dallas: Taylor Publishing Company, 1984), 22-23, 32-32.
53. Found at the Roswell Historical Society/City of Roswell Library and Archives.
54. Wilson and McKay, 11; James Dunwoody Bulloch spelled his name with double o's.
55. Wilson, 53-54.
56. Wilson and McKay, 14-16.
57. Ibid.
58. *Catalogue of the Delta Kappa Epsilon Fraternity Biographical and Statistical* (New York: Council Publishing, 1890), 266; Personal communication Christine A. Lutz, Assistant University Archivist for Public Services, Seeley G. Mudd Manuscript Library, Princeton University, 6 November 2009.
59. Cox and Walsh, 64.
60. Huddleston, Connie and Gwendolyn I. Koehler, Mittie and Thee: An 1853 Roosevelt Romance, (Roswell, Friends of Bulloch, 2015), 90, 126; Personal Communication from Walter E. Wilson with transcription of this will found at the Georgia Historical Society Research Center.

61.   W.W. MacKall, "The Late Doctor Francis Sorrell: A Picturesque Character." *Georgia Historical Quarterly*, Vol.1(1) 1917, 36-37; *Weekly Raleigh Register* 25 February 1857; Thomas Gamble, *Savannah Duels and Duellists: 1733-1877* (Spartanburg, South Carolina: The Reprint Company, 1974), 249-256; Huddleston, Connie M. and Gwendolyn I. Koehler, *Divided Only by Distance & Allegiance* (Roswell: Friends of Bulloch, 2017), xiv-xv.

62.   Savannah Anti-Dueling Association constitution and minutes, MS0680, Georgia Historical Society Research Center, Savannah, GA; Walter Fraser Jr., *Savannah in the Old South* (Athens: The University of Georgia Press, 2003).

63.   Wilson, 56.

64 .   *Desilver's Philadelphia Directory and Stranger's Guide* (Philadelphia: Desilver, 1830), 208.

65 .   Jordan, John W. (compiler), *Colonial Families of Philadelphia*, Vol. 1 (New York: Lewis Publishing, 1911), 21, 563.

66 .   A. McElroy (compiler), *A. M'Elroy's Philadelphia Directory* (Philadelphia: Isaac Ashmead & Co) Found Online (https://archive.org/details/mcelroysphiladel00mcel_0).

67 .   Mary West Roosevelt (1823-1877); Theodore Roosevelt Collection, Houghton Library, Harvard University

68 .   The Hutchison-Dawson Papers, 1815-1897, Collection No. 2226, Box 1, Folder 9, Georgia Historical Society Research Center, Savannah, Georgia.

69 .   The Hutchison-Dawson Papers, 1815-1897, Collection No. 2226, Box 2, Folder 12, Letter from R. Hutchison to Miss Mary M. Caskie, Richmond, Virginia. Transcription provided by Stephen C. Kinnaman.

70 .   "U.S., Newspaper Extractions from the Northeast, 1704-1930. Ancestry.com Found Online (https://search.ancestry.com/cgi-bin/sse.dll?indiv=1&dbid=50015&h=1099735&tid=&pid=&usePUB=true&_phsrc=SUE535&_phstart=successSource).

Chapter X:

1.   James was born in 1793. His age of 56 at death as indicated by his gravestone, places his birthday between 1 January and 18 February.

2.   Cox, Connie M. and Darlene M. Walsh, *Providence: Selected Correspondence of George Hull Camp 1837-1907* (Macon: Indigo Publishing Group, 2008), 555; Florida Bayard Seay (1834-1917) was the daughter of Nicholas Bayard and Sarah Glen. He married second Eliza King Hand, daughter of Roswell King and widow of Bayard Hand in 1846. The family lived in Primrose Cottage on the street leading to the Roswell Presbyterian Church.

3.   Fold3.com "War of 1812 Pension application by Martha Bulloch," Fold3.com Found Online (https://www.fold3.com/image/301627387?terms=james,bullock,761).
4.   The Hutchison-Dawson Papers, 1815-1897, Collection No. 2226, Box 2, Folder 12, Letter from R. Hutchison to Miss Mary M. Caskie, Richmond, Virginia. Transcription provided by Stephen C. Kinnaman.
5.   Estate of James S. Bulloch - Probate Records" Microfilm 317, Georgia Archives,

Sources Cited

Books

Adams, John (L.H. Butterfield, Leonard C. Faber, and Wendell D. Garrett, editors). *Diary and Autobiography of John Adams,* Vol. 2. Boston: Harvard University Press, 1990.

Bell, Malcolm, Jr. *Savannah, Ahoy! The Steamship and the Town in the Gala Year of 1819.* Savannah: The Pigeonhole Press, 1959.

Braynard, Frank O. *S.S. Savannah: The Elegant Steam Ship.* New York: Dover Publications, Inc., 1988.

Bulloch, J. G. B. *A Biographical Sketch of Archibald Bulloch, President of Georgia 1776-77.* Privately Published, 1907.
—— *A History and Genealogy of the Families of Bulloch and Stobo and of Irvine of Cults.* Salem, MA: Higginson Book Company, 1990.
—— *History and Geanology [sp] of the Stewart, Elliott and Dunwody Families.* Savannah: Robinson Printing House, 1895.

Catalogue of the Delta Kappa Epsilon Fraternity Biographical and Statistical (New York: Council Publishing, 1890.

Clarke, Erskine. *Dwelling Place: A Plantation Epic.* New Haven: Yale University Press, 2005.

Coleman, Kenneth and Charles Stephen Gurr (editors). *Dictionary of Georgia Biography.* Volume One. Athens: University of Georgia Press, 1983.

Colquitt, Neyle. *An Historiette of Midway.* Midway, GA: Privately published, 1915.

Cox, Connie M. and Darlene M. Walsh. *Providence: Selected Correspondence of George Hull Camp 1837-1907.* Macon: Indigo Publishing Group, 2008.

Derks, Scott and Tony Smith. *The Value of a Dollar: Colonial Era to the Civil War, 1600-1865.* Millerton, NY: Grey House Publishing, 2005.

Desilver's Philadelphia Directory and Stranger's Guide. Philadelphia: Desilver, 1830.

Evans, Virginia Fraser, *Liberty County, Georgia: A Pictorial History*. Statesville, NC: Brady Printing Company, 1979.

Force, Pete (complier). *American Archives: Consisting of A Collection of Authentik Records, State Papers, Debates, and Letters and Other Notices of Public Affairs, The Whole Document Forming a Documentary History of the Origin and Progress of the North American Colonies; of the Causes and Accomplishments of the American Revolution; and of the Constitution of Government for the United States, to the Final Ratification Thereof.* Washington, D.C., Clerk's Office of the District Court of the District of Columbia, 1843.

Fraser Jr., Walter. *Savannah in the Old South.* Athens: The University of Georgia Press, 2003.

Gamble, Thomas. *Savannah Duels and Duellists: 1733-1877.* Spartanburg, SC: The Reprint Company, 1974.

Granger, Mary (editor). *Savannah River Plantations.* Savannah, Georgia Historical Society, 1947.

Groover, Robert Long. *Sweet Land of Liberty: A History of Liberty County, Georgia.* Roswell, GA: W.H. Wolfe Associates, 1987.

Hamlin, Talbot. *Greek Revival Architecture in America.* New York: Dover Publications, 1944.

Harden, William. *A History of Savannah and South Georgia*, Vol. I. Chicago: Lewis Publishing Company, 1913.

Helmers, Lois (editor). *Early Records of Liberty County, Georgia.* Winchester OH: Badgley Publishing Company, 2013.

Hoffman, Charles and Tess Hoffman. *North By South: The Two Lives of Richard James Arnold.* Athens: University of Georgia Press, 1988.

Holmes, James. *"Dr. Bullie's" Notes: Reminiscences of Early Georgia and of Philadelphia and New Haven in the 1800s.* Atlanta: Cherokee Publishing Company, 1976.

Huddleston, Connie M. and Gwendolyn I. Koehler. *Divided Only by Distance & Allegiance: The Bulloch/ Roosevelt Letters: 1861-1865.* Roswell: Friends of Bulloch, 2017.
—— *Mittie and Thee: An 1853 Roosevelt Romance.* Roswell: Friends of Bulloch, 2015.

Ingrisano, Jr., Michael N. *The First Officers of the United States Customs Service: Appointed by President George Washington in 1789.* Washington, D.C.: United States Customs Publication 578, 1987.

Johnson, Jr., Charles J. *Mary Telfair: The Life and Legacy of a Nineteenth-Century Woman.* Savannah: Frederic C. Beil Publisher, 2002.

Jones Jr., Charles C. *Biographical Sketches of the Delegates from Georgia to the Continental Congress.* Spartanburg, SC: Reprint Co., 1972.

Jordan, John W. (compiler). *Colonial Families of Philadelphia*, Vol. 1. New York: Lewis Publishing, 1911.

Kinnaman, Stephen Chapin. *Captain Bulloch: The Life of James Dunwoody Bulloch Naval Agent of the Confederacy.* Indianapolis: Dog Ear Publishing, 2013.

Knight, Lucian Lamar. *Reminiscences of Famous Georgians*, Vol.II. Atlanta: Franklin-Turner Company, 1908.

Koehler, Gwendolyn I. and Connie M. Huddleston. *Between the Wedding and the War: The Bulloch/Roosevelt Letters: 1854-1860*. Roswell: Friends of Bulloch, 2016.

Martin, Clarece. *A Glimpse of the Past: The History of Bulloch Hall and Roswell Georgia.* Roswell: Lake Publications 1987.
—— *A History of the Roswell Presbyterian Church.* Dallas: Taylor Publishing Company, 1984.

Miller, Randall M. (editor). *"A Warm & Zealous Spirit": John J. Zubly and the American Revolution, Selection of His Writings.* Macon, GA: Mercer University Press, 1982.

Myers, Robert Manson (editor). *Children of Pride: A True Story of Georgia and the Civil War.* New Haven: Yale University Press, 1972.

Nichols, Frederick Doveton. *The Early Architecture of Georgia.* Chapel Hill: University of North Carolina Press, 1957.

Niles, Hezekiah (ed.). *Principles and Acts of the Revolution in America.* Baltimore: W.O. Niles, 1822.

Northen, William J. and John Temple Graves. *Men of Mark.* Atlanta: A.B. Caldwell Publisher, 1907.

Phalen, William J. *The Consequences of Cotton in Antebellum America.* Jefferson NC: McFarland Publishers, 2014.

Sheftall, John McKay. *Sunbury on the Medway: A Selective History of the Town, Inhabitants and Fortifications.* Norcross, GA: National Society Daughters of the American Colonists, Georgia State Society, 1995.
—— *Sunbury on the Medway: A Selective History of the Town, Inhabitants, and Fortifications* (Atlanta: Georgia Natural Resources, 1977), 61-62.

Skinner, James L. III (editor). *The Autobiography of Henry Merrell: Industrial Missionary to the South.* Athens: University of Georgia Press, 1991.

Smith, Gordon Burns. *History of the Georgia Militia, 1783-1861.* Vol. 4. Milledgeville, GA: Boyd Publishing, 2000.

Snoby, Paulette. *Georgia's Colony of Roswell: One Man's Dream and the People who Lived It.* Roswell, GA: Interpreting Time's Past, 2015.

Spratt, H. Philip. *The Birth of the Steamboat.* London: Charles Griffin & Company Limited, 1958.

Stacy, James. *History of the Midway Congregational Church, Liberty County, Georgia.* Newnan, GA: S.W. Murray, 1899.

Stevens, William Bacon. *A History of Georgia, from Its First Discovery by Europeans to the Adoption of the Present Constitution in MDCCXCVIII.* Originally published in 1847. Reprint, Savannah, GA: Beehive Press, 1972.
——*History of Georgia, From its First Discovery by Europeans to the Adoption of the Present Constitution in MDCCXCVIII*, Volume II. (Philadelphia: E.H. Butler, 1859), 295-296.

Sullivan, Buddy. *The Darien Bank: A Celebration of 100 Years 1889-1989.* Darien, Georgia: The Bank, 1989.

Taylor, Robert J. (ed.), *The Adams Papers, Papers of John Adams*, Vol. 4, February–August 1776. Cambridge, MA: Harvard University Press, 1979.

Thorp, Willard Long and Hildegarde E. Thorpe. *Business Annals: The Annals of the United States of America.* Washington, D.C.: National Bureau of Economic Research, 1926.

Totten, John Reynolds. *Thacher-Thatcher Genealogy*. New York: New York Genealogical and Biographical Society, 1910.

Walsh, Darlene M. *Natalie Heath Merrill's Narrative History of Roswell, Georgia.* Roswell, Privately Published, 1996.
—— *Roswell A Pictorial History*. Roswell, GA: Roswell Historical Society, 1994.

Wilson, Adelaide, and Georgia Weymouth. *Historic and Picturesque Savannah*, Boston: Boston Photogravure Company, 1889.

Wilson, Caroline Price. *Annals of Georgia: Important Early Records of the State Abstracted and Compiled. Volume I, Liberty County Records and A State Revolutionary Pay Roll.* New York: Grafton Press Publishers, 1928.

Wilson, Walter E. *The Bulloch Belles: Three First Ladies, a Spy, a President's Mother, and Other Women of a 19th Century Georgia Family.* Jefferson [NC]: McFarland & Company, 2015.

Wilson, Walter E. and Gary L. McKay. *James D. Bulloch: Secret Agent and Mastermind of the Confederate Navy.* Jefferson [NC]: McFarland & Company, 2012.

White, George. *Historical Collections of Georgia*. New York: Pudney & Russell, 1855.

Wood, Betty. *Mary Telfair to Mary Few: Selected Letters 1802-1844.* Athens: The University of Georgia Press, 2007.

Periodicals
Carithers, Julie, "Self-Sufficiency in the Antebellum South: A Study of Greek Revival Architecture in North Georgia and Its' Relationship to Local Industry." *The Atlanta Historical Journal* Vol. 34(3), 31.

Ford, Elizabeth Austin, "The Bullochs of Georgia," *The Georgia Review*, Volume VI:3 (1952).

Gunning, Margaret House (editor), *Historical & Genealogical Collections of the Martha Stewart Bulloch Chapter*, Volume 592, 2001.

Jordan, David Starr, "The Inbred Descendants of Charlemagne: A Glance at the Scientific Side of Genealogy," *The Scientific Monthly* Vol.13:6 (1921) 481-492.'

Katcher, Brian S., "Benjamin Rush's Educational Campaign against Hard Drinking." *American Journal of Public Health*. 83(2), (February 1993), 273–281.

Lawton, Alexander R., "An Address by Alexander R. Lawton: Delivered in the City Hall, Savannah, Georgia, April 21 1919." *The Georgia Historical Quarterly* Volume 3:2 (June 1919), 45-60.

W.W. MacKall, "The Late Doctor Francis Sorrell: A Picturesque Character." *Georgia Historical Quarterly*, Vol.1(1) 1917, 36-37.

McLeod, Rebecca, "The Loss of the Steamer Pulaski," Georgia Historical Quarterly 3:2 (1919):88.

"Original Rules and Members of the Charleston Library Society," *The South Carolina Historical and Genealogical Magazine,* Vol. 23:4 (1922).

Pauley, William E., "Tragic Hero: Loyalist John J. Zubly," *Journal of Presbyterian History* 54 (1976).

Reports of the First, Second, and Third Meetings of the Association of American Geologists and Naturalists, at Philadelphia, in 1840, and 1841, and at Boston in 1842. Boston: Gould, Kendall, & Lincoln, 1843.

Sever, Catherine Elliott, "A Memory of the South, with Introduction by Monroe F. Cockrell" *The Atlanta Historical Bulletin*, Volume 14:1.

Smith, Henry A. M. "Charleston and Charleston Neck: The Original Grantees and the Settlements along the Ashley and Cooper Rivers." *The South Carolina Historical and Genealogical Magazine,* Vol. 19:1 (1918).

Archival Collections
Chatham County [GA] Courthouse:
    Office of the Clerk of Superior Court: Deed Books
Duke University Manuscript Department:
    Papers of Charles C. Jones, Jr. Collection
Georgia Historical Society Research Center:
    Archibald Bulloch Papers (1769-1777)
    Chatham County Health Department Death Cards/Index
    Chatham County Superior Court Record Room
    Robert Hutchison Papers
    Registry of Deaths in Savannah, Georgia: Volume II
    Savannah Anti-Dueling Association Constitution and Minutes
    The Hutchison-Dawson Papers, 1815-1897
Georgia Department of Archives and History:
    Estate of James S. Bulloch
    Estate of Georgia Elliott
    William Scarbrough Collection
Hargrett Rare Book and Manuscript Library, University of Georgia Libraries:
    Reverend John Jones Family Papers
    Letters of Charles Colcock Jones, Jr.
Liberty County Courthouse (GA):
    Court of Ordinary Wills and Appraisements
    Deed Books
    John Elliott Probate File
Roswell Historical Society/City of Roswell Research Library and Archives:
    Barrington King's Ledger 1835-1838
    Barrington King's Journal 1837-1840
    Minutes of the Roswell Manufacturing Company
    Howell Brothers Store Ledger
Theodore Roosevelt Collection, Houghton Library, Harvard University
United States Census Records

Newspapers and Magazines
Augusta Chronicle
Charlotte (North Carolina) *Journal*
Columbia Museum and Savannah Advertiser
Columbia Museum and Savannah Daily Gazette
Daily Union (Washington, D.C.)
Darien (Georgia) Gazette
Gazette of the State of Georgia (Savannah),
Georgia Gazette
Harper's New Monthly Magazine

Macon (Georgia) *Weekly Telegraph*
Magazine of American History
Milledgeville [Georgia] *Journal*
Milledgeville (Georgia) *Standard of Union*
Milledgeville (Georgia) *Federal Union*
Milledgeville [Georgia] *Reflector*
Milledgeville (Georgia) *Recorder*
Milledgeville (Georgia) *Southern Recorder*
Mount Pleasant (New York) *Westchester Herald*
New York Gazette
Patriot (Savannah)
Savannah Daily Georgian
Savannah Georgian
Savannah Patriot
Savannah Daily Republican
Savannah Republican
South Carolina and American General Gazette
South Carolina Gazette
Weekly Raleigh Register

Websites
All Music.com
Ancestry.com
Archive.org
Armstrong Economics.com
Biographical Directory of the United States Congress [congress.gov]
Connecticut History.org
Digital Commons [bepress.com]
Electric Scotland.com
Fold3.com
History.com
Liberty County Historical Society.org
Library of Congress.gov
Measuring Worth.com
New Georgia Encyclopedia.org
National Archives.gov
Research Subjects: Government & Politics, The Napoleon Series.org
Savannahga.gov
The Jefferson Monticello.org

APPENDIX A:

List of Contents

Will of Peter Tondee	A-190
Will and Warrant of Appraisement of Archibald Bulloch	A-191
List of Slaves	A-193
Appraisement for John Elliott, Sr.	A-195
Will of Mary DeVeaux Bulloch	A-197
Report of the Committee of Claims, on the Petition of	
Archibald S. Bulloch and others, February 28, 1822.	A-200
Probate of Estate of John Elliott (d. 1827)	A-203
List of Slaves, Inventory and Appraisement	A-204
Marriage Settlement for Jane Elizabeth Elliott to John Law	A-210
James Bulloch Assignment of Property to Joseph Cumming	A-212
Will and Appraisement for Daniel Stewart	A-214
List of Slaves	A-214
Summary of Will and Appraisement for Sarah Stewart	A-216
List of Slaves	A-218

In all documents transcribed herein _____ indicates illegible script. A question mark in brackets denotes some doubt about the accuracy of the transcription. *Do* is shorthand for ditto. Additionally, page breaks in original documents are noted when at all possible. Documents are presented in order as noted in book.

Will of Peter Tondee (Theodore Roosevelt Collection, Houghton Library, Harvard University)

Georgia   In the Court of Ordinary

       Whereas Lucy Tondee of Savannah in the Province of Georgia widow Executrix named and appointed in a Paper purporting to be the Last Will and Testament of Peter Tondee late of Savannah aforesaid Carpenter, deceased, Hath proved and suggested in the said court by Thomas Rofs [Ross] her Proctor, That the said Peter Tondee on or about the twenty first day of October last past gave directions to the Honorable William Young Esquire since deceased to draw his will which was accordingly done. And whereas it appears by the affidavit of Peter Gandy of Savannah aforesaid Gentleman and William Pickerson of the same Place Taylor, "That on or about the day last aforesaid they the said Gandy and Pickerson together with the said William Young and Mr. Jacob Oates since deceased where at the House and in the Bed Room of the said Peter Tondee who was then very sick and weak in Bod - That the said William Young then and there produced a Paper, which Mr. Tondee said was his will, [   ] Mr. Tondee said he would sign it - That [   ] the said William Pickerson helped Mr. Tondee to sit up in Bed and he Mr. Tondee attempted to sign the said Paper but was so weak and feeble that he could only make a crooked mark, which mark is not to be seen at the end of the said paper. - That the said Peter Tondee at the time of making the mark was of sound mind memory and understanding and was particularly desirous to have the said Paper or will properly Executed, but the said William Young having thought proper to postpone the Execution thereof in hopes that Mr. Tondee would thereafter be able to sign the said in his usual manner. [   ] Mr. Tondee continued to grow worse and died the next Evening, so that the same never was closed [?]; But the said Gandy and Pickerson upon their oaths declared that they are well convinced the said Mr. Tondee meant and intonated the said Paper, and the writing therein contained as and for his Last Will and Testament," as by the said will or paper and the aforesaid affidavit [   ] in the Registers Office of the said Court, referenced being to them respectively had may and doth fully and at large appear. And Whereas the said Lucy Tondee by her Proctor aforesaid, hat humbly moved in the said Court that a Citation should [   ] requiring and admonishing the Kindred & Creditors of the said, Peter Tondee, deceased to appear in the Court aforesaid on a day to be appointed to show Cause, if any they can, [   ] the said Will should not be established and Letters Testamentary granted to the said Lucy - Those are therefore to Cite and Admonish all and singular the Kindred and Creditors of the said Peter Tondee, deceased, that they be and appear before me in the Council Chamber in Savannah, on Thursday next after the Publication hereof to show Cause, if any they have or can Why the said Paper should not be established as and for the Last Will and Testament of the said Peter Tondee deceased, and Letters Testamentary granted to the said Lucy being the Executrix therein named.

Excellency's Command James Whitefield Sec^{ry}	Given under my Hand and Seal at Savannah The Twenty fourth day of August in the year of our Lord One thousand Seven Hundred & Seventy Six — Arch: Bulloch

Papers entitled: Warrant of Appraisement for Mary Bulloch on the Estate and Effects of Arch[d] Bulloch deceased.

This is the last Will and Testament of me Archibald Bulloch of the parish of Christ Church in the province of Georgia Esquire being in good health of Body and of sound and disposing mind and memory. Duly considering that it is appointed for all men once to die, and being mindful of the uncertainty of that great change when it shall please God to call me hence do make this my last Will & Testament of and concerning the real and personal Estates where of I am in anywise seized or professed of either profession revision or remainder or any other person in trust for my or which I have any power to dispose of as followeth.

First, I give and devise to all my sons that may be living at the time of my death all my Lands and other real Estate whatsoever or wheresoever, and of what nature or kind so ever, equally to be divided amongst them, share and share alike if more than one to hold to them their heirs and assigns for ever, provided always and it is my will my eldest son shall have the first choice of his share or portion after the same is divided. Also, I give, devise, & bequeath to my dear Wife Mary Bulloch, all my Furniture, Goods, household stuff, utensils & implements whatsoever in a or belonging to my dwelling house or dwelling houses whatsoever at the time of my death. Also, I give and bequeath to my said dear wife and to all my children that may be alive at the time of my death, all the rest and residue of my personal Estate to be equally divided between them share and share alike, but it is my Will and I do hereby give my said dear Wife full power to name any four of my Negroes to be included in her share in portion the respective share of each child or children to be respectively delivered to them upon their obtaining their ages of years or days of marriage which shall first happen, and it is my further will that the proceeds of my said estate, after the maintenance of my said Wife and Children is deducted be laid out in Land or Negroes or both as my Executor herein after mentioned shall think fit and most for the benefit of my Estate. But I do order and direct and it is my Will that no part of my Estate be sold. _____ And I do hereby nominate and appoint my said dear wife Mary Executrix and my friends James Deveaux and Joseph Clay - Esquires and my dear son James to be Executors of this my will. But it is my will, and I do hereby order and direct my said Executors not to interrupt my said Wife in the management of my Estate and education of my Children as long as she continues my widow,   Archibald Bulloch.

But my further will is and I do hereby direct that in case my said Wife after my death shall happen to marry with any other husband, that and in such case that they my Executors shall take upon themselves the management of my Estate that my said wife's share or portion of the same be immediately delivered to her and Executrixship [sp] shall cease and determine. And I do hereby revoke and make void all former Wills and Testaments. In Witness thereof I the said Archibald Bulloch have to this my last will & Testament contained in two sheets of paper fixed together in the margin and sealed and to the last sheet have set my hand & Seal, and to the other Sheet my hand only, declaring it to be my last Will & Testament the eleventh day of February in the year of our Lord One thousand seven hundred and seventy five. And in the fifteenth year of the reign of his Majesty King George the third.

        Arch;[d] Bulloch [signed]

Signed sealed published and declared by the above Archibald Bulloch as and for his last Will and Testament in the presence of Us, who at his request, in his presence and in the presence of each other have subscribed our names as witness thereto. . . .

  WWY Yonge Jun[r]
  Stephen Haven
  Mary Yonge

Georgia
Chatham County

William Stephens of Savannah in the State of Georgia Attorney at Law maketh oath, that he was well acquainted with the late Archibald Bulloch esq. deceased, and his handwriting and verily believe the name "Arch;d Bulloch" subscribed to the first sheet, and the same name, subscribed to and opposite the Seal of the second sheet of the foregoing Will is the proper hand writing of the said Archibald Bulloch, and the deponent further saith, that he was well acquainted with Henry Yonge Junr; and that the name WWY Yonge Junr is the proper signature of the said Henry Yonge Junr the deponent having often seen him write his name, and further saith ___

W. Stephens

Sworn before me
1st March 1786
    Geo. Jones

Memorandum this fourth day of 1786, personally appeared before me Joseph Clay esq. one of the States Justices assigned to keep the Peace in being from the appraisers appointed to appraise the goods and chattels of Archibald Bulloch deceased, who being duly sworn made oath that they would make a just and true appraisement of all and singular the goods and chattels, ready money, only excepted, of the said Archibald Bulloch, deceased, as shall be produced by Mary Bulloch Executrix of the estate of the said Archibald Bulloch, deceased and that they would return the same, certified under their hands, unto the said Mary Bulloch within the time prescribed by law.

Sworn to, as above   Seth Cuthbert
before me the 7th   Peter Deveaux
Day of March 1786   W. Stephens
Joseph Clay

Appraisement of the personal estate of the late Archibald Bulloch esquire deceased, as shown to us by Mary Bulloch executrix, this 3 March 1786

					£1020
1	Morris (driver)	£130	19	Clarissa	70
2	Toby	80	20	Doll	65
3	Dick	80	21	Elsie	65
4	Cicero	60	22	Tenah	70
5	Hector	35	23	Sapho	40
6	Casar	40	24	Rose	30
7	Brutus	50	25	Dianna	40
8	Harry	35	26	Dora	30
9	Peter	50	27	Priscilla	15
10	Adam	70	28	Polly	15
11	Billy	50	29	Daphne	15
12	Isaac	50	30	Rachel	20
13	Saba	50	31	Kate	50
14	Charles	45	32	Lucy	75
15	Hannibal	35	33	Eve	65
16	Sampson	40	34	Charlotte	75
17	Chance	20	35	Flora	70
18	York	100	36	Bella	50
		£1020			£1880

3 cows and calves £3	£9
3 dry cows £2	6
3 bulls	5
	£20

The above mentioned thirty-six negroes appraised at the sum of one thousand eight hundred and eighty pounds and the above nine head of grown cattle and three calves appraised at Twenty pounds, this 3 March 1786.
      By   Seth Cuthbert
                                 Peter Deveaux
                                 William Stephens

Georgia   By George Jones, Esquire Register of Probate for the County of Chatham in the State aforesaid

              Geo. Jones   These are to authorise [sp] and impower [sp] you or any three or four of you, whose names are here unwritten, to repair to all such parts and places within this state as you as shall be directed unto by Mary Bulloch named Executrix in the last Will and Testament of Archibald Bulloch late of the County aforesaid deceased, wheresoever any of the goods and chattels of the said deceased are to do remain within the said parts and places, and which shall be shown unto you by the said Mary Bulloch and their view and appraise all and every the said in goods and chattels, being first sworn on the Holy Evangelists of Almighty God to make a true and prefect inventory and appraisement thereof, and to cause the same to be returned unto your hands, or any thrice or four of you, the said Mary Bulloch on or before the First day of June now next ensuing.

Dated the first day of March in the year of our Lord 1786 and in the tenth year of the Independence of the United States of America.

To Messiurs,
Seth John Cuthbert
John Milledge
Peter Deveaux and
William Stephens
      or any three or four of them

Sir

The matter between Mr. Bulloch and myself being adjusted I now withdraw the Caveat entered in your office against him by me..

6th Augt [illegible]   Mary Bulloch

                                                   James Whitefield esquire

Appraisement of John Elliott's Estate (Father of Senator) - Note: the appraisement is in pounds
(Will Books, Colony of Georgia, RG 49-1-5, Georgia Archives
Digital Collection/Colonial Will Books)

Appraisement of the good and Chattles of the Estate of John Elliott deceased made the 10th day of January 1792

Negro Fellow						
Ben	50		Wench	Deanah	20	
do	Peter	50		Bess	43	
do	John	50		Rachel	40	
do	Caesar	50		Dinah	40	
do	Cupid (?)	50		Sylvia	40	
do	Plato	50		Hagar	40	
do	Handy	45		Phillis	40	
do	Tollydore (?)	45		Hellen	40	
do	Abram	45		Delia	37	
do	Monday	40		Affey	37	
do	Tarquin	40		Bella	30	
do	Cook	40		Mazer	27	
do	Boston	38		Tinor	15	
do	Hinz	35	Wenches		£486	
do	Abraham	25	Girl	Bess	25	
do	Mingo	22		Betsy	25	
do	Tom	22		Patty	25	
do	Sam	20		Moll	17	
Fellows		£757		Sary	16	
Boy	Harry	25		Sharlotte	16	
	_____	18		Murriah	13	
	Billy	18		Sary	15	
	Stephen	17		Stella (?)	15	
	Charles	17		Henna	12	
	Prince	17		Linda	12	
	Hary	15		Amaritta	12	
	Jack	15		Prisscilla	12	
	Bob	14	Girls		£215	
	London	10				
	Isaac	10				
	Sam	10				
	Joe	15				
Boys		£201				

APPENDIX A

[page 2]
Fellows   757.00
Wenches   486.00
Boys   201.00
Girls   215.00
                                               £1659.00

Cattle   100.00
Sheep   24.00
Horses   40.00
Hogs   2.12
                                               £166.12

One Chaise & harness   18.00
One old chair   1.00
Tools   2.12.4
Desk and bookcase   10.00
Table   illegible
Mills, Pots, ____kettle   13.7.0
Firedogs ____ ironiron & gridirons   3.5.8
___ Chairs, Books, & Trumphery   22.10.5
_____, ____, & hone   4.9.4.00
Knive, pistol, sword, and old saddle   2.10..00
Curtains, Beds, & other furniture   53.5.00
A ___ of ___   11.18.80
Cases & bottle ware   2. 2
chests & 2 casks   00.11.00
_____   1   P
glass & crockery ware   9.0.4
A lot of old iron   illegible
                                              £ 151.19.11

John Mitchell June
Joseph Plummer
Wright Murphe(?)

Will of Mary DeVeaux Bulloch (Transcribed from a copy found at Bulloch Hall, Roswell, Georgia)

Georgia City of Savannah

In the name of God, Amen, I Mary Bulloch of the City of Savannah, in the State of Georgia, widow of Arch. Bulloch, heretofore of Savannah Engl, deceased, being of sound mind and understanding and knowing the uncertainty of human life do make this my last will & testament as follows: I do hereby give and bequeath, unto my sons Arch S. Bulloch & William B. Bulloch and their heirs & assigns forever all my Estate real & personal of whatever nature, kind or description, & however derived - to be equally divided between my said two son, share & share alike- It is may will, and I hereby desire, that as soon after my death as conveniently may be all may estate real & personable of what ever nature or kind, and however derived & as above bequeathed to be shared and share like to my said sons & shall be valued & appraised in the usual manner & my executor herein after named shall cause the same to be done & it is my will and I hereby desire & bequeath that my said two sons, Arch S. Bulloch & William B. Bulloch shall pay in money in equal proportions to the widow & children of my deceased son James Bulloch, one fourth part of the amount of the evaluation & appraisement of my estate, real & personal, herein before directed to be appraised & I do hereby further will and direct that my said two sons Arch. S. Bulloch & William B. Bulloch, shall pay from time to time in equal proportions, to my grand son William B. Maxwell the son of my deceased daughter Jane Maxwell, such money or sums of money, as in their discretion he may require for his support, & no more, until he shall have received equal to one fourth part of the amount of the evaluation & appraisement of my Estate real and personal and in making this arrangement for my said grand son William B. Maxwell, I have his own good in view, but should my said grand son William B. Maxwell depart this life before he shall have received the above amount, it is my will and I direct the ballance [sp] shall be divided in three parts, one third to my son Arch. S. Bulloch, one third part to my son William B. Bulloch, and one third part to my deceased son's widow and children, James Bulloch, to be equally divided between them, share & share alike, and to their heirs forever - and it is my will that all my debts of whatever kind, shall be paid out of the whole of my estate ___ to as every fourth part first divided and every ___ bear part ___ in deed as I think my debts will be small - the Negroes will soon pay them by their work. And I do make & appoint my sons Arch S. Bulloch and William B Bulloch my executors to this my last will hereby revoking all former wills by me and declare this to be my Last Will & Testament in witness hereof I do set my hand and seal this 18 May in the year of our Lord Eighteen Hundred and Eight.

Signed, sealed, published, & declared by the Mary Bulloch the testaton [?] as her last will and testament in the presence of us who at her request & in her presence and in the presence of each other have here unto subscribed our names as Witness

[illegible signatures]

I have sold and conveyed to my son William B. Bulloch my plantation on Skideway [sp] called Bloomsberry for two thousand dollars; five hundred of which I have given to him & five hundred he has paid to my son Arch S. Bulloch and he has given me his note for one thousand dollars. I enjoin upon all my heirs to acquiesce in this sale & should any of them my legatees on _____ make any dispute to the title given to him the said plantation I do hereby disinherit them and give to my other heirs nay proportion that he she or they would otherwise be entitled to - provided they did not make such contest. Savannah Feb 18, 1809.
Mary Bulloch

Witness
Catharine Matthews
Peter Millen
Witnesses

William Stephens Esquire being duly sworn saith the same Mary Bulloch whose name is above subscribed in the handwriting of the said Mrs. Mary Bulloch deceased & that the same was subscribed in his presence.   W. Stephens

Sworn to June
1st 1818
Sam M. Bond
clkco ord

Beaufort

Johny	Lucy
York	Julia
Lewis	Mary, went off
Cato	Rachel
Billy	Nelly
illegible	Eliza
Ben with A.S.B. [Archibald Stobo Bulloch]	Dianna
Sidny with W.B.B. [William Bellinger Bulloch]	Betty
	Peggy
Zackey, went off	Cloe with A.S.B. [Archibald Stobo Bulloch]
	Therysa, with Mrs. James Bulloch, which she may keep at the appraisement at the time of my

I have no charge to any of my children 30 May 1809 M.B.

Memorandum

My wearing apparel, such as are good, the others to my attendances on my Last & gold watch I leave to my GD Ann D. Bulloch, my sister Stephens & Wm Stephens picture I leave to my niece Mrs. Belcher - Brother and Mrs. Deveaux to my Niece Mrs. Alger - Mr. & Mrs Algers to My Niece M. O. Deveaux. My family ps to my Eldest son or only son if it should be so at my death - to the longest liver at any rate. All my others to my son William B. Bulloch - unless my unfortunate G S Will B Maxwell should be alive and wish for one - then let him have one if he is fit to have it - all only to say I have not forgot my neices - am sorry I don't think it in my power to do better - My D. Jane Dunwody must take something to say was mine- and with most ardent wished to meet you all in Heaven. I conclude yours ____ M. Bulloch   Sav. June 4th 1818

The subscribers appointed by the Honorable of the Court of Ordinary to appraise the estate of Mrs. Mary Bulloch deceased being duly sworn upon examination of said property to certify the value of the ____ as follows.

Lizzy	$250.00
Judy	250.00
Rachel	
Diana	1500.00 [grouped]
Peggy	
Teresa	
Charity	1000.00 [grouped]
John	1200.00
Ben	800.00
Sydney	600.00
Bob	550.00
Betty	500.00
	7250.00

The total amount of said evaluation   G. W. Owens
seven thousand two hundred fifty dollars   Rob Habersham
    illegible

Amount A. S. Bulloch's note to
    Mrs. Mary Bulloch $400

Amount W.B. Bulloch's note to
    Mrs. Mary Bulloch $800

Cash (applied as far as it went to funeral expenses.)
One hundred & six dollars & fifty cents.
Savannah 4th June 1818

    A.S. Bulloch
    W.B. Bulloch

Report of the Committee of Claims, on the Petition of Archibald S. Bulloch and others, February 28, 1822. Read and ordered to lie on the table, 11 March 1822. Printed by order of the House of Representatives. Serial Set Vol. No. 86. House Report 10.

REPORT
of the Committee of Claims on the petition of Archibald S. Bulloch, and others.

February 28, 1822
Read, and ordered to lie on the table

March 11, 1822
Printed by order of the House of Representatives

December 12, 1822
Reprinted by order of the House of Representatives

The Committee of Clamis, to whom was referred the petition of Archibald S. Bulloch, collector of the port of Savannah, James S. Bulloch, administrator of Alexander Irvine, late of the city of Savannah, naval officer, and Alexander Hunter, surveyor of the port of Savannah, have had the same under consideration, and submit to the House the following
REPORT:
The petitioners state, that, in October 1819, by information they furnished, the schooner Montevediana, alias Libertad, or Liberty, was libelled [sp] in the admiralty court for the district of Georgia; that the said was sustained so far as respected the interest of certain persons named in the decree, and the sum of $197.28, ordered to be paid over to the collector. After the first information was lodged, and before the rendition of the judgement, another libel was filed against the said vessel, for violating the laws of the United States prohibiting the slave trade. This was likewise sustained, and so much of the vessel and cargo as had not been affected by the first degree was condemned, and the sum of $1176.70, paid over to the district attorney for the use of the United States.
The petitioners further state, that they incurred great expense and trouble in prosecuting the second libel; that the act prohibiting the slave trade makes no provision for those who, like themselves, may cause offenders to be brought to justice, and they ask Congress to grant them suitable indemnity out of the sum of $1176.70, paid over to the district attorney for the use of the United States.
The act of 1799, regulating duties on imports and tonnage, gives to collectors, &c., a moiety of forfeitures, but the law prohibiting the slave trade makes no such allowance. The committee, therefore, think it inexpedient to extend the provisions of the last mentioned act; and therefore, submit the following resolution.
Resolved. That the prayer of the petitioners ought not to be granted.

Treasury Department,
18th February, 1822

Sir: I have the honor to return the petition of Archibald S. Bulloch, James S. Bulloch, and Alexander Hunter, with the papers by which it was accompanied.
It is ascertained that there has been paid into the Treasury the sum of $1176.70, of the proceeds of the sale of the schooner Montevediana and cargo, the vessel described in the petition.
By the act of the 24th of February, 1819, for the relief of Thomas Hall Jervey, one half of the nett proceeds of the Lovely Cordelia, and of the James and Elizabeth, were directed to be paid to the said Jervey, who was the surveyor of the port of Charleston. These vessels had been condemned for

violations of the laws prohibiting the slave trade. The said Jervey, in his petition, alleged that he had seized the said vessels upon his own responsibility, and against the opinion of the collector, and that the prosecution had been carried on wholly by his determination and exertions. This allegation was supported by unquestionable evidence. Hence, the other officers of the customs were excluded from any participation in the liberality of Congress.

It is highly probable that there have been other cases of a nature similar to that of the petitioners. The case of Jervey is the only case which occurs to my recollection at this time, in which relief has been given, and the facts in that case were very peculiar.

As a general principle, "it is expedient to interest the officers employed in the execution of penal statues, by giving them a part of the penalties. Where this has not been done by the law creating penalties, it is believed to be inexpedient to make such provision by law in particular cases, after the penalties have been incurred, unless where the circumstances are of a very peculiar nature, as in the case of Mr. Jervey.

It is for the committee to determine whether there is any thing peculiar in the cases of the petitioners.

> I am, with respect,
> Your most obedient servant.
> WM. H. CRAWFORD

Hon. Lewis Williams,
Chairman Committee of Claims.

> Treasury Department,
> Register's Office, February 6th 1822.

The Register begs leave, respectfully, to report to the Secretary of the Treasury, that, on an examination of the accounts of Archibald S. Bulloch, collector of the port of Savannah, there does not appear to have accrued to the United States any portion of the fine or forfeiture incurred by the Portuguese schooner Liberty, so far as the accounts of the said collector have been received in his office, which is to the 31st March, 1821. The whole amount of duties accruing to the United States on goods imported in said vessel, appears, from the collector's abstract of merchandise imported during the fourth quarter of 1819, to amount to fourteen dollars and ten cents.

> JOSEPH NOURSE, Register.

To the Honorable the President and Members of the Senate, and the Speaker and Members of the House of Representatives, of the United States of America Congress assembled.

The petition of Archibald S. Bulloch, collector of the port of Savannah, James S. Bulloch, administrator of Alexander Irvine, late of the city of Savannah, naval officer, and Alexander Hunter, surveyor of the port of Savannah.

HUMBLY SHEWETH:

That, in the month of October, 1819, a certain schooner, called the Montevediana, alias Libertad, or Liberty, arrived in the port of Savannah, from sea, laden with an assorted cargo; that, soon after her arrival in said port, it was discovered by the officers of the revenue, that the person, or persons, having charge of the said vessel, were in the act of smuggling goods from on board the same; that information of this fact was immediately given, by your petitioners, to the attorney of the United States, who, thereupon, filed a libel in the court of admiralty, against the said vessel, her tackle, apparel, and furniture, and the goods so unladen, alleging that the same became forfeited to the United Sates, under the act of Congress, entitled "An act to regulate the collection of the duties on imports and tonnage," passed the 2d day of March, 1799; that the said libel was, by a decree of the district court, sustained, so far as the same respected the interest of certain persons in the said decree named, and the sum of one hundred and ninety-seven dollars and twenty-eight cents ordered to be paid over the to the collector of the port of Savannah, all which will more fully appear to your honorable bodies by the exemplification of the proceedings in the cause, which is most respectfully submitted herewith.

That shortly after the filing of the said libel against the said vessel and goods, and long before the decree of the court hereon, it was discovered by the officers of the revenue of the port of Savannah, that a certain African slave was introduced into the said port by the person, or persons, having charge of the said vessels, in the said vessel with intent to sell the same, contrary to the provisions of the several acts of Congress to prohibit the slave trades; that the said African was seized, but made his escape; was secreted by the person, or persons, having charge of the said vessel, and was removed by them into the country, at a distance from the city and port aforesaid; that, after great trouble and expense, your petitioners succeeded in apprehending the said African, and lodging him with the jailer of the said city for safe keeping, to abide the order of courts; that information of this further violation of the law was immediately given by your petitioners to the attorney of the United States, who, thereupon, filed another libel against the said vessel, under the act of Congress, entitled "An act to prohibit the importation of slaves into any port and place within the jurisdiction of the United States, from and after the first day of January, in the year of our Lord one thousand eight hundred and eight," passed on the second day of March, eighteen hundred and seven; that the last mentioned libel was, by a decree of the court aforesaid, sustained, against so much of the cargo of the said vessel as was unaffected by the decree of condemnation against the vessel and part of the cargo, under the libel for smuggling; that, by the last decree, after certain sums were ordered to be paid into the registry of the court for its further order, the sum of eleven hundred and seventy-six dollars and seventy cents was decreed to be paid over to the district attorney, for the use of the United States. Your petitioners humbly shew, that the expenses incurred and borne by them in the prosecution of the said libels, amount to a sum of larger that the sum of one hundred and ninety-seven dollars and twenty-eight cents, decreed to the collector under the libel for sumggling, and that, as your petitioners, under the last decree on the libel under the slave act, have no provisions made for them. They have, by their information and testimony, procured the condemnation of the said vessel and goods, for a violation of the laws, without any remuneration thereof. Our petitioners humbly and respectfully contend, that they are entitled, in justice, to some compensation for their labors, and although in this particular case, there may be no law which authorizes the payment to them of a moiety of the forfeiture, yet your petitioners fully believe that your honorable bodies will grant them a reward for their exertions, and relief in the premises.

Your petitioners, therefore, humbly pray the passage of an act or resolution of your honorable bodies which will authorize the payment to them of a moiety of the said forfeiture, or of such other sum as may seem right and just.

                And they will ever pray, &c
                A. S. Bulloch,
                Collector,
                James S. Bulloch,
                Adm'r estate A. Irvine, naval officer,
                A. Hunter
                Surveyor Revenue.
                Port of Savannah, January 3 182

Probate File for John Elliott (Probate Court, Liberty County Courthouse, Hinesville, Georgia)

State of Georgia   10 December 1827
Liberty County

Know all men by these present that we James S. Bulloch, Anne Powell, John B. Gaudry, John Bacon, William Ward are held and firmly bound and obligated unto the Honorable the Justices of the Inferior Court of Liberty County for the time being, acting as a Court of Ordinary in the sum of Seventy thousand dollars, to be paid to the said Justices, their supors in office, or assigns for which payment will and truly to be made and done, we find ourselves, jointly ____ and each of our heirs, executors of administrators, firmly by these presents. Sealed with our seals, and dated 10th this tenth day of December in the year of our Lord one thousand eight hundred and twenty seven. The condition of this obligation is such, that if the above bounden James S. Bulloch administrator of the goods, chattels, & credits of the Estate John Elliott deceased, do make or cause to be made, a true & perfect inventory of all & singular the goods, chattel & credits, of the said deceased, which have or shall come to the hands, possession or knowledge, of the said James S. Bulloch or into the possession of any other person for him, and the same so made do exhibited unto the said Court of Ordinary, when he shall be thereunto required, and such goods, chattels, & credits, do well & truly administer accordingly to Law, & make a just and true account of his actings and doings therein when required by the Superior Court, or Register of Probates for the County: and all the rest of the goods, chattels, & credits, which shall be found remaining upon the account of the said administration, the same being first allowed by the said court, shall deliver and pay to such persons respectively as are entitled to the same by law; and if it shall hereafter appear that any last will & testament was made by the said deceased, and the same be proved before the court, and the executors obtain a certificate of the probate thereof and the said James S. Bulloch do in such case if required render and deliver up the said Letters of Administration, then this obligation to be void, else to remain in full force.

Sealed & delivered	James S. Bulloch
In presence of	Anne Powell
Elias Tort (?) ____	John B. Gaudy
Sealed and delivered	Jno Bacon
by John Bacon & William Ward	William Ward
in open court in presence of	
E. Baker _____	

Inventory and Appraisement of John Elliott (Will Record B, 1824-1850, page 41, Probate Court, Liberty County Courthouse, Hinesville, Georgia.) [Spacing maintained as the slaves appear to be grouped by families]

Inventory & Appraisement of the goods & chattel belonging to the Estate of John Elliott, deceased, or exhibited ___ by James S. Bulloch, admir. of said deceased this 11 December 1827 in L. County.

Negroes			Amt. brought forward		$10400
			Polly	400	
James, driver	600		Nancy	300	
James	200		George	300	
Jim	200		Tandy	250	
Just	450		Daphne, old	100	
___	450		Nanny	400	
Lydia	300				
___	325		Caesar	200	
Titus	225				
Dambo	175		Amelia	200	
Isaac	50	2975			
			Titus	50	
Isaac, carpenter	600		Boston	200	2400
Hannah	400				
Rose	225		Diana	100	
Mindy	175		Polly	225	
Bob	100				
			Will	450	
Luke	450		Charlotte, at Nabs	400	
			Patience	400	
Pheobe, old [?]	125				
Libby	350		50 Lenah, old	50	
Maria	350		Tom, driver	300	
			Katy, cook	250	2175
Judy	50	2825			
			Bob	425	
June	325				
Cupid	450		Henry	350	
			Elsey	325	
Ben, tailor	450				
Leah	400		Amarintha	225	
Lucy	400				
Ben	325		Maurice	200	
Mary	275				
Sue	225		Nanny	150	
Elizabeth	150				
Frances	50	3050	Binah	125	1800
K _ ish	400		Stephens, carriage driver	450	
			Vermont, carpenter	450	
Davy, [___]	450		William	400	
			Henry	350	
Rose	400		James	300	
			Sarah	275	
			Isabella	200	
Sally	300	1550			
carried forward		10400	Stephens	50	2475
			carried forward		$19250

APPENDIX A - 204

Amount brought forward		$19250	
Harry	375		
Betty	300		
Charles	450		
Delia	400		
Peggy	400		
Moll	300		
Affy	275		
Renty	225		
Paul	450		
Murriah	300		
Billy	225		
Titus	200		
80 December	150		
Lucy	50	4100	
Caesar	350		
Elijah	300		
Charity	275		
Sue	200	1125	
Ben	400		
Sally	400		
Cretia	400		
Amey	400		
90 Grace	325		
Fanny	300		
Pompey	200		
Betty	150		
Will, cripple	300		
Nancy	275		
Tenah	400		
Frank	325	3875	
Isaac	300		
Dinah, old	25		
100 London	100		
Bob, diseased	200		
Vaughn	300		
Rinah	300		
Margaret	200		
Handy, old ____'s husband	300	1725	
Dick	300		
Nelly	375		
Sylvia	325		
Clarissa	250		
110 Ginda	225		
Andrew	200	1675	
Amount carried forward		$31750	

Amount brought forward		31750	
Jack	400		
Daphne, crippled	50		
Katy, diseased	100		
Phillis	250		
Jupiter	225		
Stephen	450		
Bess	275		
Bill, diseased	200		
120 Rachel	400		
Mary	50	2400	
Harry	450		
Phoebe	400		
Anthony	200		
Edward	50		
Jason	400		
Dye	350		
Hannah	225		
Tarquin	175	2250	
130 Clarinda	350		
David	250		
Ben	225		
Molly	200		
London, shoemaker, crippled	300		
Sylla	400		
Flora	400		
Nancy	150		
Tom	400		
Affy	400		
140 Finch	50		
Prime, Brothers	450		
Joe	450		
Peter	450		
Tom, Congo	300		
Flora	400		
Toney	200		
Fortune	150		
Clarissa	50		
Moll	350		
150 Peggy	300	3100	
Dinah	350		
Amelia	150		
Caesar, diseased	150		
Dublin	250		
Hagar	25		
Harriet	400		
Beck	50	1375	
		$44000	

Amount brought forward		$44000	Amount brought forward	$56485	
Charlotte	200		Elsey, dropsey	175	
Patty	200		Bob, cripple	10	
160 June, old	300		Titus	450	
Will, old	50		Isaac	250	
Tom, old	10		Billy	350	
William	300		Patty	100	
Phillis, old nurse	50		[Billy and Patty are also grouped with Matilda and Hetty]		
Titus	450		210 Matilda	200	
Nat, driver, aged	350	1910	Hetty	50	
Charlotte	400		Ned	450	
Riky	275		Jim	150	2185
Sarah	225		Jane	400	
170 William	175		Phillis	350	
George	50		Julian	400	
Leah, Rose ___ daughter	250	1375	Joe	75	
173 Jacob	250		Bob, carpenter	800	
Binah, old	100		Miley, cook	200	2625
Moll, driver Nat's wife	400		[Actual total is $61295]		$61245

Furniture

Celia	400	Secretary & book case	65.00
Catharine	125	Piano forte & stool	120.00
Phillis	50	backgammon box	1.00
Sandy, Celia's husband	450	1 Tea table	6.00
180 Adam	450	1 Sideboard	30.00
Delia	400	2625	1 Liquor case	6.00
Primus	400	1 Mahogany dining table & cover	10.00
Maria	400	1, do	10.00
Peter	400	12 chairs, yellow	15.00
Joe	275	1 set marble mantel piece ornaments	12.00
William	225	4 plated candlesticks, with	
Franklin	50	2 glass lamps	5.00
Jim	350	1 Brass fender	10.00
Sophia	350	1 set andirons, shovel & tongs	12.00
190 Sandy	400	1 large figured carpet & rug	10.00
Stephen	325	1 portable secretary	12.00
Molly	275	1 lot glassware, tumblers, wines,	
Bella	225	Decanters, tea	10.00
Pussy	175	1 set casters, plated	6.00
Bonny	50	3900	1 large stone pitcher	.75
Tim, husband to Patience _ 69 negroes	425	1 broken set dining crockery	12.00
Jacob	450	1 broken set tin ware, waiters,	
Tally, invalid	200	lamps, _____	5.00	82.75
Cato	200	1 old bedstead	3.00
200 Mingo	450	1 crib	1.25
Minda	100	1 toilet glass	4.00
March	450	1 washstand & sink, basin & pitcher	2.50	10.25
Gentle Jack	400	2675		
Amount carried forward	$56485	Amount carried forward	$61613.60

APPENDIX A - 206

Amount brought forward	$6613.00	
1 set china ornaments	.50	
1 feather bed & mattress	45.00	
1 bedroom carpet	5.00	
1 set andirons, shovel & tongs	10.00	
1 bedstead	3.00	
1 toilet glass	1.25	
1 room carpet	5.00	
1 set andirons, shovel, & c.	3.00	
1 mattress, pillows & bolster	12.00	
1 mahogany bedstead	12.00	96.75
1 featherbed, mattress, pillow & bolster	45.00	
1 toilet glass	4.00	
1 wash hand stand, basin & pitcher	2.50	
1 set andirons	3.00	
1 bed rug	.50	55.00
1 low front stained wood bedstead	1.25	
2 set chimney ornaments, yellow	2.00	
1 old sofa	15.00	
1 print "The Annunciation"	3.00	
2 prints from Shakespeare	8.00	
2 do. Adam, Cain, & Able	8.00	
2 do. Maternal Love	6.00	
1 Bellows and hearth broom	1.00	
1 lot kitchen furniture	12.00	
Lot empty bottles	2.00	
Lot trumpery in cellar	3.00	51.25
Lot knives & forks	5.00	

Books
210 volumes neatly bound books, with a lot of state papers & broken volumes thrown in	315.00	
43 Not. Ed. Review	10.75	
6 Large maps	30.00	

1 four wheel carriage & harness	180.000	
1 gig & harness	80.00	
1 pair carriage horses	300.00	
1 horse Buncombe	75.00	
1 do. Burke	20.00	
1 do. Charley	100.00	$1115.75
1 do. Rock	40.00	
1 do. Bachelor	80.00	
1 Male Buck	70.00	
4 Plantation waggons	140.00	
1 livery do.	15.00	345.00

Amount carried forward $63276.75

Amount brought forward $63276.75

1 double barrel gun	100.00	
1 singe do. do.	10.00	
1 gold watch	50.00	

Stock	159 head cattle	795.00	
	44 do. sheep	66.00	
	42 do. Hogs	63.00	1084.00
	Total	$64360.75	

Inventory and Appraisement of the goods & chattel belonging to the Estate of John Elliott deceased, as exhibited to us by James S. Bulloch, admin. Of said deceased, in Chatham County.

1 Sideboard	200.00	
1 set dining tables	100.00	
1 pair card tables	60.00	
Do.	60.00	
1 centre table	60.00	
2 Mahogany bedsteads	100.00	
1 doz. Do. Chairs	100.00	
1 doz. Do. Do.	100.00	
2 Bureaus	54.66	
1 do.	27.34	862.00
2 dressing tables	80.00	
1 ditto	32.00	
2 wash stands	30.00	
1 crib	18.00	
1 stained wood bedstead	12.00	
1 trunnel do.	10.00	
1 mahogany stand	2.00	
1 do. bedstead	20.00	
1 old Mahogany stand	2.00	
1 wash hand stand	2.00	208.00
1 set drawers, old	9.00	
1 do.	9.00	
1 pair old card tables	20.00	
1 old Mahogany stand	2.00	
1 old tea table	6.00	
1 parlor carpet	68.00	
1 do. Rug	14.00	128.00

Amount Carried forward 1198.00

Amount brought forward	$1198.00		Amount brought forward	2878.11	
20 curled maple chairs, & settee	130.00		1 Tea set, butter tub, & cup plates	24.25	
1 Drawing room carpet	110.25		1 broken set, dinner	12.00	
1 ditto	110.25		1 Dinner set, new	102.25	
1 rug	15.00		1 do.	102.25	
1 rug	15.00		1 set cut decanters	18.00	
1 Scotch carpet, nursery	33.00		2 doz. tumblers	10.00	
1 do., bedroom	63.93		2 ½ doz. wines 4 ½	11.25	
1 Ditto	54.56		1 ½ doz cordials 4	6.00	
1 matting parlour	20.00		1 pair white pitchers with ivory	7.00	
2 do. Bedrooms	36.25		1 do. Without	3.00	
	1786.24		1 do. Rafall[?] jugs	4.00	
			1 do.	1.75	301.75

1 ditto   ditto   18.12
1 stair case carpet   18.75
1 entry   do.   10.00
4 Feather beds, bolsters &
    pillows   180.00   226.87

    1 Pyramid ____   10.00
    1 large cut glass bowl 12.00
1. 1 pair glass pitchers 20.00
    1 pair do. Dish   13.00
    1 pair   Ditto   10.00

4 mattresses, each $20   80.00
1 children's do.   5.00
1 lot table linen   31.50
1 lot bed linen   66.50
14 quilts   35.00
11 blankets   33.00
2 sets bed curtains   16.00
1 parlour ditto   12.00
1 Set ivory knives & forks 37.50
1   Do.   37.50
1 lot knives & forks, dish
        covers   20.00
1 Lot waiters & bread basket 12.50
1 Set cream waiters   35.00
1 Pair plated candlesticks 15.50
1 do. do. old   7.00
1 Pair mantle piece lamps 5.00
1 set casters   28.00
1 Cordial stand & 4 bottles 25.00
1   Do. 3   "   "   18.00
1 mantle lamp   57.50
1   do.   57.50   281.00

    1   Do.   10.00
    1 odd do.   6.00
2. 2 pair do   12.00
    2 pair glass bowls on stand 12.00

1 lot tumblers, wines, decanters, & c.
20.00   125.00

2 doz. champaign glasses 10.00
2 doz. Claret   7.00
1 set old sherry   15.00
1 set tea china, old   24.35
1 pair gravy spoons   8.00
1 large silver ladle   13.00
1 smaller do.   5.00
4 do. do. 2 1/4   9.00
2 dozen silver spoons   80.00
2 do. dessert   56.00
2 do. tea   28.00   255.25

1 Pair astral lamps   55.00
1 do.   32.00
1 entry lamp   8.00
1 pair mantel ornaments 33.00
1 ditto   45.00
1 tea set
   2 doz. Coffee, 2 doz. Tea
   2 doz plates, 2 cake plates 57.00   230.00

   Amount carried forward $2878.11

7 old silver spoons, 1 silver teapot,
1 silver sugar dish & tongs, 1 milk pot,
1 cream bowl & stand, coffee urn 57.00
4 plated decanter stands 2.00
1 lot kitchen furniture 31.00
1 saddle & bridle   28.00
1 set parlour ornaments 12.00
1 do. Ornam.   7.00
1 do.   Do.   10.00
1 do.   do.   8.00
1 toilet glass   4.00
1 set andirons   3.00
1 Sender [or Lender]   5.25   167.25

Amount carried forward $3727.36

Amount brought forward $3727.36
1 cow & calf   25.00
1 wheelbarrow   5.00
1 four wheel carriage   500.00
            Total $4257.36

Say four thousand two hundred & fifty seven 36/100 dollars $4257.36

Done by us qualified appraisers, this 27 February 1828

Jos. Jones
William Ward   Qualified appraisers
Oliver Stevens

Inventory of bank _____, bonds, notes, & accounts, found among the papers of the late Mr. John Elliott, and which have come in possession of James S. Bulloch, administrator of estate of said John Elliott.

States bank stock _____, 50 shares at 100 $ 5000.00
Notes Altho in the name of J. Elliott, it is the property of his niece
Mrs. Catherine E. Russell.

Edward B. Baker bond, dated 25 Oct. 1822 & due 1 Jan. 1823 $710.10
Samuel Jones & Jno. W____ bonds, dated 4 Jany. 1818,
due 16 June 1827   630.44
Eli Mc _____, note, dated 20 March 1827, & due 1 July 1829   200.00
Alex McIvers, ditto 1 June 1827, & due 1 Jany. 1828   127.50

                                                             6668.04

                    Savh. 19th February 1828

                    James S. Bulloch, admin est. J. Elliott
                          Recorded 9 April 1828
                          E. Baker _____

Marriage Settlement for Jane E. Elliott. James S. Bulloch and John Dunwody, trustees (Liberty County Deed Book I, page 299)

Recorded 22 May 1828

State of Georgia
Chatham County

This Indenture of three parts, made the thirtieth day of April in the year of our Lord one thousand eight hundred and twenty eight, Between John S. Law of the City of Savannah in the County of Chatham and State of Georgia aforesaid practitioner of medicine of the one part, Jane E. Elliott, of the City and State aforesaid spinster of the second part, and James S. Bulloch, of the City and State aforesaid, and John Dunwody of the County of Liberty and State aforesaid, Esquires of the third parts. Whereas John Elliott late of Liberty County in the State of Georgia aforesaid being seized and possessed of considerable real and personal estates, did depart this life, intestate, and the said Jane E. Elliott, is entitled to receive, have and possess an undivided seventh of all the estate, real and personal, of the said John Elliott, deceased, in her own right, as one of the children and heirs of the said John Elliott deceased: And whereas a marriage is intended to be shortly had and solemnized between the said John S. Law and Jane E. Elliott; and upon the contract of said intended marriage, it was agreed to make a settlement of the estates, real and personal, as well that in possession or in expectancys, for the uses herein after particularly expressed: Now this indenture witnesseth, that in consideration of the said intended marriage, and in pursuance and performance of the before mentioned agreement, and in consideration of the sum of five dollars to the said Jane E. Elliott in hand, paid, the receipt where of is hereby acknowledged, and for divers other good causes and valuable considerations the said Jane E. Elliott hereunto moving, She the said Jane E. Elliott with the consent and approbation of the said John S. Law, testified by his being a party to and sealing and delivering these presents, Hath granted bargained, sold, aliened released, conveyed, and confirmed, and by these presents doth grant, bargain, sell, alien, release convey, and confirm, unto the said James S. Bulloch and John Dunwody, their executors and administrators, All that undivided one seventh part of all the estate, both real and personal, of which her late father John Elliott died seized and possessed, and which one seventh she then said Jane E. Elliott, as one of his heirs, has inherited, pursuant to the laws of the State of Georgia; an inventory of the personal part of said estate being on file in the office of the Clerk of the Court of Ordinary of the County of Liberty. To have and to hold, receive and take, this said undivided seventh part of all the estate both real and personal, of the said John Elliott deceased, unto the said James S. Bulloch and John Dunwody, and the survivor of them, and the executors and administrators of the survivor of them, in trust to and for the joint use, benefit, and advantage of the said John S. Law and Jane E. Elliott, during their joint lives, and on the death of either of them, then for the use and benefit of the survivor during his or her natural life; and on the death of the survivor, to the issue of the marriage, if any, in case of no issue of the marriage, then to the sole use, benefit, and behoof of this survivor, his or her heirs and assigns forever. Provided, and it is hereby declared and agreed by and between all the said parties to these presents, that it shall and may be lawful to and for the said James S. Bulloch and John Dunwody and the survivors of them, and the executors and administrators of such survivor, at any time, or times hereafter at the desire of the said John S. Law, and with the approbation of the said Jane E. Elliott, expressed in writing to make sale of, or to convey in exchange for or in lieu of other property, either real or personal, of equal or better value, all or any part of the said undivided seventh part herein before mentioned, and the fee simple and inheritance thereof, to any person or person whomsoever, either together or in parcels, for such price or prices in money, or for such other equivalent in slaves, bonds, tenements, or other property, real or personal, as shall seem reasonable; and upon payment of the money arising from the sale of any part or parts of the said undivided share before mentioned, where any part or part thereof shall be sold and disposed of by them or him for a valuable consideration in money, to sign and give proper receipts for the money for which the same shall be sold, which receipts shall be a sufficient discharge to any purchaser or purchases for so much of the purchase money as shall be therein acknowledged or expressed to be received. And that when any part of the said undivided seventh, herein made saleable and exchangeable as aforesaid, shall be sold or exchanged in pursuance of these presents, that then and from henceforth all and every part of the said premises so sold or exchanged shall be and remain forever freed and discharged of and from all and every the uses, trusts, limitations, and agreements in and by these presents limited, expressed and declared. And that all and every this sum and sums of money which shall arise from such sale and sales shall, with all convenient speed, be paid out and invested by the said James S. Bulloch and John Dunwody, or the survivor of them or the executors or administrators of such survivor, by and with the consent and approbation of the said John S. Law and Jane E. Elliott, in the purchase of other property, real or personal, and as well the said property, so to be purchased, as all which may be acquired in exchange shall be respectively settled and conveyed by the said James S. Bulloch and John Dunwody, or the survivor of them, or the executors or administrators of such survivor, to such and the same uses and upon such and the same trusts, and for such and the same intents and purposes, and by, with and under the same powers, provisions, and agreements, as are herein before, expressed and declared of and concerning the said undivided seventh herein before mentioned to be hereby granted and released as aforesaid, or as near thereto as the death of the parties, or other contingencies, will them admit of. In witness whereof the parties to these presents have hereunto interchangeably set their hands and seals the day and year first above written.

Sealed and delivered in the presences of us   Jane E. Elliott
                                                Jno. S. Law

                                                H. A. Dunwody   James S. Bulloch
                                                R. S. Baker   John Dunwody

State of Georgia
Liberty County   Richard S. Baker Jun. Being duly sworn, disposeth, and saith, that   he is a subscribing witness to the within instrument of writing, which he saw duly executed by the within named Jane E. Elliott, John S. Law, James S. Bulloch   and John Dunwody, in the presence of H. A. Dunwody, the other subscribing witness.

Sworn to before me, this Richard S. Baker Jun.
19 May 1828
                E. Baker C.S.C. L.C.
Recorded 26 May 1828

E. Baker . . .

Assignment by James S. Bulloch of his portion of the estate of John Elliott to Joseph Cumming (Deed Book K, page 11, Liberty County)

State of Georgia: To all to whom these presents shall come, James S. Bulloch, of the City of Savannah, merchant sends greeting.

Whereas John Elliott, late of the County of Liberty in the State aforesaid, departed this life intestate, leaving a considerable estate, real and personal, within the said State of Georgia: and whereas the said James S. Bulloch, by virtue of his intermarriage with Hetty A. daughter of the said John Elliott, is now entitled to one seventh part of the estate, real and personal of the said John Elliott; and whereas the said James S. Bulloch hath, in due form of law, been made and qualified as administrator of all and singular the goods and chattels, lands, and tenements, rights and credits, which were of the said John Elliott deceased, and is as such administrator, in possession of said estate; Now know ye, that the said James S. Bulloch for and in consideration of the sum of ten thousand dollars to him in hand paid by the said Joseph Cumming, the receipt whereof is hereby in full acknowledged, Hath bargained, sold and assigned and by these presents, Doth freely, clearly, and absolutely bargain, sell and assign, unto the said Joseph Cumming his heirs, executors, administrators and assigns, All such part, share and proportion of the estate, real and personal, of the said John Elliott deceased, as is now, or shall at any time or times hereafter, become due to him the said James S. Bulloch, and all the right, title, interest, equity, benefit, claim and demand of him the said James S. Bulloch of, in or in the same. To have, hold, receive, take and enjoy the said premises, and every part thereof, unto the said Joseph Cumming, his heirs, executors, administrators, and assigns, to his end and their proper use and behoof forever. And the better to enable the said, Joseph Cumming, his executors, administrators and assigns to have and receive the same, he the said James S. Bulloch doth hereby make, constitute, and appoint the said Joseph Cumming, his executors, administrators, and assigns his true and lawful attorney and attorneys irrevocable in the name of him the said James S. Bulloch, as administrator aforesaid, or in his and their own name or names and to his and their own proper use, to receive, retain, keep and enjoy the share or portion of the said James S. Bulloch in the said estate, real and personal, and to grant a full receipt and discharge for the same, as fully and amply, to all intents and purposes, as he the said James S. Bulloch might or could do if these presents had never been made. And the said James S. Bulloch for himself, his heirs, executors, administrators, and assigns, doth covenant and agree to and with the said Joseph Cumming, his heirs, executors, administrators, and assigns, by these present, that he the said James S. Bulloch, his executors, and administrators, shall and will from time to time and all times hereafter upon the reasonable request, and at the costs and changes in the law, of the said Joseph Cumming, his executors, administrators, and assigns, make, do and execute, or cause and procure to be made, . . . and executed, all such further and other lawful and reasonable . . . and things, conveyances and assurances in the law whatever, for the further and better assigning and assuring the said promises to the said Joseph Cumming, his executors, administrators or assigns as by his or their . . . learned in the law shall be reasonably advised, devised, or required. In witness, whereof the said James S. Bulloch had hereunto set his hand and seal this thirtieth day of April in the year of our Lord one thousand eight hundred and twenty eight.

Signed, sealed, and delivered   James S. Bulloch
in presence of
P.D. Woolhopter
A. Porter JPC.C.C.
Savannah, 13 June 1830. The object of the above assignment being accomplished, I, Joseph Cumming, for & in consideration of the sum of one dollar to me in hand paid, the receipt whereof is hereby acknowledged, have bargained, sold, released, and confirmed, and by these presents so bargain, sell, release, and confirm, unto the said James S. Bulloch, his heirs, and assigns, all the interest, right, property, and demand of the said James S. Bulloch in the estate of the said John Elliott

deceased, which by the above deed is conveyed to me.   In Witness, whereof I have hereunto set my hand and seal this day and year aforesaid.

Witness W.W. Gordon Not. Pub.   Jos. Cumming
Isa Davenport

                                              Recorded 18 August 1830
                                              E. Baker Clk

Will and Appraisement of Daniel Stewart's Estate (Liberty County, Georgia, Court of Ordinary, Wills and Appraisements. As transcribed in Historical & Genealogical Collections of the Martha Stewart Bulloch Chapter: Volume 592 2001.)

You, Thomas Bacon Senr., R. S. Baker & E.W. Russell, do swear, that you will make a true appraisement and inventory of all and singular the goods, chattels and credits of General Daniel Stewart, late of Liberty County deceased, as shall be produced and therein to you by Col. Josiah Wilson, executor of the will of said deceased; and that you will return to same, certified under your hands, to the said executor within the time prescribed by law.

Sworn before me this 15th July 1829 Thos. Bacon Sen.
                Wm. J. Way, J.P.   R.S. Baker
                                     E.W. Russell

Negroes		Amt. brot. Forward	$4205
Hannah	375	Sylvia	150
Hampshire	275	Diana	375
Luke	175	Daphne	125
Abram	125	Elsey	375
Will	250	Robin	300
Kate	125	Katy	150
Adam	700	David	75
Harry	280	Phillis	350
Bristol	400	Moses	150
Prince	450	James	150
Sandy	350	Joseph	50
Flora	300	Old Leah	200
Clarinda	175	Old Bob	200
Leah	275		
Carried forward	$4205	Amount carried forward	$6685

Amount brought forward	$6685	Amount brought forward	$7297
wives furniture		Mahogany _____	50
1 small ____ table	8	1 Large dining table	20
1 sofa	25	Tea Table	6
1 dining table	10	1 dozen chairs	6
1 small slab	35	Secretary, book-case & Books	42
1 breakfast table	25	Sofa	15
1 dozen chairs	12	Andirons & _____	15
1 round dining table	13	Andirons in room	4
6 wood chairs	4	Large Bible	15
1 set china & tray	20	1 set table china?] for dinner	
glassware, pitchers & glass	15	25	
3 dozen silver spoons	80	Dish covers	6
Waiters & Trays	12	1 Double Barrel Gun	30
Rug & carpet	20	1 Four wheel Carriage & Harness	300
Lamps & candlesticks	6	1 Sorrel Mare	25
Stand	5	1 Grindstone	2
2 Mattresses & Beds	40	Kitchen furniture	12
5 Quilts & Coverlets	30	Crockery ware	15
18 Sheets	32	11 Demijohns	7
Bedtest & trimmings	20	8 Stone Jars	3
Chest & Drawers	6	Waggon & gear	30
Room furniture, wash stand & pitchers	8	1 Old Gig & Harness	50
1 Wire safe	4	1 Saddle	7
1 Bed, mattress, pillows	60	1 Bay Horse	60
12 Blankets	24	1 Gray Horse	5
2 Carpets & Rugs	25	1 Pair Mules	140
1 Stained Bedstead	8	80 head Cattle @ $5	400
1 Small Crib & Mattress	2	42 Do. Sheep @ $2	92
1 Bureau	14	1 Large Grindstone	5
Toilet & glass	4	1 Pair Andirons	2
Pine bedstead	2	1 Slab	30
Wash Stand	1		
Bed, Mattress & bedstead	40		$9153
Andirons	2		
Amount carried forward	$7297		

We certify, that the above is a true inventory and appraisement of the goods and chattels of the estate of Genl. D. Stewart, as showed us by the executor Col. Jos. Wilson.

                Thos. Baker Senr.
                R.S. Baker
                E.W. Russell

July 25th 1829 Recorded 28 August 1829   E. Baker Clk.

Summary of Sarah Stewart's Will, 1829, as found at:
Citation: "Georgia Probate Records, 1742-1990," images, FamilySearch (https://familysearch.org/ark:/61903/3:1:3QS7-L93L-P97?cc=1999178&wc=9SYT-PT5%3A267679901%2C268032901 : 20 May 2014), Liberty > Wills, appraisements and bonds 1790-1850 vol B > image 476 of 689; county probate courthouses, Georgia.

[Will Summary]

Court of Ordinary, 4 January 1830
The last will and testament of Sarah Stewart, deceased, proved on the 19th of October 1829 by the affidavit of Raymond Harris was exhibited to the Court for examination. The Clerk requested the particular attention of the Court to the three first items in said instrument, expressing his doubts whether they did not tend in some degree to the manumission of the slaves therein named. Ordered that the two first items in said instrument be disallowed, and the third, together with the remainer [sp] of said instrument be admitted to record.

Extract from the minutes
E. Baker clk.

October 5th, 1829. Memorandum of the last will and testament of Mrs. Sarah Stewart, who being in sound mind, but unable to converse much, did declare the following.

3. Harry, carpenter, under control of same person [Charlton Hines], and to pay ten dollars per month, for the benefit of the Sunday School of Walthourville.

4. Sylvia and her three children I wish to be given to Mrs. Martha Elliott, her and her three children by Mr. John Elliott, with my particular request that she be ever treated with particular care and kindness.

5. I give Marriah to my niece Harriet H. Lewis, her and her heirs forever.

6. I give Bella to my niece Mary Eliza Lewis, to her and her heirs forever.

7. I give the girl Eliza to Ann Drusilla Lewis, her and her heirs forever.

8. I give the girl Lucy to Caroline Lewis, to her and her heirs forever.

9. I give two hundred dollars, to be used in the purchase of a watch and chain, for my brother C. Hines.

10. I give Jenny and Stephen in trust to my brother Charlton, for the use and benefit of my brother David Hines during his natural life, and at his death to be sold and divided among his children.

11. I give to my niece Eliza my chest of drawers & glass & other appurtenances, now at Tranquil, together with my hexagon quilt.

12. All the other quilts to be equally divided amongst the children of the late Samuel Lewis. I give each of the children of Saml. Lewis a bed and mattress.

13. All my plate I wish equally divided between my nieces Harriet and Eliza Lewis.

14. I give to my brother William, Lancaster, Amey, and her children Lancaster and Prince, Old Affy and Hannah, to him and his heirs forever.

15. To my brother Charlton Hines, I give Jack and his brother London, to him his heirs and assigns forever.

16. I give to Wm. J. Way young Pluto, to him and his heirs forever.

17. I give to my niece Susan Russell, and her children Big Sylvia and her son Mike and her infant.

18. All the residue of my estate, I leave to be taken in charge of my brother Charlton, to be worked by him, and the avails to be appropriated to benevolent and charitable objects.

19. I give my watch to my niece Harriet Lewis.

Witnesses: R. Harris, John Dunwody

Probated by Raymond Harris on 19 October 1829.

Estate of Mrs. Sarah Stewart
Warrant of Appraisement
Recorded in Book B pages 76 [illegible] This 23 January 11830
E Baker CCO

The State of Georgia
Liberty County
By the Honorable The Court of Ordinary of Liberty
To Wm N. Way John Way Senr.   Jos. Way
These are to authorize you, or any three of you, to repair to all such parts and places, with the County and State aforesaid, as you shall be directed unto, by Charlton Hines Esq. executor of the last will & testament of Mrs. Sarah Stewart, late of said county deceased, wherever any of the Goods and Chattels, of the said Sarah Stewart are or do remain within the said parts or places; and the Goods and Chattels, which shall be there shown you by the said executor you shall view and appraise according to their just value; being first sworn to make a true and perfect inventory and appraisement of the said Goods and Chattels. And you shall cause the same inventory and appraisement to be returned to the said executor under your hands, or under the hands of any three of your, on or before the fourth day of April next ensuing the date hereof.
Given under my hand, and seal of office this fourth day of January in the year of our Lord one thousand eight hundred and thirty.

You Wm N. Way John Way Senr.   Jos. Way
do swear that you will make a true appraisement and inventory of all singular the Goods, Chattels and Credits of Mrs. Sarah Stewart, late of Liberty County deceased, as shall be produced ad shown to you by Charlton Hines Esq. executor of the last will & testament of said deceased; and that you will return the same, certified under your hands, to the said executor within the time prescribed by law. Sworn before me; this seventy day of January, 1830. Wlm. I Way. J.J.C.

A true appraisement and inventory of all and singular the goods chattels and credits of Mrs. Sarah Stewart late of Liberty County decd as shown and produced to us by Charlton Hines Esq. Exec. of the last will and testament of said decd to wit.

Plato Driver	250	Lucy	125
Sylvia	400	Mike	150
Plato	400	Harry	75
Jack	400	Betsy	275
Rose	375	Bellah	275
Leomon	400	July	400
Lavinia	175	Eliza	200
Hagar	150		$10575
Charles Byron	100		
Affey	150	32.5 head stock cattle @5	162.50
Lancaster	400	20 do Sheep @1.50	30.00
Tom	275	1 - 2 horse wagon	15.00
Amy	300	1 lot ploughs & harrow	3.00
Prince	125	1 small grindstone	2.00
Lancaster	100	1 large do	5.00
Hannah	250	2 pr hand mill stones	14.00
Winter	400	1 pr [ ]yards	2.00
Pattey	150	1 whip saw & c,	2.00
Jim	400	1 lot silver spoons & tongs	600.00
Ginney	350	1 bell & snuffer tray	2.00
Stephen	400	2 sets caster 10 + 15	25.00
Dublin	350	2 broken pr. candle sticks	6.00
Ben	275	2 Beds & mattresses 50	200.00
Big July	400	9 quilts	30.00
Old Dublin	000	1 bureau &slats & [ ]	70.00
Bob	250	10 foot [ ] @3 $	30.00
Carpenter Harry	1000	2 horses & carriage	300.00
Big Sylvia	350		958.50
Mariah	225	Amt. brot. [ ]	1057.75
John	175	Total	$11533.50

We certify the above to be correct [ ] our hands this [ ] the seventh of Jany. 1830
                             Wm [ ] Way
                             John Way Sr.
                             Joseph Way

Recorded 23 January 1830.

APPENDIX B:

List of Contents

Guardianship of Elliott Children	B-220
Marriage Settlement for Martha Elliott	B-221
Papers from the Estate of Anne Irvine Bulloch Powell	B-223
Inventory and Appraisment of the Property of Anne Powell	B-224
Papers related to the estate of Anne Powell, dated from 1833 to 1848	B-225
Vermont Chronicle (Fellows Falls, Vermont) 4 April 1834	B-228

In all documents transcribed herein ____ indicates illegible script. A question mark in parentheses denotes some doubt about the accuracy of the transcription. Do is shorthand for ditto. Additionally, page breaks in original documents are noted when at all possible. Documents are presented in order as noted in book.

Guardianship of Elliott Children (Liberty County, Georgia, Court of Ordinary, Wills and Appraisements. As transcribed in Historical & Genealogical Collections of the Martha Steward Bulloch Chapter: Volume 592 2001.)

State of Georgia
Liberty County

Know all men by these presents, that we, Martha Elliott of Chatham County, and James S. Bulloch & Jno. Bacon of Liberty County are held firmly bound unto the Judges of the Court of Ordinary for the said County of Liberty, and their successors in office, in the just & full sum of four thousand dollars for the payment of which sum to the said Judges, and jointly & severally, firmly by these presents, sealed with our seals, and dated this nineteenth day of April in the year of our Lord eighteen hundred & thirty two.

The condition of the above obligation is such, that whereas the said Martha Elliott hath been appointed by the Honorable the Court of Ordinary for the said County of Liberty, guardian to Susan A. Elliott, Georgia A. Elliott, and Daniel Elliott, orphans of the Honorable Jno. Elliott, deceased; Now if this said Martha Elliott do well & truly demean herself as Guardian aforesaid to the said orphans, agreeably to letters of guardianship, to be issued by the Clerk of the Court of Ordinary for this County of Liberty aforesaid & agreeably to law, the above obligation to be void, otherwise to remain in full force & virtue.

Witness	
John Dunwody	Martha Elliott
Witness to Signature of M. Elliott	James S. Bulloch
Jas. Cleland J.P.	Jno. Bacon

I Martha Elliott do solemnly swear that I will do & perform the duties required of me as guardian to Susan A. Elliott, Georgia A. Elliott & Danl. Elliott, orphans of John Elliott deceased, to the best of my knowledge & understanding. So help me God.

                                                                   Martha Elliott

Sworn to & subscribed before
This 19th day of April 1832
Jas. Cleland   J.P.
Recorded 26 April 1832   E. Baker Clk

Marriage Settlement for Martha Elliott (Chatham County, Deed Book K, page 52,)

State of Georgia
Chatham County

This Indenture tripartite, made this eighth day of May in the year of our Lord one thousand eight hundred and thirty two, Between James S. Bulloch, of the County of Liberty in the state aforesaid, Planter of the one part, Martha Elliott, of the County of Chatham and State aforesaid, Widow, of the second part and Daniel M. Stewart, of the County of Glynn and State aforesaid, & John Dunwody, of the County of Liberty and State aforesaid of the third part: Whereas a marriage is intended to be shortly had and solemnized between the said James S. Bulloch and said Martha Elliott: and whereas the said Martha Elliott, as one of the heirs of her late father, General Daniel Stewart, is entitled in her own right to receive, have and possess an undivided part or portion of all the real estate of her late father; and whereas the said Martha Elliott, as the widow of her late husband, the Honorable John Elliott, is also entitled to receive, have and possess one undivided part or portion of all the real estate of her late husband ; and where as the said Martha Elliott is also possessed in her own right of the following Negro slaves, thirty nine in number, herein after particularly mentioned and described: And whereas, upon the contract of said intended marriage, it was agreed to make a settlement of the estate, both real and personal, as well as that in possession as in expectancy, which the said Martha Elliott is entitled to receive and enjoy, to and for the uses and trusts herein after particularly expressed: Now this Indenture witnesseth, that in consideration of the said intended marriage, and in pursuance and in performance of the before mentioned agreement, and in consideration of the sum of five dollars by the said Daniel M. Stewart and John Dunwody parties of the third part, to the said Martha Elliott in hand paid, the receipt whereof is hereby acknowledged, and for divers other good causes and valuable considerations, the said Martha Elliott hereunto moving, she the said Martha Elliott, with the consent and approbation of the said James S. Bulloch, testified by his being a party to, and sealing and delivering these presents, Hath granted, bargained, sold, aliened, released, conveyed and confirmed, by these presents Doth grant, bargain, well, alien, release, convey and confirm, unto the said Daniel M. Stewart and John Dunwody, and the survivor of them and the executors and administrators of such survivor, All the undivided interest, portion or part of or in the real estate of her late father, General Daniel Stewart, late of Liberty County in the State of Georgia, deceased, to which she the said Martha Elliott is now, or may at any time hereafter, become entitled, as one of the heirs of her said father, pursuant to the laws of the State of Georgia: also all the undivided portion, interest or part of in the real estate of the late John Elliott of Liberty County in said State, deceased, to which the said Martha Elliott, as widow of the said John Elliott, is now, or may hereafter, become entitled, under and by virtue of the laws of said State: also all the following named negro slaves, thirty nine in number; namely Bob (carpenter), Rose, Leah, Monroe, Sylvia, Bristol (carpenter), Lavinia, Byron, Hagar, Sarah Ann, Old Sylvia, Adam (carpenter), Luke, Cupid, Jacob, June, March, William, Daphne, Nanny, Caesar, Malia, Polly, Nancy, George, Sandy, Sally, Paul, Maurice, Billy, Lucy, Hagar, Paul Jr., James (shoemaker), Phillip, Moses, James, Joe, and Moll together with the future issue and increase of the said female slaves. To have and to hold, receive and take the said undivided interest, portion or part of or in the said real estate of the late General Daniel Stewart, deceased, to which she the said Martha Elliott is now, or may at any time hereafter, become entitled, as one of the heirs of her late father, the said General Daniel Stewart, deceased: And also all the said undivided portion, interest, or part of or in the real estate of the late John Elliott, deceased, to which the said Martha Elliott, as widow of the said John Elliott, is now or may hereafter, become entitled. And also to have and to hold all the said Negro slaves, thirty nine in number namely Bob (carpenter), Rose, Leah, Monroe, Sylvia, Bristol (carpenter), Lavinia, Byron, Hagar, Sarah Ann, Old Sylvia, Adam (carpenter), Luke, Cupid, Jacob, June, March, William, Daphne, Nanny, Caesar, Malia, Polly, Nancy, George, Sandy, Sally, Paul, Maurice, Billy, Lucy, Hagar, Paul Jr., James (shoemaker), Phillip, Moses,

James, Joe, and Moll together with the future issue and increase of the said female slaves, unto the said Daniel M. Stewart and John Dunwody, and the survivor of them, and the executors and administrators of such survivors . In trust, and to and for the joint use, benefit, and advantage of the said James S. Bulloch and Martha Elliott, during their joint lives, but to be in no event subject to any debts which the said James S. Bulloch may have heretofore contracted, or may hereafter contract, but the said property, real or personal to be held freed or discharged from all liability to the debts of the said James S. Bulloch. Provided, and it is hereby declared and agreed by between the said parties to these presents, that it shall and may be lawful for the said Martha Elliott, by her will, duly executed in writing, to dispose of the said property, or any part thereof; and in and by her said will to alter, change, or revoke any of the trusts declared in this Indenture, in said manner as she may think proper; thereby exercising complete control by her will over said property as fully as she might or could do, if the same were her property, solely and absolutely, and not made subject to the trusts expressed in this Indenture. And in the event of the death of said Martha Elliott, without making any disposition of said property by will as aforesaid, or otherwise, as hereinafter authorized & empowered, then the said property, or any part thereof, not disposed of by the said Martha Elliott by her will, or otherwise, to be held in trust for the use & benefit of the said James S. Bulloch during his natural life, but to be in no event subject to any debts he may have heretofore contracted, or may hereafter contract: And on the death of the said James S. Bulloch, then in trust for the use, benefit and advantage of the heirs of the said Martha Elliott, their heirs and assigns for ever. And provided also, and it is hereby declared and agreed by and between the said parties to these presents, that it shall and may be lawful for the said Daniel M. Stewart and John Dunwody, or either of them, or the survivor of them or the executors and administrators of such survivor, at any time or times hereafter, at the desire of the said Martha Elliott, expressed in writing, to make sale of or to convey in exchange for or in lieu of other property, real or personal, of whatsoever nature or description the said Martha Elliott may desire, whether stock, bonds, or any other description of property, the said undivided parts of portions of the real estates herein before mentioned, or any part thereof; and also all or any part of said negro slaves, to which the said Martha Elliott is now, or may hereafter, become entitled; and to invest the proceeds of such property as may be sold as aforesaid in such other property as the said Martha Elliott may desire, to be held under & by the same uses & trusts as the property sold or exchanged by virtue of these presents: and the conveyance of any part of said property, real or personal, by the said Daniel M. Stewart and John Dunwody, trustees, or either of them, at the desire & with the consent, of the said Martha Elliott, testified by her being a party to and signing and sealing said conveyance, shall forever free and absolutely discharge, said property, to conveyed of and from all and every the uses, trust, limitations and agreements, in and by these presents limited, expressed and declared: and the receipt of the said Martha Elliott, signed also by the said Daniel M. Stewart and John Dunwody, or either of them, for any money or moneys to be received for a part of said property, or sold or conveyed in manner aforesaid, shall forever discharge the purchaser or purchasers of said property from the payment of so much of the said purchase money.
In witness whereof the said parties to these presents have hereunto, interchangeably set their hand, & affixed their seals, the day and year first above written.

Signed, sealed and delivered
in the presence of
Geo. Gchley   Not. Pub.
W.H. Bulloch Not. Pub.

James S. Bulloch
Martha Elliott
Daniel M. Stewart
John Dunwody

Recorded 12 June 1832
E. Baker Clk.

Papers from the Estate of Anne Irvine Bulloch Powell - Found Liberty County and Ancestry.com

State of Georgia
Liberty County
By the Honorable the Court of Ordinary, of Liberty County.
To Nathaniel Varnidal (?), William Jones ad William Wilson
These are to authorise you, or any three of you, to repair to all such parts and places, within the County and State aforesaid, as you shall be directed unto, by John Dunwoody, Esq. executor of the last will and testament of Mrs. Anne Powell, late of Liberty County deceased, wherever any of the Goods and Chattels, of the said Anne Powell are or do remain within the said parts or places; and the Goods and Chattels, which shall be there shewn to you by the said executor you shall view and appraise according to their just value/ being first sworn to make a true and perfect inventor and appraisement of the said Goods and Chattels. And you shall cause the same inventory and appraisement to be returned to the said Executor under your hands, or under the hands of any three of you, on or before the second day of August next ensuing the date hereof.
Given under my hand, and seal of office, this second day of May in the year of our Lord one thousand eight hundred and thirty one.

You Nathaniel Varnidal [sp], William Jones, and William Wilson do swear that you will make a true appraisement and inventory of all and singular the Goods, Chattels and Credits of Mrs. Anne Powell, late of Liberty County deceased, as shall be produced and shewn to you by John Dunwody Exor. Of the deceased; and that you will return the same, certified under your hands, to the said executor within the time prescribed by Law.

Sworn before me this 25th day of May 1831.

[Note: On the following page the slaves are grouped by family units with a value for the entire family listed between the names and personal values. On the orginial this was achieved with underlines between the family units]

Inventory and Appraisment of the Property, ___ and personal belonging to the Estate Anne Powell as Exhibited to us by John Dunwody Exor. said Estate

Cedar Hill Plantation & appurtenances	4,500	Amt. brot. forward	$12026
1. Old Jack	50	31. Elsey	50
		2. Steven	500
2. Billy	350	3. John	500
3. Jenny	150	4. Israel	450
4. Ned $1500	600	5. Hagar $2525	400
5. Lucy	400	6. Tenan (Jonah*)	250
		7. Elsey	75
6. Phoebe	300	8. Mary	300
7. Harry $675	175		
8. Billy	125	9. Old Hester	1
9. Diana	75		
		40. Rose	175
10. Betty	400	1. Edmund	300
1. Peter $600	125		
2. Frank	75	2. Tom	500
		3. Charlotte	200
3. Patty	400	4. Hannah $1050	150
4. Sandy	300	5. Nancy	125
5. Bob $1060	250	6. William	75
6. Sue	110		
7. Affey	400	7. Hester	150
		8. Binah	400
8. Ben	500	9. James $850	200
		50. MaryAnn	150
9. Peter	325	1. Noble	100
20. Rosana $825	250		
1. L. Steven	250	2. Doll	250
		3. Sylvia	110
2. Illegible (William*)	300	4. Jack	50
3. Peggy	350	5. Caroline $1535	350
4. Hester	300	6. Clarifso [?]	275
5. Jenny	275	7. Alfred	500
6. Delia $1615	250		
7. Will	200	8. William	100
8. Doll	150	one pair rone[sp] horses	100
9. Tom	90	65 head stock cattle 4$	<u>260</u>
30 Old Sue	1	Say nineteen thousand and ___ seventy two dollars	$19072
Carried forward	$12026		

* identified in Security Deed for Cedar Hill

APPENDIX B - 224

Papers related to the estate of Anne Powell, dated from 1833 to 1848 (Filed with the estate papers of James S. Bulloch. Transcribed from copy found at Bulloch Hall, Roswell, Georgia)

Georgia
Liberty County

Know all men by these presents that I, James S. Bulloch of said State and County, Planter, am held and firmly bound with John Dunwody, trustee in the last will of Anne Powell deceased, for William Gaston Bulloch and Jane Bulloch, children of John Bulloch deceased and Charlotte Bulloch, in the full and just sum of nine thousand three hundred and sixty six dollars and fifty two cents.

The conditions of the above obligation is such that of the above named James S. Bulloch his heirs and assigns, shall pay on moiety or half of the the sum of four thousand six hundred and eighty three dollars and twenty six cents to the above named William G. Bulloch, and Jane Bulloch, each as they serially become of age, and annually the interest on the above sum of four thousand, six hundred and eighty three dollars and fifty two cents at six percent per annum for the maintenance and education of the above named William G. Bulloch and Jane Bulloch, when and in that case the above bond or obligation to be null and void otherwise to remain in full force.

In testimony where of I have hereunto put my hand and seal on this the ninth day of May eighteen hundred and thirty three.

Signed sealed and delivered in presence of
Geo. ____
                                          James S. Bulloch

Second page:
Liberty County, 9th May 1833 Rec. From James S. Bulloch, the interest to say two hundred eighty 99/1000 dollars being the first annual payment of interest due 25th January 1833.
                                    John Dunwody Trustee

Liberty County 12 March 1834 Rec. from James S. Bulloch the interest day two hundred & eighty 99/100 dollars being the second annual installment of interest due 25 January 1834.John Dunwody, Trustee

Liberty County 19 May 1835 Rec. from James S. Bulloch the interest say two hundred eighty 99/100 being the 3rd annual interest due 25 January 1835.
                                    John Dunwody, Trustee

Liberty County 5 February 1836 Rec. from James S. Bulloch the interest say two hundred & eighty 99/1000 dollars being the 4th annual amount interest due 25 January 1836.John Dunwody, Trustee

Liberty County 25 January 1837 Rec. from James S. Bulloch the interest say two hundred & eighty 99/1000 dollars being the 5th annual amount interest due 25 January 1836.John Dunwody, Trustee

Liberty County 25 January 1838 Rec. from James S. Bulloch the interest say two hundred & eighty 99/1000 dollars being the 6th annual amount interest due 25 January 1837.John Dunwody, Trustee

Rec. L. C.9 May 1838 from Jno. Dunwody, Trustee of Wm. G. Bulloch & Jane Bulloch the sum of two hundred & eighty dollars being for the schooling & maintenance of said. Wm. G & Jane Bulloch. J.S. Bulloch

Ditto Ditto 12 March 1834 from Jno Dunwody the same amount for said purposes.
J. S. Bulloch

Ditto Ditto 19th May 1835 from John Dunwody the sum of two hundred & eighty 99/100 dollars for the same purposes.   J. S. Bulloch

Ditto Ditto 5 February 1836 from John Dunwody the sum of two hundred eighty 99/100 dollars for the said purposes.   J. S. Bulloch

Ditto Ditto 25 January 1837 from John Dunwody the sum of two hundred eighty 99/100 dollars for the said purposes.   J. S. Bulloch

Ditto Ditto 25 January 1838 from John Dunwody the sum of two hundred eighty 99/100 dollars for the said purposes.   J. S. Bulloch

James S. Bulloch
Bond to Jno. Dunwody,
Trustee
Wm. G Bulloch
&
Jane Bulloch
Voucher
No 14
$1509.36_____ Wm. G. Bulloch _____James S. Bulloch

1837   To Balance due me as per ____ current
25 Jany this day & to be written off my bond $1455.14
                                 Ins. 1 yr. ____ mos. $155.20

25 Jan   To cash _____Oakes for gold watch
                                        ____old one sold on ____ 95.50

1838
16 March To cash remitted Prof. _____ being
                                 3rd _____ fee _____ 105.50

                     Balance due _____ Bulloch   11.28 $2022.62

1838
25 Jany   By cash recd. From Jno. Dunwody
            Trustee int. on Bond due Wm. &
            Jane Bulloch 4683.26   280.99

       ___ ½ of said bond Wm. Bulloch
      _____   2341.63 $2622.62

Savannah 7th day of May 1838 Received from James S. Bulloch Eight hundred & eleven 28/100 dollars in full to be written off his bond to John Dunwody, Trustee of Wm G. Bulloch. $811.28

Account Current
Wm. G. Bulloch with
J. S. Bulloch
1838_____ Jane D. Bulloch in ___ with James S. Bulloch

1839
January 20th To amt: paid Mr. Potter tuition bill ___ Smith $146.00
February 5th check on _____ Bank Phila emporium 144.00
  "   8th check sent Jane on Phila postage 7.29
March 30th sent Jane _ Mrs. Potter 10.00
May 23rd   sent Mrs. Glen _____& postage 27.25
June 8th   by misc. rec. traveling _____ 10.00
July 1st   _ Smith tuition, board due to date Germantown 288.19

1840
January 16th   sent Mrs. Evans postage 25.50
May 13   check on _____ for Mr Boldon emporium 267.50
June 3   check Phila Misses Smith & 275.34
 "   sent by Doct. Bulloch for clothing 27.00
October 20   sent Mr. Bolson 300.00

[Note: This accounting continues until James Bulloch's death in Feb. 1849; however, the copy is mostly illegible.]

Vermont Chronicle (Fellows Falls, Vermont) 4 April 1834.

Instruction of Slaves.
From the annual Report of the Association in Liberty Co. Georgia, published in Charleston Observer.

Officers for 1833. Rev. R. Quarterman, President: Rev. S.S. Law, Vice President: James S. Bulloch, Secretary and Treasurer.
Executive Committee. T. Bacon, T. Mallard, J.O. Baker, J. Dunwody, O. Stevens, B. King.
Missionary Rev. C.C. Jones

Field of Labor. The county contains a population of 1544 whites and 5729 blacks, which gives a proportion of 3.23 black to one white, according to the census of 1830.
The County is divided into the 15th, 16th, and 17th Company Districts. There are only 28 slaves in the 16th District—in the 17th, 276—and in the 15th, 4577. The total of taxable slaves in the County is 4880.
Your agent has directed his efforts exclusively to the 15th District. Near fifty plantations have been returned by members of the Association, as open for religious instruction: which shows how extensive is the field, and it may be further enlarged.

Classes of Instruction. A class of instruction for professors of religion of all denominations, was formed, the last winter, at Newport, embracing male and female , over 400 members. The afternoon of the Sabbath was appropriated to this class. The men and women occupied different seats. I gave them familiar lectures on the doctrines and duties of Christianity. Such classes, well conducted, will be productive of great good; and I hope to form at some future time, a regular course of instruction for them. The station at Newport I resigned to Rev. S. S. Law, in the spring. His meetings have been very nearly every fortnight, well attended and interesting.
I have established a class of instruction for children and youth at the station on Fraser's Plantation. It is deeply interesting, and varies in number from 25 to 50. I meet this class between morning and afternoon services, and my hope is to establish such a class at all the stations. Without pausing to lay before the Association my reasons, I will say, that such classes are, above all others, to be desired, and upon the rising generation of negroes, our hope of success mainly depends.
The children and youth have been, to all appearances, much interested. I instruct them from a catechism which I am attempting to prepare for them. I also instruct them from Scripture cards. The parents of these children take deep interest in their instruction and express gratitude for it.

[Note: This report continues for two more columns of the newspaper, detailing all the missions and their levels of instruction.]

APPENDIX C:

List of Contents

Tranquil Plantation (next to Riceboro) Sale to James S. Bulloch	C-230
Tranquil Plantation Sale to Martha Stewart Elliott Bulloch	C-231
Tranquil Plantation Sale to Samuel Spencer by James S. Bulloch	C-232
Mortgage on Slaves by James S. Bulloch	C-233
Security Deed on Cedar Hill	C-234
Purchase of Cedar Hill tract by James S. Bulloch	C-236
Security deed on Cedar Hill and Clifton Plantations w/Negro House Settlement	C-237
Warranty Deed on Cedar Hill to William LeConte	C-239
Division of John Elliott's Slaves, Will Record B, 1824-1850	C-241

In all documents transcribed herein ____ indicates illegible script. A question mark in parentheses denotes some doubt about the accuracy of the transcription. Do is shorthand for ditto. Additionally, page breaks in original documents are noted when at all possible. Documents are presented in order as noted in book.

Tranquil Plantation (next to Riceboro) Sale to James S. Bulloch (Liberty County Deed Book K, page 142)

State of Georgia
This Indenture made this twentyeth [sp] day of March in the year of our Lord eighteen thousand and thirty three said of the Independence of the United States of America the fifty seventh, between Daniel M. Stewart, executor of the last will and testament of Daniel Stewart, late of this county of Liberty and State aforesaid, deceased, of the one part and James S. Bulloch of the State & county, Planter, of the other part. Witnessed that whereas by virtue of an order granted by the Honorable the Court of Ordinary of said county, on the first Monday in November last to the said Daniel M. Stewart to sell a tract on plantation of land, containing eight hundred and fifty five acres more or less. Situated lying and being in said county on the waters of North, Newport river and in and in the vicinity of the village of Riceboro. Bounded North by the estate of John Lambert. East by Major Woods land South by lands of Henry R. Rufase and West by lands belonging to the estate of Sam. J. Alyson [?] and Quarterman _____and after the said was duly advertised in the public Gazette, in conformity to law, it was put up and exposed to public sale to the highest bidder at the door of the Court house of said County, within the legal hours of sale on the first Tuesday in February last by the said Daniel M. Stewart executor a aforesaid when the same was [acknowledged] knocked of to the said James S. Bulloch at the price or sum of fifteen hundred dollars, being the highest & last bidder. Now for and in Consideration of the sum of fifteen hundred dollars in ___ paid to him the said Daniel M. Stewart by the said James S. Bulloch, at and before the sealing and delivery of these presents, the receipt whereof is hereby acknowledged , he the said Daniel M. Stewart, executor as afforsaid said. Hath granted, bargained, and sold, and by these presents Doth grant, bargain, & sell unto him the said James S. Bulloch, the before named and bargained land with all the improvements and ____thereunto belonging, or in any wise appertaining unto him the said James S. Bulloch his heirs and assigns to his and there own proper use and benefit and behoof forever in fee simple; And the said Daniel M. Stewart, Executor as aforesaid, the ___ land with all improvements and ____thereunto belonging or in any wise ____ unto him the said James. S. Bulloch his heirs and assigns. Shall and will warrant and forever defend the legal and Equitable title against himself and all ____ every other person or persons, whatever, as far as in law or equity ____may be bound to do as executor as aforesaid. In ____whereof the said Daniel M. Stewart, Executor of the last will and testament of Daniel Stewart, deceased hath hereunto set his hand and seal this day and year first above written.

Signed sealed and delivered
in presence of
James S. Bonds   Not. Pub.   D M Stewart Ex.
Charles Stebbins
Roberto Mellen   Recorded 21st day of March 1834
                                                        Thos. J. Shepard Clk

Tranquil Plantation Sale to Martha Stewart Elliott Bulloch (Liberty County Deed Book K, page 146)

State of Georgia
This Indenture made this twentyeth [sp] day of March in the year of our Lord Eighteen Hundred and thirty three, and of the Independence of the United States of America the fifty seventh, Between Daniel M. Stewart, executor of the last will and testament of Daniel Stewart, late of the County of Liberty and State aforesaid, deceased, of the one part and John Dunwody and Daniel M. Stewart, trustees for Martha Bulloch, wife of James Bulloch of said State & County of the other part ____whereas by virtue of an order granted, by the Honorable the Court of Ordinary of Liberty County on the first Monday in November last to the said Daniel M. Stewart to sell a certain tract of land containing sixty nine acres and three tenths of an acre belonging to the estate of the said Daniel Stewart, which said tract of land is situated in said County in or near to the Walthourville settlement and bounded west by the Estate of Andrew Wathour and in all other sides by lands of the Estate of William Anderson; and after the said land was duly advertized, in one of the public gazettes in conformity to law. The same was put up and exposed to public sale to the highest bidder at the door of the court house in said county, within the legal hours of sale on the first Tuesday in February last by the said Daniel M. Stewart Executor of aforesaid where the same was knocked off to the said John Dunwody and Daniel M. Stewart, trustees as aforesaid, at the price or sum of five hundred and thirty dollars. They having the highest and best bids for the same ____for and ____ consideration of the said sum of five hundred & thirty dollars in hand paid to the said Daniel M. Stewart, executor as aforesaid, at and before the sealing and delivery of these presents, the receipt whereof is hereby acknowledged, he the said Daniel M. Stewart as executor as aforesaid Hath, granted, bargained, and sold and by these presents Doth grant bargain and sell unto the said John Dunwody, and Daniel M. Stewart, trustees as aforesaid, and to the survivor of them, and to the executors or administrators of such survivors, the before described tract or parcel of land, with all the improvement and ____thereunto belonging , or in any way ____ to the proper use and behoof of the said Martha Bulloch, for all the purposes and subject to all the limitations, promises and restrictions, mentioned in a certain deed of trust, or marriage settlement, executed by the said Martha Bulloch (then Martha Elliott) and James S. Bulloch her present husband the date of which is the eight day of May in the year of our Lord Eighteen Hundred and thirty two, and which said deed is recorded in the Clerks office of the Superior Court of Liberty County in Book K pages 53.54&55. And the said Daniel M. Stewart, Executor as aforesaid, the before described tract of land with all the improvements and appurtainances [sp], thereunto belonging or in any wise appertaining unto the said John Dunwody and Daniel M. Stewart, trustees as aforesaid, to the survivor and to the Executors or administrators of such survivors, for the use and purpose aforesaid, shall and will warrant and forever defend the legal and equitable title against himself and all and every other person or persons, whatsoever as far as in law or Equity he maybe bound to do as Executor of the late will and testament of the late Genl. Daniel Stewart, deceased. In Witness whereof the Daniel M. Stewart, executor as aforesaid, hath hereunto set his hand & seal this day & year first above written.

Signed Sealed and delivered in presence
of   James S. Bonds, Not. Pub.

                                            DM Stewart, EX

    Charles Stebbins
        Robert Millen   Recorded 2nd April 1834
                                   Thomas J. Shepard, Clk

Tranquil Plantation Sale to Samuel Spencer by James S. Bulloch (Liberty County Deed Book K, page 189)

Georgia Liberty County
This Indenture made this first day of December in the year of our Lord one thousand eighty hundred and thirty four: Between Samuel Spencer of said County of the one part and James S. Bulloch of the said county of the other part; Witnessed that the said Samuel Spencer hath this day made and delivered to the said James S. Bulloch his four ___ promissory notes in writing inscribed with his hand being ever ___with the presents, for eleven hundred dollars and payable to the said James S. Bulloch on order [?] _____ Two hundred dollars on the first day of Janu. (1837), one hundred dollars on the first day of Janu. (1838), four hundred dollars on the first day of Janu. (1839) & one other note for four hundred dollars and payable on the first day of Jan. (1840) all for value received. The said four notes amounting to the said sum of Eleven hundred dollars _____and all and each of said notes drawing interest from the date of these presents, now for and in consideration of the sum of five dollars by the said James S. Bulloch to the said Samuel Spencer in hand paid by the receipt whereof is duly acknowledged as well as for _____the payment of the aforesaid notes the said Samuel Spencer hath granted, bargained, and sold and ____ by these presents grant, bargain and sell ___ the said James S. Bulloch his heirs, executors, and administrators and assigns all that certain tract or part of land, known as Tranquil Plantation _____ eight hundred & forty five acres more or less situated laying and being in the said County on the waters of North Newfort River and in the vicinity of the village of Riceboro bounded north and east by the Estate of John Lambert, East by Major Jacob Woods land South by lands of Henry R. Russell and west by lands belonging to the estate of Samuel J. Afson and Estate of Quarterman Coay [?], to have and to hold, the said tract or parcel of land to him the said James S. Bulloch his heirs, executors, administrators and assigns and to his and their proper use benefit, and behoof forever in fee simple. And the said Samuel Spencer for himself his heirs executors administrators and assigns the said tract or parcel of land unto the said James S. Bulloch his heirs executors administrators and assigns will warrant and forever defend against all legal claims provided _____that if the aforesaid Samuel Spencer his heirs executors administrators and assigns shall will and truly pay unto the said James S. Bulloch, his heirs, executors administrators and assigns, the sum of money mentioned in the aforesaid notes on the day appointed for the payment thereof in the said presents ____notes mentioned with lawful interest for the same, according to the terms of the said notes, then and from henceforth as will this present indenture hold the right to the property thereby conveyed as the said promissory notes shall cease _____be void and to all intents and purposes
In Testimony whereof the said Samuel Spencer hath hereunto set his hand and seal the day and year first above written.

In presence of   Samuel Spencer
John _____
W.B. Fleming J.J. C.L.C

                                                   Recorded this 28th day of December 1834
                                                         Thos. J. Shepard CLK

Mortgage on Slaves by James S. Bulloch (Liberty County Deed Book K, page 246)

State of Georgia

To all to whom these presents shall come I James S. Bulloch of Liberty County in the State aforesaid send greetings, whereas I the said James S. Bulloch by my certain promissory note bearing date the day of the date of these presents payable five years after date for the sum of fifteen thousand nine hundred dollars with legal interests payable Annually payable to A. Low & Co. ____ to the said A. Low & Co. in the sum of money in their said ex____ Know ye that I the said James S. Bulloch for the letter securing of the said sum of fifteen thousand nine hundred dollars & interest unto the said A. Low & Co. their heirs executors administrators and assigns together with lawful interest for the same at or before the maturity thereof as aforesaid have bargain [sp] & sold & By these presents do Bargain [sp] & Sell unto the said A. Low & Co. their heirs executors administrators and assigns the following Negro slaves named Sue, Henry, Jane, No, Buk, Dick, George, Stephen, Edmond, Abraham, Jack Robbin, Fillig [?], Samuel, Frank & Hoby, Ira [?] & their issue & _____of the females. To have and to hold the said sixteen slaves named Sue, Henry, Jane, No, Buk, Dick, George, Stephen, Edmond, Abraham, Jack Robbin, Fillig [?], Samuel, Frank & Hoby for the ____of the ___unto the said A Low & Co. their heirs executors administrators and assigns forever provided ____. That if the said [remainder of line illegible][beginning of line illegible]heirs executors or administrators, shall and do well & truly pay or cause to be paid unto the said A. Law & Co. their heirs executors administrators and assigns the full and just sum of fifteen thousand nine hundred dollars at or before the expiration of five years from the date of these presents, according to the true intent & meaning of the aforesaid promissory note & of these presents together with lawful intents for the same, then this deed of Bargin [sp] and Sale and all and every clause article & thing therein contained, shall cease determine & be utterly void & of none effect, anything herein before _____to the contrary thing in any wise notwithstanding. And it is hereby declared by & between the said parties, and the said James S. Bulloch for himself his heirs executors administrators and assigns, to the covenant promise and agree to & with the said A. Low & co, their heirs executors administrators and assigns, by these presents, that if default shall happed to be made of or in payments of the said sum of fifteen thousand & nine hundred dollars, at or before the maturity of the said note as aforesaid or of the interest of the same, then & in such case it shall & may be lawful to & for the said A. Low & Co. their heirs executors administrators and assigns, attorneys or agents from time to time and & all times hereafter, to take the said sixteen negro slaves unto their custody & possession & the same to have and detain to their own use & behoof, as their own proper goods & chattels from thenceforthwith & forever, or the same to sell & discharge of at their will and ____the ____ if any shall happen to be after payment of the said sum of fifteen thousand nine hundred dollars interest & ____the said James S. Bulloch, his heirs executors administrators and assigns.

In Witness whereof the said James S. Bulloch hath hereunto set his hand & seal, this nineteenth day of May in the year of our Lord one thousand eight hundred & thirty five and in the _____ year of the Independence of the United States of America.

Signed Sealed & delivered   James S. Bulloch
in presence of
W.W. Gordon
Not. Public   Recorded 25 day of June 1835 by
                         Thos. J. Shepard Clk

Security Deed on Cedar Hill (Liberty County Deed Book K, page 248)

This Indenture made the nineteenth day of May in the year of our Lord one thousand Eight hundred and thirty five. Between James S. Bulloch of Liberty County & State of Georgia of the first part and Andrew Low & Robert Hutchison of Savannah State aforesaid merchants unto & copartining [sp] The firm of A Low & Company of the second part. Witnesseth that the said party of the first part as well for the letter securing the parties of the second part, the faithful payment of the debt which he [blank section] justly owed to the hands of the seconds part in manner hereafter mentioned as in consideration of the sum of one dollar to him in hands paid by the parties of the seconds part, the receipt which is hereby acknowledged, hath granted bargined [sp], sold, alieneds, [sp] released and confirmed & by these presents doth grant, bargin [sp], sell, allien, release, and confirm unto the parties of the second part and to their heirs and assigns forever, all that plantation, ____or parcel of lands, lying being & situated in the county of Liberty State aforesaid, near Riceboro called Cedar Hill Plantation, containing nine hundreds & fifty five acres more or less and also the following forty three negro slaves named, Joe, Sam, Grace, Crawfords, Nancy, Sam (?), Tobby, William, Ben, Sally, Cinter & her infants, Amy & her child, Grace, Fanny, Betty, Titus (?), Betty, Prince, Mariah, Peter, Joe, William, Franklin, Tom, Affey and her child, Frank, Bill, Rachell & her child, Phoebe, Mary, Hagar, Hartwell, Ned, July, Daniel, Ben, Dublin, Joe and Simon, also all the undivided one six part of the real estate of the late John Elliott, consisting of a plantation or tract of land situated lying & being in the county of Liberty aforesaid called Laurel View, and also all the interests property letter claim possessions and demands of him the said James S. Bulloch being ____the undivided one third thereof absolutely and in fee simple, and one other undivided third part thereof for the life time of him the said James S. Bulloch of in and to the following fifty two negroes of the Estate of the late Ann Powell, named Elsey, Stephen, John , Jannie, Hagar, Jonah, Eloy, Mary, Phoebe, Hester, Hason, ... , Deanna, Betty, Peter, Frank, Patty, Sandy Bob, Sue & sam, Affey, Peter, Boson, Ben, Stephen, William, Peggy, Hester, Jinsey, Delina, Will Doll, Tom, March Peggy, Donny, Fortune, little (?) March, Rose, Lucy, Jack, Rose, Edmond, Tom, Charlotte, Hanah Nancy, William, Billy, Jinny, Lucy & Ned & the future issue of the female slaves, above mentioned all of which, said land and negroes are under mortgage executed by the said James S. Bulloch to one Charles W. Rizing having date the 12th of May 1831 & recorded in Book 22 folio 316 of the clerks office of the Superior Court of Chatham County and which said mortgage is a _____at the time of the _____of these presents. Together with all and singular the [Edway] holdings, rights & _____ & appertaining to the same belonging; or in any way appertaining; and all the Estate, rights, _____interests, property claims and demands Whatsoever of the said party of the first part of issue to the [Page 249] same, and the _____and account, demands & remands thereof To have and to hold the said premises hereby Granted & released with the eighty nearby, _____ and appertaining thereunto – belonging, and every part & parcel thereof, unto the said parties of the second part, their heirs and assigns, to the only Proper use and behoof of the said parts of the second part their heirs and assigns forever. Upon condition nevertheless that if the said James S. Bulloch of the first part, his heirs, Executors, Administrators or assigns shall faithfully pay to the party of the second part their Exec utors, administrators or assigns and to the survivor of them the sum of fifteen thousand nine hundred dollars at or before the Expiration of five years from the dates of these presents with lawful intent of the State of Georgia, the said interests to be paid _____according to this tenure & true intent & meaning of his certain promissory note bearing date the same day of the date of these presents, _____duly made and executed by the said James S. Bulloch party of the first part to the party of the second part, then this present indenture & the Estate hereby granted, and every action and clause herein contained as well as the said promissory note shall cease & become utterly void. And it is hereby mutually committed and agreed between the parties to these presents that if default shall be made in the payment of the principal deemed to be paid to the said A Low & Company party of the first party, and the interest which shall accrue therefore, at any time or thing on which they shall be due or of any part

of such principal or interest that then and from hence forth it shall [or] lawful for the party of the second part then bring. Executors, administrators or assigns to grant forgive sell and dispose of the said hereby granted _____, and all benefits & Equity of Redemption of the said party of the first part then being Executors, Administrators, or assigns, therein according to the direction of the act of the Ligator in that case made & provided Rendering the _____ of the purchase money to be _____ for the same, after full satisfaction of the principal & interest to be due on such promissory note in _____ aforesaid and the charge of advertized & sale if any surplus there shall be, unto the said James S. Bulloch party of the first part, his heirs, executors, Administers, or assigns.   In witness where-
of the parties to these presents have
hereunto interchangeably set their hands and seals on the
day and year first above written
Sealed and delivered in the presence of us
Jas McHenry
W.W. Gordon   James S Bulloch
Not Pub
    Recorded 23 June 1835 by
      Thos Shepherd, CLK

Purchase of Cedar Hill tract by James S. Bulloch (Liberty County Deed Book K, page 386-387)

Georgia
Know all men that I Thomas W. Quarterman of the State and County afforsaid planter for & in consideration of the sum of two hundred dollars to me in hand paid by James S. Bulloch the reciept whereof is hereby acknowledged do give, grant, sell and convey unto the said James S. Bulloch his heirs and assigns forever all that tract of land situated lying and being in the afforsaid county and state, containing six or seven more or less acres being a part of a tract of lands consigned to me the said Thomas W. Quarterman by Jacob Woods Esquire of McIntosh County, and hath such _____ buttings and boundings as an ___ in the above plat. Now be it known that I Thomas W. Quarterman do hereby for myself my heirs and assigned quit all _____, _____ or dismissed whatsoever in law or equity of in or to the above _____. In behalf of the said James S. Bulloch to him his heirs, and assigns to there only proper use & behoof and I the said Thomas W. Quarterman do covenant . . . with the said James S. Bulloch that I will ____ and defend the said above premises to the said James S. Bulloch to his heirs and assigns from the lawful claims of me or my heirs and assigns. Thomas W. Quarterman have hereunto set my hand and seal this tenth day of March one thousand eight hundred and thirty seven.

Signed sealed and delivered
in presence of   Thomas W. Quarterman
Wm Jones
Thos J. Shepard C.S.C.L.C

Recorded this 4th day of April
A. D. 1837

Thomas J. Shepard Clerk Security Deed on Cedar Hill and Clifton Plantations w/Negro House Settlement (Liberty County Deed Book L, page 16)

GeorgiaThis Indenture, made the First day of January in the year of our Lord one Thousand eight hundred & thirty eight Between Daniel M. Stewart of the County of Chatham & State of Georgia of the first part & James S. Bulloch of Said county & state of the second part ------ Witnessed, that the said party of the first part, as will for the better securing to the party of the second part, the faithful payment of the debt which he the said Daniel M. Stewart justly owes to the party of the second part, in manner hereafter mentioned, as in consideration of the sum of one dollar, to him in hand paid by the party of the second part the receipt whereof is hereby acknowledged, HATH granted, bargained, aliened, sold, released & confirm and by these presents DOTH grant, bargain, sell, alien, release & confirm unto the party of the second part & to his heirs & assigns, forever, ALL that tract or parcel of Land, situate lying & being in the County of Liberty & State aforesaid, containing nine hundred & sixty five acres, including Cedar Hill & Clifton Plantations, adjoining the town of Riceboro, & also that other tract or piece of Land in the said County, adjoining Cedar Hill & Clifton Plantations containing six acres, more or less, & known as the Negro House Settlement and the said Daniel M. Stewart doth also hereby bargain & sell unto the said James S. Bulloch, the following Negro Slaves with their future issue and increase Voz Tom, Joe, Dick, James, Noble, George, Edmund, William, Fran, Old March, Little March, ___, Stephen, Tom, Anderson, Prince, Peter, Joe, William, Morgin, William Will, Tom, Abraham, Ben, Fortune, David, Ben, Sanders, Jacob, Cain, Aaron, Jim, Samuel, Peter, Little Stephen, Doublin, Hary, Billy, Ned (Carpenter) Billy, Sam, Burke, Titus, Old Sue,Tabby, Affy, Beck, Bina, Mary Ann, Rosetta, Big Mose, Ka__, ___, Mary, Phoebe, Rosannah, Charlotte, Hanna, Nanny, Sylla, Maria, Sue, Peggy, Delia, Amy, Sarah, Grace, Sally Betty, Cretia, Phillis, Fanny, Harriet, Old Hagar, Hester, Jenny Lucy, Dianna, Susan & Daphney. TOGETHER with all singular, the edifices buildings, rights members there ____ & appenertaining [?] to the same ___ belonging, or any wise appertaining; and all the estate, right,title, interest, property claim & demand whatsoever, of the said party of the first part, of in or to the same; & the ___ & revisions remainder & remainders there of TO HAVE & TO HOLD the said premises hereby granted & released, with the rights, members, hereditaments, & appurtenances thereunto belonging; and in every part & parcel thereof unto the party of the second part his heirs & assigns, to the only proper use & behoof of the said party of the second part, his heirs & assigns forever.
UPON CONDITION NEVERTHELESS, That if the said Daniel M. Stewart of the first part, his heirs, executors, administrators, or assigns, shall faithfully pay to the said party of the second part, his executors administrators, assigns, the sum of thirteen thousand three hundred & thirty nine dollars & twenty eight cents, on or before the first day of January which will be in the year of our Lord, one thousand eight hundred, forty five, with lawful Interest from the date according to the ___ and true intent & meaning of a certain Promissory Note ____ date with them presents & duly made & executed by the said

[Page 17]
Daniel M. Stewart of the first part, to the said party of the second part, Then this present Indenture & the estate hereby granted and every article and clause herein contained, as ___ As the said Promissory Note shall cease & become utterly void. And it is hereby mutually covenanted and agreed between the parties to these presents, that if default shall be made in the payment of the principal secured to be paid to the said James S. Bulloch and the interest which shall accrue therefore, at any time or times, on which they shall be due, or of any part of such principal or interest that these & from henceforth, it shall be lawful for the party of the second part his heirs, executors, administrators, or assigns to grant, bargain, sell and dispose of the said hereby granted premises, annual benefits and equity of redemption, of the said party of the first part his heirs, executors, administrators, or assigns, therein according to the directions of the ___ of the ___ in that case made ___ the ___ of the purchase money to be obtained for the same, after full satisfaction of the principal & interest to

be due on such Promissory Note in the manner aforesaid and the charges of advertisement and (if any overplus there shall be) unto the said Daniel M. Stewart part of the first part his Heirs executors, administrators, or Assigns. In Witness whereof, the parties to these presents have hereunto interchangeably set their hands & seals the day & year first above written.

Sealed & delivered in
The presence of   Daniel M. Stewart
Levi L. _____ Lyon
A Porter J.J.C.C.C   Recorded 2nd July 1838
                                E. Way clerk

Warranty Deed on Cedar Hill to William LeConte (Liberty County Deed Book L, page 78-79)

Georgia   This Indenture, made the seventeenth day of January in the year of our Lord one thousand eight hundred and thirty-nine, Between Daniel M. Stewart of the County of Liberty & said State Planter of the second part WITNESSETH, That the said Daniel M. Stewart, for & in consideration of the SUM of ten thousand two hundred and fifty dollars to him in hand paid by the said William LeConte at or before the sealing & delivery of these presents, the receipt whereof is hereby acknowledged, HATH granted, bargained, sold, aliened, remised, released & confirmed ___ By these present DOTH grant bargain, sell, alien, release & confirm, unto the said William Leconte, and to his heirs, and assigns, the following plantation or tracts of land, one called Cedar Hill bound North by North Newfort River & Land now owned by David Anderson, East by the Town of Riceboro to Land recently owned by Wm. Roberts also by land now owned by Raymond Cay and Estate Morgan Manor, South by Lands owned by Samuel Way, William Jones and Thomas Quarterman, West by Land owned by Thos. Quarterman & David Anderson, containing nine hundred & fifty one acres more or less. The other a plantation recently purchased of William Robarts, bounded North by North Newfort East by Land now owned by Rev. C. C. Jones & Lands of the Estate of Morgan Mara South by Land of Estate Morgan Mara, West by Land of Raymond Cay & Cedar Hill Tract aforesaid, all which will more fully appear by the plats annexed TOGETHER with all and singular the House, out Houses, edifices, buildings, stables, yards, gardens, privileges, easements, commodities, _____, hereditaments, rights, numbers, & appurtenances, whatsoever therein to belonging; or in any wise to pertaining: AND the reversion and reversions, remained & ____unto issues & profits: AND all the estate, rights, title, interest, property, or pro____ claims, and ____ Whatsoever, in law or in Equity of him the said Daniel M. Stewart of , in or to the sum, or any part or parcel thereof, with the appurtenances: TO HAVE AND TO HOLD, THE SAID Plantation or tracts of land, and all and singular, other the premises hereby granted bargained, sold, aliened, & confirmed, with the hereditaments and appurtenances, unto the said William LeConte, his Heirs and assigns to the only use & behoof of the said William LeConte, his heirs and assigns, forever, and to and for no other use intent or purpose, whatsoever: AND LASTLY, the said Daniel M. Stewart, his heirs the said Plantations and Tracts of land and premises unto the said William LeConte, his heirs and assigns, against him the Said Daniel M. Stewart, his heirs and against all and every other person or person whatsoever shall & will WARRANT and forever DEFEND by these presents. IN WITNESS WHEREOF, the said Daniel M. Stewart HATH hereunto set his HAND & SEAL this day and year first above mentioned.

Signed and delivered
In presence of us   Daniel M. Stewart.
??? W. Harris
James S. Bulloch
A. Porter J.J.C.C.C   Recorded this 23rd day of March 1839
                                                                    By E. Way   Clerk

Received of W. LeConte on the day and year ??? written the sum of
Ten thousand, two hundred & fifty dollars being the full consideration money
within expenses To be paid.   Daniel M. Stewart
Recorded this 23rd day of March 1839   E. Way   Clerk

Savannah 29 January 1839
To the Clerk Superior Court Liberty County
E Way, Esquire

You will please enter satisfaction in full on mortgage of record, Daniel M. Stewart to James S. Bulloch of Cedar Hill tract of Land.

            Your Obt Servant
            James S. Bulloch

Recorded this 23rd March 1839 E Way Clerk

The tract of land referred to in the above release (D. M. Stewart to Jas S. Bulloch) mortgage of Cedar Hill Plantation you will refer back to folio 16 & 17 of this book.

            E. Way Clerk

Division of John Elliott's Slaves, Will Record B, 1824-1850, page 370, Probate Court, Liberty County Courthouse, Hinesville, Georgia

You William Maxwell, A.B. Busby, and W. S. Baker do swear that you will make a true appraisal and inventory and division of all _____ the goods chattel and _____ John Elliott deceased as shall be produced and shown to you by James S. Bulloch administrator in estate of the deceased and that you will return the same to the said J S. Bulloch within the time prescribed by law.
Sworn before me Wm Maxwell
this 20th April 1844 B.A. Busby
 G. M. D _____ Ill
 W. S. Baker

Appraisement and division of the negroes belonging to the estate of Jno. Elliott deceased as exhibited to us by James S. Bulloch admin by order of the Justice of the Superior court of Liberty county, and even allotment of one third to Susan A. Elliott, one third to Georgia A. Elliott and one third to Daniel Elliott to wit.

Lot No 1		Lot No 2		Lot No 3	
Jacob (Driver)	500	Harry	200	Alex	600
Molly	550	Charles (Driver)	700	N____	500
Merry	600	James	550	Randy	550
John	600	Deliah	550	Mary Ann	550
Crawford	550	Peggy	500	Hetty	500
Affy	400	_____	350	Tom	500
C____	400	Betty	250	Phas___	250
Jim	300	Affy	550	Dick	175
Amanda	250	Charles	200	Betty	75
Daniel	200	Edward	75	B____ford	225
0 Affy	1	Moll	550	Charlotte	75
Vermont		Reueby	550	Sandy	600
(Carpenter)	1000	Benjamin	600	Goliah	600
Titus	600	_____	600	Charity	450
Die	550	Sibby	550	Sue	550
L Ha_____	650	Tuck	450	Henry	600
Mary	350		7125		6450
	6401				

[Should be 7401]

[Should be 6950, as it appears that Tom at 500 is added to the list and not calculated into the total.)]

Amt of No 1 held over 6401		Amt of No 2 held over 7125		Amt of No 3 held over 6450	
Lass	175	Cato	450	Tenah	550
Tayton Ben (____)	50	Stephan	150	Dinah	100
Leih	250	William	600	Ch_____	275
Big Sue	550	Lucy	550	Carp William	1000
Lizzy	550	George	450	Raky	550
Henry	500	Jamy (bricklayer)	1000	George	450
Truman	550	Sarah	550	Charles	450
Polly	550	Isabella	550	Sarah	125
Celia	450	Jacob	600	Peggy	75
Catherine	550	Bella (diseased?)	100	Long Hoss	300
Isaiah	200	Pufsey	550	_____	550
Peter	600	Billy	400	Charlotte	425
Julia Ann	550	Phillis	550	Big Hannah	500
Di _____	175	Mariah (diseased?)	100	R_____	450
Affy	50	Kaziat	500	Minty	550
Omar	550	Flora (diseased?)	50	O Moll	25
Joe	450	O Pheobe	00	Joe	500
O Billy	200	O Sophia	00	Giles	450

34 negroes No 1	14350
34 negroes No 2	14275
35 negroes No 3	14275
	42900

34 negroes   14275

35 negroes   14275

Files in this office 1 May 1844
and recorded 25 May 1844

J.S. Bradwell
Clerk

The foregoing three lots being appraised and arranged by us , Lot no 1 was allotted to Susan A. Elliott,
Lot no 2 to Dan'l Elliott & Lot no 3 to Georgia A. Elliott
and we award lot no 1 to ____to
lots no 2 & 3 twenty five 33/100 in cash.

W. Maxwell   _____
B.A. Busby   Appraisers &
William Baker   Dividers

APPENDIX C - 242

APPENDIX D:

List of Contents
Estate of Georgia Amanda Elliott   D-244
Estate of James S. Bulloch - Probate Records   D-246

In all documents transcribed herein ____ indicates illegible script. A question mark in parentheses denotes some doubt about the accuracy of the transcription. Do is shorthand for ditto. Additionally, page breaks in original documents are noted when at all possible. Documents are presented in order as noted in book.

Estate of Georgia Amanda Elliott - Georgia Archives, Cobb County Probate Records, Microfilm Drawer 317

Appraisement of Division of the Negroes belonging to Miss Susan A. Elliott and Miss Georgia A Elliott deceased as joint property and also of the half awarded to Estate Miss Georgia A Elliott as exhibited to us by James S. Bulloch, Executor & by order of the Justice of the Inferior Court of Cobb County and our allotment of our half to Miss Susan Elliott one fourth to Mrs. Martha Bulloch and one fourth to Daniel Elliott as bequeathed by ____ to said Parties by will dated 22nd September 1848.

1. Vermont   Carpenter   700
2. William   do   1100
3. [Old] Charlotte   300
4. Rake   350
5. Sarah   300
6. Peggy   250
7. [Little] Charlotte   150
8. George   600
9. Charles   500
                              $425

Lot No 1 for Miss Susan A. Elliott		Lot No. 2 Estate Miss Georgia A. Elliott	
Vermont	700	Raky	350
William	1100	Sarah	300
Old Charlotte	300	Peggy	250
	$2100	Charlotte	150
		George	600
No 2 Lot to Pay No. 1 $25		Charly	500
			$2150

Miss Susan A Elliott
Lot No 1   Raky   350
                        Little Charlotte 150
                        Charly   500   1000

Mrs. Martha Bulloch
Lot No 2   Sarah   300
                        Peggy   250   550

Mr. Daniel Elliott
Lot No. 3   George $600

The foregoing three lots of Negroes being appraised and arranged by us Lot No. 1 was allotted to Susan A. Elliott Lot No 2 to Martha Bulloch and Lot No 3 to Daniel Elliott No 2 to pay No 1 Eighteen dollars & 75/100 No 3 to pay No 1 Sixty eight 75/100 dollars

John Dunwody

N. J. Bayard
B. King

_____ B. King, N. J. Bayard, & John Dunwody before me Harrison T. Martin a Justice of the Peace for the first district of the County of Cobb do swear that you will make a
just and true appraisement of Division of all and singular the goods and chattels (ready money excepted) of Georgia A. Elliott deceased, as shall be produced by James S. Bulloch, the Executor of the Estate of said G. A. Elliott deceased and that you will upon the same _____ under your hands unto the said James S. Bulloch, Executor within the time prescribed by Law.

Sworn to this day	B King
21st November 1848	N. J. Bayard
H. T. Martin J. P.	John Dunwody

State of Georgia   By the Honorable the Inferior
Cobb County   Court of Said County, when sitting
                                    for ordinary purposes.
To Barrington King, John Dunwody, and N. J. Bayard, Arch. Smith and John Dunwody

These are to authorize and empower you, or any three of you, whose names are here above, ____ to attend and appraise the goods and chattels of Georgia A. Elliott, late of this county, deceased, in dollars and cents, so far as the same shall be provided to you by James S. Bulloch, the executor of said estate, or come to your hands knowledge or sight, you having first taken the oath before some justice of the peace, for said county, will and truly so to do. A certificate of which you are required to return annexed to the appraisement; and when the sum you have so appointed, you are to return an inventory thereof signed by any three or more of you, unto the said court, within the time prescribed by law, together with this warrant.

In testimony of which, I have officially put my hand and seal, by order of said court, this 6th Nove. 1848.

J. M. Anderson, C.C. O.   Seal

Estate of James S. Bulloch - Probate Records - Microfilm Georgia Archives Drawer 317

State of Georgia, By the Honorable the Inferior Court
Cobb County of said County when Sitting for
Ordinary purposes

To John Dunwody, Jr., Nicholas J. Bayard, Barrington King, Archibald Smith, and William Fuller esq.

These are to authorize and empower you or any three of you, whose names are here above written to attend and appraise the goods and chattels of James S. Bulloch, late of this county, deceased, in dollars and cents, so far as the same be produced to you by Robert Hutchison, administrator [illegible] to your knowledge or sight, ready money excepted, you having first taken an oath before some Justice of the Peace for said County, well and truly so to do, a certificate of which you are required to return annexed to the appraisement and when the same you have so appraised you are to return an inventory there of signed by any three or more of you unto the said Court within the time prescribed by law together with the warrant. In testimony whereof I have officially at my hand and seal by order of the said Court the 7th day of May 1849.

J. M. Anderson CCC

State of Georgia, Cobb County:

KNOW ALL MEN BY THESE PRESENTS, that we Robert Hutchison
Principal, John Dunwody and Barrington King securities are held and timely bound unto the Justices of the Inferior Court, when sitting for ordinary purposes for said county, and their successors in office, in the just and full sum of twelve thousand dollars, for the payment of which sum, to the said Justices and their successors we bind ourselves , our heirs, executors, and administrators, in the whole, and for the whole sum, jointly and severally and firmly, by these presents: sealed with our seal, and dated this 7th day of May eighteen hundred and forty nine

The condition of above delegation sworn, that if the above bound Robert Hutchison administrator of the goods, chattels, and credits of James S. Bulloch late of this county, deceased, do make a true and perfect inventory of all and singular, the goods, chattels, and credits, both real and personal of the said deceased, which have or shall come to the hands, possession or knowledge of the said Robert Hutchison or into the hands or possession of any other person or persons for him; and the same so made, do exhibit into the said Court of Ordinary, when he shall be thereunto required and such goods, chattels and credits do well and truly administer according to law, and do make a just and true account of his actings and doings thereon, when required by the Superior Court, or Register of Probates for the county. And all the rest of the goods, chattels, and credits, both real and personal, which shall be found remaining upon the account of the said administration, the same being first allowed by the said Court, shall deliver and pay to such persons, respectively, as are entitled to the same by law, and if it shall hereafter appear that any last will and testament was made by the said deceased, and the same be proved before the Court, and the executors obtain a certificate of the Probate thereof, and the said Robert Hutchison do, in such case, if required render and deliver up the said letters of administration, then this obligation to be void; else, remain in full force

J. M Anderson	Robert Hutchison	Principal [L S]
C.C.C.	John Dunwody	Security [L S]

B. King   Security [L S]

Dated June 20, 1849

Inventory & Appraisement of the Estate of James S. Bulloch
Registered in Book B Pages 218-219-220& 221 June 20th 1849
J. M. Anderson C.C.C.

Est. of J. S. Bulloch
Robert Hutchison Bond

Registered in Book of Bonds Page 183
June 21st 1849
J. M. Anderson C. C. C.

You, Nicolas J. Bayard and John Dunwody, Junior, and Archibald Smith, do swear that you will make a just and true appraisement of all and singular the goods and chattels of James S. Bulloch, deceased, as shall be produced by Robert Hutchison, Administrator of the Estate of the said James S. Bulloch, deceased, and that you will return the same, certified under your hands, unto the said Robert Hutchison, Administrator, within the time prescribed by law, so help you God.

Inventory and Appraisement of the Estate of James S. Bulloch, deceased

Item	Value	Item	Value
No. 1 Lounge	5.00	Centre Table	20.00
No. 2 Ditto	4.00	Pine Table	3.00
No. 3 Ditto	3.00	Ditto	.50
1 doz. Chairs	18.00	Ditto	.50
No. 1 Rocking Chair	2.00	Sideboard	20.00
No. 2 Ditto	2.00	Mahogany Stand	5.00
4 Bedroom Chairs	5.00	Mahogany Desk	10.00
6 Old Chairs	6.00	Stained Wood Bedstead	8.00
1 Matt	4.00	Ditto	8.00
No. 1 Carpet	12.00	Ditto	7.00
No. 2 Carpet	5.00	Black Walnut Bedstead	15.00
No. 3 Carpet	7.00	Mahogany Bedstead	25.00
Hearth Rug	3.00	Pine Bedstead	2.00
No. 1 Andirons, Shovel & Tongs	5.00	Chest Drawers	15.00
No. 2 Ditto	10.00	Ditto	15.00
No. 3 Ditto	7.00	2 Ditto @ 10 each	20.00
No. 4 Ditto	7.00	3 Pine Wash Stands	5.00
1 Brass Fender	10.00	1 Black Walnut ditto	10.00
1 Wire ditto	1.00	Sofa	20.00
Dining Table & Ends	25.00	Set Bed Curtains	2.00
Table in Library	<u>8.00</u>	Window Curtains	<u>3.00</u>
	149.50		362.50

1 Lot Bed Linens	25.00	2 Cake Baskets (plated)	10.00
6 Linen Table Cloths	30.00	4 Small Ladles	10.00
4 Beds	60.00	1 Soup Ladle	4.00
6 Mattresses	60.00	1 Silver Bowl	10.00
8 Pillows, 4 Bolsters	14.00	1 pair plated Candlesticks	6.00
Room Crockery	5.00	Books	150.00
1 Dinner Set China	40.00	1 Knife Case	10.00
1 Broken ditto	5.00	1 Spoon Case	10.00
Stair Carpet & Rods	6.00	Wine Safe	5.00
Entry Lamp	10.00	1 Set Dish Covers	6.00
2 Maps	10.00	Candle Mould	3.00
Solar Lamp	5.00	1 doz. Silver Forks	25.00
2 Pair Brass Candlesticks	1.00	2 Silver Milk Pots	6.00
Set Glass Ware	12.00	Dressing Table	8.00
2 Preserving Kettles	10.00	Small Mahog. Table	3.00
Kitchen Furniture	15.00	Lot Tin Bathing Tubs	10.00
1 Lot Earthen Jars	3.00	Saddle & Bridle	5.00
23 Table Spoons	46.00	Wardrobe - pine	4.00
2 doz. Dessert ditto	36.00	1 Yoke Steers	25.00
2 doz. tea ditto	20.00	16 Head Cattle @ 4.00	74.00
4 small spoons	2.00	48 Head Hogs @ .50	24.00
1 Large Ladle	5.00	12 Head Sheep @ 1.00	12.00
1 Fish Knife	3.00	Log Chain	4.00
2 Butter Knives	4.00	Cart	15.00
4 Large Gravy Spoons	12.00	Wagons - $50, $45, $20	115.00
2 Sugar Tongs	4.00	5 Ploughs @ 2.00	10.00
1 pair Salt Spoons	1.00	Horse, Billy	25.00
Set Casters	10.00	Horse, Old Gray	10.00
Branch Candle Stick	20.00	Horse, Bay	50.00
Syphon	2.00	3 Mules @ $50	150.00
Wine Strainer	1.00	Mule Colt	<u>12.00</u>
Bronze Urn	3.00		1667.50
2 Sugar Dishes	<u>8.00</u>		
Bronze Urn	1.00		
Silver Tea Pot	6.00		
	828.50		

[Third Page]		Corn Sheller	8.00
Straw Cutter	10.00	lot of Plough Castings	<u>5.00</u>
1 Grain Cradle	4.00		$1672.50

State of Georgia
Cobb County

We do certify and upon cath that as far as was produced to us by the executor or administrator the above and foregoing contains a true appraisement of the goods, chattels, and credits of the estate of James S. Bulloch deceased to the best of our judgement and understanding. Given under our hands and official signatures this June 8, 1849.

        John Dunwody Junior
        Archibald Smith
        Nicolas J. Bayard
        APPRAISERS

I do certify that the above appraisers were sworn to perform their duty as appraisers according to law this 8th of June 1849.

        William Fuller J. P.

Warrant of Appraisement
To Jno Dunwody, Jr.
Nicholas J. Bayard
B. King
A. Smith &
Wm Fuller J. P.

INDEX

Adams, President John 11-12, 15-16, 21, 50, 70, 83
Adams, President John Quincy 56, 78
American Temperance Society 83
Argyle Island GA 23, 72
Atwood, Henry 140
Atwood, Jane Margaret 158
Augusta, GA 44, 72, 81-82, 87, 93, 130, 139, 145

Bacon, John 96
Bacon, Augustus 125
Ball, Willis 131-134
Bank of Darien 79, 81, 122, 132
Barrington Hall 132
Bayard, Florida 153
Bayard, Nicholas J. 156
Beard, Edward 113
Beard, Joseph 113
Benjamin, Asher 131
Boston, MA 7, 12, 15, 56, 58, 115, 144
Boston Massacre (MA) 7
Boudinot, R.S. 148
Boyd, Priscilla 113
Boyd, Sam 113
Building and Insurance Bank 79
Bull, William 2
Bulloch & Dunwody 61, 75, 77
Bulloch, Anna Louisa n, 111, 121-122, 129, 139-140, 153
Bulloch, Ann/Anne (1793 - ?) n, 26-27, 38
Bulloch, Anne Ferguson n, 3
Bulloch, Anne Graham n, 3
Bulloch (Powell), Anne Irvine n, 26, 37, 56, 75, 96, 99, 111-112, 125
Bulloch, Archibald n, 3, 5-12, 15-16, 19-22, 24, 159
Bulloch, Archibald Stobo n, 7, 19-25, 52, 75, 77
Bulloch, Charles Irvine n, 133-136, 146
Bulloch, Charlotte Glen n, 51, 111-112
Bulloch, Christina n, 3, 5
Bulloch Hall 128, 130-132, 153-154, 156, 158
Bulloch, Hester Amarantha "Hetty" Elliott n, 27, 41-42, 45-46, 57, 73, 85-89, 93-94, 98, 104-107, 111, 142-143
Bulloch, Irvine Stephens n, 139-140, 153
Bulloch, James (1701-1780) n, 1-7, 26, 27, 41, 51, 159
Bulloch, Captain James (1765-1807) n, 21-37, 39-42. 51, 159

Bulloch, Major James Stephens n, 37-38, 41, 51, 87-96
    attempted holdup 87
    banker 79-81
    business 56
    civic leader 81-83
    death 153
    education 56
    estate 156-158
    executor/attorney 75-77
    factor 56-63
    guardianship of free Negroes 113-114
    investor 63-74
    Liberty County investments 123-126
    marriage to Hester Elliott 85-86, 106
    marriage to Martha Stewart Elliott 107-108
    military service 53-55
    move to Connecticut 112-122
    move to Liberty County 110
    move to Roswell 129
    Nancy Jackson case 115-119
    pirate 77-79
    religious education of slaves 114, 146
    temperance 83-84
Bulloch, Jane Dunwody n, 111-112, 140, 157
Bulloch (Maxwell), Jane n, 7, 23-25
Bulloch (Dunwody), Jane n, 26-27, 39, 42, 51, 88, 108, 132, 146
Bulloch, Jean Stobo n, 2
Bulloch, Jean (1730-1777) n, 3, 5
Bulloch, John Elliott n, 87
Bulloch, John Irvine n, 51, 104, 111, 138
Bulloch, Martha "Mittie" n, k, 113, 121-122, 129, 139-140, 148, 150, 153
Bulloch, Martha Stewart Elliott n, 42, 45, 49, 85-89, 92-95, 97-98, 101, 103-104, 106-107,
    110-115, 122-125, 129, 131, 135, 139, 142-143, 146-147, 151, 157-158
Bulloch, Mary DeVeaux n, 7, 24, 26, 39, 45, 58, 65
Bulloch, Mary Jones n, 6
Bulloch, Matilda "Till" 115
Bulloch, William Bellinger n, 7, 23-25, 51, 54, 58, 61, 90, 113
Bulloch, William Gaston n, 111-112, 142, 157, 149
Burke County 88
Butler's Tract Plantation 46

Camp, George Hull 148, 158
Campbell, Lt. Col. Archibald 6
Cedar Grove Plantation 46
Cedar Hill Plantation 49, 101, 110-111, 120-121, 123-126
Central Rail Road & Banking Company 104, 122, 143
Charleston, SC 2, 7, 19, 49, 59, 62, 66-68, 102, 104, 106, 110, 144, 148, 155
Charleston (SC) Library Society 2
Chatham Academy 105
Chatham Artillery 54-55, 68, 82

Chatham County GA 25, 29, 36-37, 44, 75, 106, 110, 122, 124, 142
Chatham Rangers 54
Chattahoochee River 130
Cherokee People 109, 129-130, 143
Christ Church 29, 32
Christ Church Parish, GA 3
Clay, Joseph 22
Clifton Farm (Cobb County) 126, 130 135-136, 146, 156, 158
Clifton Plantation (Liberty County) 125, 130
Cobb County, GA 130, 142, 144-145, 156
Cobb County Agricultural Society 145-146
Coe, William H. 142
Colleton County, SC 2
Cooper River 2
Continental Congress 9-10, 12, 16-17
Cornwallis, General Charles 25
Council of Safety 9, 16, 42
Crawford, Senator William H. 51
Creek (Muscogee) People 2, 9, 49
Cumming, Joseph 98-99

Daniels, Thomas 148
Darien, GA 47, 59-61, 106
Darien Presbyterian Church 146
Declaration of Independence 12, 15-21, 27, 83
DeVeaux, James 7, 23, 39
Drayton, John 2
Dunwody (Elliott), Esther Dean (d. 1815) 42-43, 46
Dunwody, Esther Dean Splatt 42-43
Dunwody, Dr. James 42-43
Dunwody, James Bulloch 43, 51
Dunwody (Stanhope, Glen), Jane Marion 43, 108, 135, 146
Dunwody, John Dean 37, 42-43, 51, 56, 61, 75, 77, 79, 95, 99, 106, 108, 110, 111-112, 114,
    130, 133, 139, 140, 153, 156, 158

Elliott, Amarintha R. N. Quarterman 44-45
Elliott, Betsy Hayward Thecher 45, 88
Elliott, Catherine Elizabeth 88
Elliott, Caroline Matilda 45-46, 88, 90, 92, 97
Elliott, Charles James 45-46
Elliott, Charles William 45, 88, 94
Elliott (Hutchison), Corinne Louisa 45-46, 88, 90, 94, 97-98, 104-105, 107, 110, 112, 114,
    120-122, 126, 134-135
Elliott, Daniel Roberts 44-45, 88
Elliott, Daniel Stewart 45, 94, 98, 104-105, 110-113, 120, 122, 124, 127, 129, 135, 137-139,
    148, 151
Elliott, Georgia Amanda 45, 88-89, 104-105, 110-111, 115, 119-120, 122, 124, 126-127,
    129, 148, 151, 153, 156-157,
Elliott, Hester Amarinthia (See Hester Bulloch)
Elliott (Sever), Jane Amarinthea 88, 137

Elliott, Jane Elizabeth 45-46, 88, 90, 94, 97-100, 105, 110, 124
Elliott, Captain John 44-45
Elliott, Colonel John 44-45
Elliott, Senator John n, 27, 42, 44-47, 57, 79, 85-93, 111, 137, 139
      Estate of . . . 94-99, 103-107, 110, 123-124, 127, 142
Elliott, John Whitehead 45, 88
Elliott, Rebecca Jane 45-46
Elliott, Rebecca Jane Maxwell 44-45
Elliott (West), Susan Ann 45, 48, 88-89, 97-98, 104-105, 110-111, 115, 120, 122, 124, 126-127, 129, 137, 139, 146-152, 156, 158
Erwin, Rev. Stanhope W. 43, 135

Fairlawn Plantation 46
Founders' Cemetery 136, 152, 154
Frederick & Mary Oakes Boarding House 112

Gaudry, John B. 96, 106
George alias "Charles White" 37
Gildersleeve, Rev. Cyrus 44
Glen, Chief Justice John 51
Georgia Militia 25, 36, 44, 49, 55, 135
Glynn County 46
Gold Lottery of 1832 109, 146
Greek Revival architecture 130-131, 158
Gwinnett, Button 12, 21, 27

Habersham, Joseph 64-65
Hall, Lyman 12, 27
Hampton, VA 23, 120
Hancock, John President 17
Hand, A.H. 133, 139, 146
Hand, Bayard E. 140, 142
Hand Eliza 131, 133
Hand, John Bayard 146
Harrison, General William Henry 145
Hartford, CT 112-117, 119-121, 138, 149
Hartford Academy 112-113
Hartford Female Seminary 113
Henry, J. P. 64, 79
Herman Briggs & Company 121
Hester's Bluff Plantation 46
Hodge, James T. 144
Holmes, Dr. James 86-87
Houston, John 20
Howell, Archibald 140, 158
Howell Brothers Store 140
Howison, Lt. Neil M. 147
Hunter, Alexander 75-76
Hutchison, Mary Caskie 150-151, 156-158
Hutchison, Robert 107, 110, 114, 119, 121-122, 124-125, 134-135, 150-151, 156

Irvine, Alexander 75-76
Irvine, Anne Elizabeth Baillie 75
Irvine, Dr. John 26, 75
Irvine, Sarah 99
Isaac, Robert 64-65, 79
Isaac Webb's Private Boarding School

Jackson, President Andrew 54, 56, 70, 80, 82, 121
Jackson, Nancy 82, 112, 115-117, 121-122
Jay, William 63
Jefferson, President Thomas 21, 50, 53, 70, 145
Jones, Charles Colcock 42, 49, 103, 114
Jones, John 114-115
Jones, Joseph 95
Jones, Mary 49- 103
Jones, Noble Wymberley 6-7, 20, 51
Jones, Sarah 51

Keep, Dr. Imla 37-38
King, Barrington 130, 134, 139, 142, 153, 156
King, Ralph 140
King, Roswell 81, 122, 129, 131, 140
Knight, Lucian Lamar 18
Knoll Plantation GA 27

Laurel View Plantation 42, 85, 88-89, 93, 96, 105, 148
Law, Elizabeth Stevens 99
Law, John Stevens 27, 99-100, 105
Law, Colonel Joseph 99
Lebanon, GA 140, 142, 144
Lebanon Baptist Church 146
LeConte, William 125-126
Lee, General Charles 19
Lee, Mrs. Efrom 90, 92
Liberty County, GA 4, 26-27, 29, 37-38, 42, 44, 46-47, 49, 61, 85-87, 89, 95-99, 101-102,
    106, 110-114, 118, 124, 126, 129-130, 133-134, 146
Liverpool, England 62-63, 73, 121, 150
Low, Andrew (and Company) 57, 64, 74, 124-125
Lumpkin County, GA 109

McDonald, Charles J. 135
McIntosh, Colonel Lachlan 9, 17, 69, 71
McWhir, Reverend William 27
Mount Vernon, VA 90, 92
Madison, President James 50, 56, 70, 79, 102
Marietta, GA 129, 131, 145, 153, 155-158
Marietta Presbyterian Church 134
Maxwell, James Benjamin 23, 25
Maxwell, John 46
Maxwell, Sr., William B. 39, 46, 93

Medway River 27, 44, 46, 61
Merrell, Henry 130, 141
Middleton, William 2, 71
Middletown, CT 113
Midway, GA 27, 42, 44, 47-48
Midway Cemetery 49-50, 94, 106
Midway Congregational Church 28-29, 42, 44, 46, 48, 50, 86, 89, 99
Monroe, President James 56, 63, 70, 78, 82
Morel, Marshall John H. 78
Mulberry Grove Plantation 3, 5, 7, 41, 55

New York, New York 16, 56, 63, 65-66, 68, 74, 89, 94, 104, 112, 114, 118, 120, 122, 124, 129, 138, 148-149, 151, 155
New York Anti-Slavery Society 118

Oak Grove Plantation 2
Oglethorpe, James 25-26, 66

Palmetto Bluff, SC 135
Philadelphia, PA 9, 11-13, 15, 41, 56, 58, 60, 88, 90-91, 114, 140, 144, 147, 149-150, 152
Phoenix Hall 131-131, 139
Pinkney, Charles 2
Planter's Bank 47, 79, 93, 104, 122
Pleyel, Ignatz Joseph 92
Plymouth, MA 88, 137, 144
Pon Pon Plantation 2
Powell, James Thomas 37, 46
Pratt, Nathaniel A. 135, 139, 146, 151
Pratt, Fanny 138
Primrose Cottage 131, 146
Princeton University 49, 138, 148

Quarterman, Thomas 44, 125

Rabun, Governor William 65
Ramoth Gilead Plantation 99
Republican Blues 53
Revolutionary War 20, 23, 26-27, 29, 41, 47, 49, 92, 102
    Battle of the Rice Boats 10
    Battle of Monmouth 19
    Cornwallis, General Charles 25
    First Battle of Savannah 6
    Fraser's Highlanders 6
    Muter's Virginia State Garrison Regiment 23
    Treaty of Paris   25
Revolutionary War Claims 114
Riceboro 59-61, 106, 110-111, 114
Richmond, VA 150
Rizing, Charles W. 124
Rogers, Captain Moses 66, 68, 73

Rogers, Dr. Charles W. 46
Roosevelt, Silas Weir 149-151
Roosevelt, President Theodore k, 21, 26, 42, 55
Roswell, GA 84, 126, 129-132, 134-141, 147-148, 151-152, 155-156, 158
Roswell, Academy 139-140
Roswell Manufacturing Company 126, 129-130, 135, 140-142
Roswell Presbyterian Church 131, 139, 146, 153, 155
Rural Felicity Plantation 46

Sadler, George 57
St. Johns Parish 22, 27, 44
St. Marys, GA 55
St. Marys Parish 3
Sayles Company Mill 149
Savannah Anti-Dueling Association 148
Savannah, GA 3, 5-7, 9-11, 14, 16-21, 23, 25-27, 29, 31, 35-37, 46-47, 51, 53-55, 57-58, 61-68, 73-83, 86-90, 92-100, 104-106, 108, 110, 112-119, 121-122, 129, 131, 134-135, 138, 140, 142-144, 147-148, 155
    fire of 1796 29-31
    First Battle of... 6
    Battle of the Rice Boats 10
Savannah Heavy Artillery 51
Savannah Marine and Fire Insurance 79
Savannah River 3, 9, 16, 55, 63, 68, 144
Savannah Steam Ship Company 64-65, 74
Schooner Montevediana 76
Second Bank of the United States 79-80
Sever, Catherine 137, 139
Sever, Jennie 137, 139
Shaftesbury Plantation, GA 23
Skidaway Island, GA 23, 33, 39
Smith, Archibald 139-141, 156
Smith's Fire Proof Stores 62
South Hampton Plantation 134
State Bank of Georgia 51
S.S. Pulaski 134
S.S. Savannah 51, 63, 65-69, 73-74, 79
Scarbrough, William 63-66, 68, 72, 74, 79
Stephens, Oliver 95
Stephens, William 25-26, 39
Stephens, Margaret DeVeaux 25-26, 39
Stewart, General Daniel 42, 46-50, 56, 88, 92, 101-102, 123
Stewart, Daniel McLachlan 49-50, 103-104, 110, 125-126
Stewart, Eliza Win Bacon 48, 104
Stewart, Georgia Drusilla 48-49
Stewart, Martha Pender 48-49
Stewart, Mary Eliza Eigelberger 48, 104
Stewart, Sarah Caroline 48-49
Stewart, Sarah Hines Lewis 48-50, 102-104
Stewart, Sarah Susannah Oswald 48-49

Stewart, Sarah Quarterman Nichols 48-49
Stewart, Susannah Bacon 47-48
Stobo, Reverend Archibald 3
Stobo, Elizabeth Park 3
Sunbury Academy 27, 37, 42, 44, 56, 59-61, 85
      Commissioners 42
Sunbury, GA 27, 44, 46-47, 49-50, 59-61, 87-88, 106, 110

Telfair, Mary 107
Texas 38
Texas War of Independence 55
Tondee's Long House (Tavern) 7, 9, 19, 20
Tondee, Peter 7, 9
Townsend MA 37-38
Trail of Tears 129
Tranquil Plantation 48-49, 123-125, 126
Tyler, Edward R. 115, 117-118
Tyler, Senator John 145

USS Delaware 147
USS Erie 147
USS Pennsylvania 147
USS Shark 147
USS United States 147

Vickery Creek 81, 129

Walterboro, SC 2, 5
Walthourville GA 42
Walton, George 7, 9, 11, 20
Ward, William 95-96
War of 1812 41, 47, 49, 51, 55-56, 65
      Battle of New Orleans 54-56, 70-71
      Battle of Point Peter 54
      60th Battalion 1st (Johnson's) Regiment 55
Waynesborough, GA 88
Webb, Isaac 113
      Private Boarding School 113
West, Hilborne 149, 151-152
West, James 149
West, Rebecca Coe 149
Western & Atlantic Rail Road 129
West Point (U.S. Military Academy) 120-121
Whitehead, Captain John 88
Whitney, Eli 41
Williamsburg, VA 23
Wilson, Col. Josiah 103
Wilson, Walter E. 113, 148

Yale University 44
Yorktown, VA 23, 55
Yonge, Christina 33, 75
Young Spartan 78-79

Zubly, John L. 16

Enslaved Persons:

Abraham 33

Ben 96
Billy 112
Bob 96, 103

Cato 3
Charity 39
Charlotte 97
Charlotte Monroe 129

George 147
George 151
Grace 130

Hagar 104
Hannah 96

Isaac 96, 142
Isaac Elliott 142

James 60
Jenny 112
John Maxwell 146
Judy 3
June 142

Lavinia 104
London 96
Lucy 112
Luke Monroe 84, 129, 153

Kate 96

Mariah 147
Mindy 96
Miley 96

Nat 96
Ned 112

Old Jack 112
Old Simon 33

Patience 97
Paul 146
Phebe 33
Phillis 96

Rose 147

Sandy 147
Stephens, Diana 39
Stephens, Peggy 39
Stephens 96
Stephen 147
Susan 146
Sylvia 103-104

Teresa/Therysa 39
Tim 96-97
Tom 96

Vermont 96

William 130

About the Author

Connie M. Huddleston is the author of eight history volumes (three with co-author Gwendolyn I. Koehler) and six historical fiction volumes. She also compiled a group of short stories for middle grade to young adult readers entitled *Winter Wonder*. Her fiction volumes have all garnered awards, excepting the newly released *Caintuck Lies Within My Soul: The Jemima Boone Story*, a novel based on the life of Daniel Boone's daughter. Her Adventures in Time series is written for middle grade readers and supported by educational materials on her website.

Connie is a former elementary school teacher, archaeologist, historic preservation consultant, and interpretive designer. She retired in 2017 after closing her own historic preservation company and now writes full time from her home in rural Kentucky.

Readers wanting to learn more of the Bulloch family story can look for:
Mittie & Thee: An 1853 Roosevelt Romance
Between the Wedding and the War: The Bulloch Roosevelt Letters: 1854-1860
Divided Only by Distance and Allegiance: The Bulloch/Roosevelt Letters: 1861-1865
Seldom Told Stories: Daddy Luke, Maum Charlotte, Maum Grace, and Daddy William of Bulloch Hall

Fiction Books written under the name C.M. Huddleston:
Middle Grade
Greg's First Adventure in Time (ebook free on Amazon and Barnes and Noble)
Greg's Second Adventure in Time
Greg's Third Adventure in Time
Greg's Fourth Adventure in Time
Winter Wonder (ebook free on Amazon and Barnes and Noble)

Young Adult to Adult
Leah's Story
Caintuck Lies Within My Soul: The Jemima Boone Story

All books are available on Amazon, Barnes and Noble, and Ingram.

Learn more about Connie at: www.cmhuddleston.com
Follow her on Goodreads at: https://www.goodreads.com/author/show/9860539.Connie_M_Huddleston

www.ingramcontent.com/pod-product-compliance
Lightning Source LLC
Chambersburg PA
CBHW081227080526
44587CB00022B/3851